Empirical
Inquiry

by the same author

The Logic of Inconsistency
(with Robert Brandom)

Scepticism

Cognitive Systematization

Leibniz

NICHOLAS RESCHER

Empirical Inquiry

ROWMAN AND LITTLEFIELD
Totowa, New Jersey

HOUSTON PUBLIC LIBRARY

An
WOLFGANG STEGMÜLLER
GELEHRT DOCH IMMER LERNEND

Copyright © 1982 by Rowman and Littlefield

All rights reserved. No part of this publication may be reproduced or transmitted, in any form or by any means, without the permission of the Publishers.

First published in the United States in 1982 by Rowman and Littlefield, 81 Adams Drive, Totowa New Jersey 07512.

Library of Congress Cataloging in Publication Data

Rescher, Nicholas.
  Empirical inquiry.

  Includes indexes.
  1. Inquiry (Theory of knowledge) 2. Empiricism.
I. Title.
BD183.R47   121   81-8557
ISBN 0-8476-7027-9   AACR2

Printed in the United States of America

Contents

PART ONE: CONCEPTS

Contents

PART TWO: KNOWLEDGE

PART THREE: QUESTIONS AND INQUIRY

Preface

This book is an exfoliation of ideas implicit in several of my earlier ones. As regards questions, it roots in *Dialectics* (Albany: State University of New York Press, 1977); as regards inquiry, it roots in *Methodological Pragmatism* (Oxford: Basil Blackwell, 1977); and as regards knowledge, it roots in *Scepticism* (Totowa: Rowman and Littlefield, 1980) and in *Induction* (Oxford: Basil Blackwell, 1980). Accordingly, the book represents an endeavor to develop and elaborate a systematic position in the epistemology of empirical inquiry by extending and weaving together themes and ideas present embryonically in these earlier books.

The substance of the book was presented in a series of public lectures on "The Epistemology of Questions" which I delivered at the University of Pittsburgh during the winter term of 1980. A revised and abbreviated version of these lectures was delivered during Trinity Term of 1980 in the School of Literae Humaniores of the University of Oxford at the kind invitation of the Sub-faculty of Philosophy. I much appreciate the kind hospitality of Corpus Christi College in affording me an academic home away from home during my visit in Oxford on this as on many previous occasions.

I am grateful to John Horty and to Lily Knezevich for reading this book in draft form and offering useful suggestions for its improvement. And I wish to thank Joyce Murphy for her work on the typescript and for helping me to see it through the press.

Pittsburgh
October, 1980

Introduction

The contemporary theory of knowledge approaches its problems predominantly with a view to the confirmation and testing of claims and assertions; its prime concern is with matters of knowledge and belief, acceptance and probability. Proceeding within the well-entrenched Cartesian tradition, its attention has been directed predominantly to the justification of belief and the establishment of knowledge claims. Recent philosophy of science, in particular, has focused upon theory-change, and the issues of the acceptance and rejection of theories, of their confirmation and testing, have played the paramount part. Its approach has been claim-oriented, not problem-oriented. The issues of scientific epistemology have accordingly been treated from the angle of the consolidation of answers rather than from that of the formulation of questions.

The present discussion alters this course of procedure. Putting factual questions at center-stage, it will consider how they give rise to one another, how lines of questioning are opened up and developed. Its focus is on how the process of empirical inquiry operates, and how we are to view the products that it delivers into our hands.

The book falls into four parts. Chapters I–III consider the conceptual stagesetting within which our factual questions arise. Chapters IV–V discuss cognitive change and its ramifications as part of the essential stagesetting of inquiry. Chapters VI–VIII examine some of the major issues of the epistemology of questioning in the scientific domain. Finally, Chapters IX–XIII deal with the issues of truth and reality in exploring the implications of a question-oriented approach for our understanding of the nature and status of the information we develop in the course of empirical inquiry. In sum, the book is an attempt to examine a wide variety of major issues in the epistemology of empirical inquiry from a perspective that assigns to questions a central and formative role within the cognitive venture.

Such an approach views inquiry as no less a process of question-posing than one of contention-substantiation, and seeks to accord to questions that parity with answers which is their proper epistemological due. It is the spirit of Kant, Dewey, and Collingwood, rather than that of Descartes, Brentano, and Carnap that is astir in these pages. For the key issues of the epistemology of inquiry come to be approached in terms of the best answers we can find to our questions, and not in terms of the issue of what sorts of structures we can erect upon a foundation of irrefrangible certitude.

PART ONE
Concepts

I

Meaning and Assertability

SYNOPSIS

(1) An exposition of the far-reaching distinction between truth-conditions and use-conditions. (2) A further clarification of the issues involved in this distinction. (3) Operating throughout the range of our objective discourse about "the real world," this distinction reflects an unavoidable Epistemic Gap between the data (or evidence) at our disposal and the actual assertoric content of our claims. (4) This gap is crossed (and can only be crossed) by an *imputational* leap that is built into the very ground-rules of operation of language through the evolutionary process of its development. Such a leap is ultimately justified not by any theoretical considerations, but on *pragmatic* grounds of functional efficacy. (5) Our (factually laden) concepts cannot survive hypotheses that abrogate the factual basis of their meaningfulness as reflected in the coordination of truth- and use-conditions. Such hypotheses will engender Kant-reminiscent paralogisms. (6) A due heed of the distinction between truth-conditions and use-conditions is essential if we are to effect cognitive entry into the linguistic resources of other conceptual schemes.

1. TRUTH-CONDITIONS VS. USE-CONDITIONS

Any adequate theory of language must recognize the crucial distinction between use-conditions and truth-conditions. The use-conditions are user-oriented indications of the circumstances in which a sentence is warrantedly assertable; the truth-conditions detail the ontological (world-oriented) circumstances that must obtain for a sentence to be true. The former afford the *operative criteria* for making the assertions at issue, the latter the inferential consequences of making them—the whole gamut of what must be

3

taken to follow their application. Use-conditions govern the
here-and-now *applications* of our descriptive or classificatory
terms. But once this issue of warranted applicability is settled, the
content-oriented question of all that follows from the assertions
being made still remains, and it is to this issue that truth-conditions
address themselves.

The truth-conditions of a language specify what range of the
objective circumstances (actual or possible) must obtain if its
statements are to be made *correctly*. The truth-conditions of a
statement thus fix its assertive content—the consequences that can
be derived from it (the set of all ontological circumstances in which
what it says is true). By contrast, the use-conditions of a language
fix the warranting norms of assertability of its statements, and
specify the sorts of circumstances whose determination enables
these statements to be made *appropriately* (or defensibly). These
use-conditions specify the circumstances under which certain
claims are in order—including what sorts of further circumstances
abrogate such entitlements.[1] They encompass—*inter alia*—the
ground-rules of plausibility and presumption that indicate the
standard bases on which claims stand "in the absence of coun-
terindications," and that inventory the types of moves which defeat
such claims. As truth-conditions are a matter of the semantics of a
language, its use-conditions are a matter of its pragmatics.

Its use-conditions are intrinsic components of the language—a
part of what every child learns about the use of his native tongue
"at his mother's knee." Truth-conditions do not have a monopoly
on "meaning"—this concept is broad enough to encompass both
sorts of conditions. After all, the use-conditions and their correlative imputational ground-rules are every bit as much an aspect of
the "meaning" of our words as are the truth-conditions. These two
aspects of "meaning" (consequences via truth-condition, antece-
dents via evidence = use-conditions) stand in a symbiotic in-
tertwining. For a crucial part of learning what a word *means* is to
learn how it is *used*—i.e., to get a working grasp of the types of
conditions and circumstances under which its use in certain ways
is *appropriate*. And here it is necessary to realize that this involves
an "inductive" component—an implicit view of "the way in which
things work in the world."[2]

Satisfaction of the conventions of use or assertability emphatically does *not* automatically determine (or guarantee) the truth of the statements at issue. These conditions simply determine the appropriateness (the justifiability or defensibility) of making these statements—the warrant, in context, for employing the terminology at issue. Truth transcends warrant. It is perfectly possible that—even when we conform to them in full—things may so eventuate that a duly authorized statement will ultimately have to be withdrawn.

To be sure, it would be misleading to speak of assertability-conditions in such a way as to invoke the idea of "rules" in this connection. For what is at issue is not, strictly speaking, a matter of *rules* at all; the use-conventions at issue are not formulated and codified; doubtless they are not fully codifiable, any more than are the "rules" for hitting a forehand in tennis. What is at issue is a matter of the characterizing conditions of a practice, of how-to-do-it guidelines, of tricks of the trade or skills, of what is learned largely through observation, imitation and habituation rather than through mastery of and adherence to explicitly specifiable rules. (There are, obviously, some things we must be able to do without using rules—following rules, for example—since otherwise we would be in the paradoxical situation of needing rules to govern the use of rules.)

2. THE "LOGIC" OF USE-CONDITIONS

The employment of some symbolism will help to clarify further the characteristic content-gap that opens up between use-conditions and truth-conditions:

$u(S, P)$ = "the situation S satisfies the use-conditions for the claim P"

$t(S, P)$ = "the situation S satisfies the truth-conditions for the claim P"

In the usual range of epistemic circumstances, the situations satisfying the use-conditions turn out to be a subset of those satisfying the truth-conditions. For $t(S,P)$ may be presumed to carry $u(S,P)$ with it—at any rate by and large and in the ordinary course of things. (If the cat is on the mat, a normal observer would, in normal circumstances, see it to be there, etc.) The test-conditions for something's being an apple—its having a core, for example—are in general circumstances that follow from actual applehood. And so we are warranted in taking the stance that, by and large, $t(S,P) \rightarrow u(S,P)$. But the converse thesis is somewhat more problematic. As we have seen, the involvements of $t(S,P)$ go well beyond those of $u(S,P)$. Yet we unhesitantly (and appropriately) claim that $t(S,P)$ has been determined to obtain, acting on the *presumption* that when the circumstances are such that we are authorized (given the rules of language) to assert that P, then P is indeed true. A use-condition has the implicational force that if a certain epistemic situation S is such that the use-conditions for a statement P are satisfied—symbolically, when $u(S,P)$—then P is to be asserted:

If $u(S,P)$ and S, then $\vdash P$

And on this basis we commit ourselves to $t(S,P)$. In general, we conduct our cognitive business with respect to factual assertions "as if" it were the case that

$$(\forall S)[u(S,\ P) \supset t(S,\ P)]$$

were a law of nature. We undertake, that is to say, a commitment to the substantive presupposition that such a transition is acceptable: it represents a material (or substantive rather than formal or logical) rule of inference that is built as a working hypothesis into the *modus operandi* of our language. The transition from u-satisfaction to t-satisfaction is, in short, an inferential step authorized by the operative conditions of language use, an implication that obtains on "practical" rather than "theoretical" grounds. And so while we recognize, *in abstracto,* that it is by no means the case that this transaction is legitimate, we proceed *in concreto* as though this were so. Our policy of language-use is such that we take the truth-conditions and the use-conditions of statements as ordinarily *de facto* coordinated.

In the final analysis, we espouse a *substantive* and *factual* assumption or presupposition that "coordinates" the criteria for applying our concepts with the inferential consequences that— given the meaning of these concepts—ensue upon these applications. Such commitments are a characteristic aspect of the fact-ladenness of the conceptual scheme with which we operate. They are a matter of the operating presumptions of our language.

It should, accordingly, be noted that the preceding thesis that P follows from the combination of S and $u(S,P)$ is part of the "practical politics" of epistemic life. It does not inhere in a logico-conceptual necessitation of the form $[u(S,P) \& S] \rightarrow P$. Our working authorization to treat P as true neither assumes nor presupposes a circumstantial *demonstration* of P's truth. The principle

If $(\exists S)[S \& u(S, P)]$, then P

represents a merely *practical* commitment, rather than an actual entailment on grounds of theoretical general principles. In this respect it is crucially different from

If $(\exists S)[S \& t(S, P)]$, then P

which is indeed a logico-conceptual truth.

Now it might be asked: Does not this latter entail the former, given

$(\forall S)[u(S, P) \equiv t(S, P)]$

to which, after all, we do stand committed? The answer is: not quite. For what we actually stand committed to is not the preceding thesis, but rather

$(\forall^* S)[u(S, P) \equiv t(S, P)]$.

And here $\forall^*$ is *not* universal quantification as such (viz. $\forall$), but only admits to the limited, substitutional interpretation of the quantifer—so that we are, in effect, dealing with a schema encompassing various particular cases rather than a generalization as such. What we have is merely a general formula for dealing with individual cases, and not a universal truth at the level of general principles.

We have no alternative to seeing the truth as our language enables us to see it. With respect to our own, seriously adopted language L, we stand committed to the principle

If $(\exists S)[S \;\&\; t_L(S, P)]$, then P

whose "truth" is "the-truth-as-L-sees-it." So far, so good. But it is also of interest to consider the converse of this principle:

If P, then $(\exists S)[S \;\&\; t_L(S, P)]$

This is the general semantical principle to the effect that if P is actually true, then some actual circumstance or state of affairs indeed satisfies the truth-conditions for P. Given this principle, we would have:

P iff $(\exists S)[S \;\&\; t_L (S, P)]$

We could now employ our practical principle

$(\forall S)[t_L(S, P) \equiv u_L(S, P)]$

to arrive at

P iff $(\exists S)[S \;\&\; u_L(S, P)]$

This is the doctrine of truth-as-assertability, one of the cardinal tenets of the pragmatic theory of truth. However, the present argumentation for this thesis rests on a mistake. It invokes the limited relationship

$(\forall^* S)[t_L(S, P) \equiv u_L(S, P)]$

as being available without the indicated quantifier limitation, transmuting the practical policy of equivalence in particular cases into an *in abstracto* equivalence at the level of general principles. This is a clearly illegitimate move.

One further matter. Any "logically normal" language L will have to satisfy the Implication Condition:

(IC)   If $P \rightarrow Q$, then $(\forall S)[u_L(S, P) \supset u_L(S, Q)]$

In such a language, entitlement to assertability flows along the channels of logical consequencehood. Now in this connection, the following objection might be offered:

Suppose that $u_L(S, P)$ obtains in cìrcumstances where $P \rightarrow Q$. Then by (IC) we shall have $u_L(S, Q)$. Now since, relative to L, the "practical principle"

$u_L(S, Q) \rightarrow t_L(S, Q)$

it will transpire that each and every implicit consequence of P must be assertable. Does this not preclude the prospect of any and all content-gap between $u(S, P)$ and $t(S, P)$?

The answer here is negative. To be sure, in asserting P, we become committed to asserting Q when (ex hypothesi) $P \rightarrow Q$ holds. But this emphatically does *not* mean that—in circumstances S—we are entitled to assert P only if $u(S, P)$ establishes explicit epistemic control over each and every implicit consequence of P. The fact that $P \rightarrow Q$ obtains does *not* render the set of situations under which $u(S, Q)$ a subset of the set of those under which $u(S, P)$. Practical warrant for calling some liquid *water* does not require practical warrant for every claim that follows if it indeed is water. (In this regard, use-conditions vary decisively from truth-conditions.)

3. THE RATIONALE OF DIFFERENTIATION: THE EPISTEMIC GAP

The preceding section has stressed the fact *that* the use-conditions of discourse differ significantly from its truth-conditions in being weaker and less demanding. The question arises as to *why* this should be so, and indeed *appropriately* so.

Throughout our discourse about the real world—not only in scientific contexts but in the most ordinary circumstances of everyday life—the claims at issue go beyond the evidence actually at our disposal. An inevitable "evidential gap" separates the *assertoric content* of an objective claim—the range of what we become committed to in making it—from the *supportive data* we ever actually obtain for it. And this represents a fundamental fact of epistemic life.

It is necessary to distinguish from the very outset between objective factual assertions that make descriptive claims about "the real world" and those contentions that are merely subjectively phenomenological and appearance-oriented. Objective assertions deal—or purport to deal—with how things actually and objectively stand; phenomenological assertions merely deal with how things appear to people or with what people think about them. (The relevant range of locutions here includes such qualifying expressions as "it seems to me," "it strikes me as," "it appears to me that," "I take it to be," "it reminds me of," etc.) Such phenomenal judgments do not deal with how things stand *in the world,* but with how they stand *with us.* They are strictly subjective—egocentric and appearance-oriented. They deal with *experiences* rather than with what is *experienced.* Experience, however, always places us on the subjective side of the fence; it is inevitably personal and phenomenal, since all experience must be somebody's experience of a certain phenomenal sort.

This distinction between objective and subjectively phenomenal judgments brings us to the very far-reaching point that the assertoric content of objective factual claims is *always* so extensive as to render these claims such as to transcend the "data of experience." This state of things is evident with regard to all *general* factual statements—and so specifically for all laws ("All elms are deciduous," "Lions have tails"). Here the data-in-hand always relate to a limited group of particular cases, whereas the claim at issue is generic and unlimited. Moreover, data transcendence also holds for *particular* statements of concrete objective fact. There are three main categories of these:

(1) thing-kind classifiers ("This is an apple" or "That is a lump of coal").

(2) property-ascriptions ("This is sour" or "That lump of coal is black").

(3). relatedness-ascriptions ("This is heavier than that" or "This is to the right of that").

And all such particular-oriented statements carry a significant admixture of nomic generality. To be an apple (or a lump of coal) is to behave in certain characteristic ways across a potential infinitude of cases. The same holds for having a sour taste or being black in color. All objective facts have a dispositional aspect. To be heavier than (or to the right of) something is also to behave in a certain lawful way. The aspect of nomic generality thus invades all particular characterizations of *objective* fact. And it inevitably outruns the necessarily finite reach of our data-in-hand. The claim/evidence relation that obtains here is inevitably characterized by what W. V. Quine has called the disparity between "the meager input and the torrential output" inherent in our factually assertoric discourse.[3]

At this point we come to face the important fact that there is an *inevitable* "epistemic gap" that separates our objective claims form the experiential evidence we do—or ever can—actually obtain as backing for them. All discourse about real things as they actually exist in the world accordingly involves an element of *experience-transcending* commitment to claims that go beyond the acquirable information, but yet rejection of these claims would mean that we would have to withdraw the thing-characterization at issue.

The experienced portion of a thing is like the part of the iceberg that shows above water. All things necessarily have hidden depths, and the existence of this latent (hidden, occult) sector is a crucial feature of our concept of a thing. Neither in fact nor in thought can we ever simply put it away.

To say of the apple that its only features are those it actually manifests is to run afoul of our very conception of an apple. To deny—or even merely to refuse to be committed to the claim—that it *would* exhibit such-and-such features *if* certain things were done (e.g., that it would have such-and-such a taste if eaten) is to be driven to withdrawing the claim that it is an apple. A real apple must, for example, have a certain sort of appearance from the (yet uninspected) other side, and a certain sort of (yet uninspected) subcutaneous make-up. And if anything goes wrong in these respects, my claim that it was *an apple* I saw (rather than, say, a clever sort of apple-substitute, or something done with mirrors and flashes of colored light) must be retracted.

The claim to see *an apple,* in short, cannot achieve a *total* logically airtight security on the basis of experience. Its content is bound to extend beyond whatever evidence is actually—or even potentially—in hand, and does so in such a way that the claim becomes vulnerable and defeasible in the face of further evidence. If, on the other hand, one "goes for safety"—and alters the claim to "It *seems to me* that I see an apple" or "I *take myself* to be seeing an apple"—this resultant claim in the language of appearance is effectively immune from defeat. Security is now assured. But such assertions purchase this security at the price of content. As C. S. Peirce stressed, direct experience of phenomenal subjectivity is objectively vacuous:

> Direct experience . . . affirms nothing—it just *is.* There are delusions, hallucinations, dreams. But there is no mistake that such things really do appear, and direct experience means simply the appearance. It involves no error, because it testifies to nothing but its own appearance. For the same reason it affords no [objective information] . . . [4]

No volume of claims in the language of subjectivity and appearance—however extensively they may reach in terms of how things "appear" to me and what I "take myself" to be seeing, smelling, etc.—can ever issue in any logically secure guaranteeable result regarding what *is actually the case* in the world. While they themselves are safe enough, appearance-theses—like theses about one's thoughts, beliefs, perceptions, etc.—will inevitably fall short on the side of objective content.[5]

Accordingly, objective factual claims are in general such that there is a wide gap between the *content* of a claim and the *evidence* we can possibly have at our disposal to warrant this claim. The milkman leaves a suitable-looking bottle of white liquid on the doorstep. One does not hesitate to call it "milk." A small cylinder of hard, white earthen material is lying next to the blackboard. One does not hesitate to call it "chalk." The *content* of such claims clearly ranges far wider than our meager evidence and extends to chemical compositions, sources of origin, behavior under pressure, etc., etc. And this story is a standard one. For the fact is that all of our statements regarding matters of objective fact (i.e., "That *is* an apple" as opposed to "Something appears to me to be an apple") are such that the *content* of the claim—its overall set of commitments and implications—moves far beyond the (relatively meager) evidence for it that is actually at our disposal. All such objectively factual claims have ramifications over whose obtaining we have no cognitive control in the absence of specific verificatory checks—verifications we cannot ever carry out *in toto* and with respect to which we can obtain only a few specific samples drawn from an infinite range.

Given the very *modus operandi* of language, these two issues of declarative content and warranting criteria—of *truth-conditions* and *use-conditions*—cannot be equated with another.

The evidence we can ever actually have at our disposal *inevitably* falls short of covering the full content of the objective factual claims at issue. Objective factual discourse—be it general or particular—always involves claims that are data-transcending in that their contentual commitments go beyond the observational and phenomenal evidence we do (or can) actually have at any particular juncture. If one understands an "hypothesis" in the more or less usual way, as a claim that moves beyond the evidence at hand, then our objective factual claims will inevitably fall into the category of the hypothetical.

It follows that there simply is no alternative to allowing the use-conditions to fall short of the truth-conditions in relation to such claims. If we want to be in a position to convey information about the real world, then we *must* endorse and accept contentions whose content outruns the data at our disposal. The reason for this resides in the lack of any alternative, and its justification lies in its inevitability. In the final analysis, it is thus the pressure of functional considerations that accounts for the disparity between use-conditions and truth-conditions. If our linguistic praxis is to do the job we intend for it, we simply *have to* work with a family of assertability-conditions whose assurances fall short of the assertion-content of the claims we undertake on their basis.

Accordingly, the experiential data actually at our disposal to serve as grounds for an objective factual claim will never actually *entail* that claim (in the logician's sense of this term). The falsity of an objective factual claim is always *logically and theoretically compatible* with all the evidence at our disposal.

The "evidential gap" between the assertoric content of objective claims and the experientially accessible supportive data we can ever obtain for them is thus a fact of epistemic life with which any adequate theory of knowledge must come to terms. And this fact that the *content* of an objective claim always far *outruns* our *evidence* for it means that the use-conditions of assertion-entitlement for our objective judgments—their evidential warranting conventions—will encompass only a modest sector of the range envisaged by the conditions for their actual truth.

Given this "evidential gap," it is crucial to the very viability of language that the demands at issue in its truth conditions involve more than its conditions of appropriate usage can possibly manage to assure. As we have seen, the "evidential gap" at issue with objective factual claims means that the *content* of every such claim involves such a variety of implications and ramifications that it would be in principle impossible to check them all. And since omniverification is impossible, it becomes, through this very fact, an irrational demand. It is *inevitable* that the truth-conditions should outrun the use-conditions for objective claims.

4. LEGITIMATION THROUGH THE TELEOLOGY OF COMMUNICATION

The aim of the linguistic enterprise, after all, is to convey information as to how things stand in the "real world." And so, the use-conditions of natural languages are bound to be of a rather rough and ready sort. Language has evolved as an instrument of communication among hunters and gatherers, and its most fundamental uses were of a rough, pragmatic sort—identification of friend or foe, signaling the presence of a quarry, coordinating the efforts of people engaged in a common venture and the like. If language-use authorization were not forthcoming on the footing of a very sparse and indeed (theoretically) *grossly* inadequate data-basis, language would never have developed into a useful instrument of communication. The language of our descriptive discourse regarding the matters of objective fact is in its very nature a vehicle for evidence-transcending imputations.

Given the epistemic gap between the evidential circumstances encompassed in the use-conditions and the asserted content of our factual claims, the question remains as to just exactly how we manage to cross this gap?

In its very nature, this "evidential gap" is (clearly) not to be closed by any evidence at our disposal. It is, in fact, simply *leapt over by an evidence-transcending imputation*[6]—by staking a claim of a postulational or conventional nature that steps beyond the probative resources at our command. We do not cross the evidential gap by some particular *method* or some peculiar cognitive device: We do not cross it by any sort of *theoretical* device at all, but simply by a *leap*.

Now the important point here is that imputation is not *inference*. It is not a matter of a move from given premises to a resulting conclusion elicited from them by the extraction of implicit commitments. We do not somehow *derive* or extract "objective theses" from "observed data"; to speak in such terms would be gravely misleading. Observation does not provide an *inferential* basis for making an "inductive leap" over the gap at issue, but merely furnishes our assertion-authorizing *cues and signals* on the basis of which, given the assertion-norms that govern language-employment (its use-conditions), certain claims are appropriate and in order. An element of presumption is thus involved in all our factual statements about real objects. But in making the trans-evidential leap at issue, we at the same time stand committed to what we have leapt over: we are always committed to more than we have in hand (epistemically speaking) by way of actually secured data. We always assert more than we have a strictly logical authorization for saying relative to the evidence actually available—and that is where assertability conditions come into play.

Such an imputation or presumption is accordingly not idiosyncratic or haphazard. It is not a personal act, but a shared resource built into a social framework, based upon a communally available linguistic praxis whose groundrules are a matter of public property. Such imputations are not a matter of human psychology (this is where Hume's resort to habit goes wrong), but rather are built into the conceptual scheme codified in language. The conceptual scheme embodied in the language incorporates a "theoretical" stance towards the world that embodies certain factual (and inevitably data-transcending) imputations. The language of our objectively descriptive discourse is in its very nature a vehicle for such evidence-transcending imputations.

A closer look at the justification of our evidence-transcending imputations is warranted. Such imputations are not something reckless, unfounded, and fortuitous; they are warranted through a fundamentally linguistic rationale of legitimation. As the preceding considerations suggest, the authorizing warrant for the imputational component of our objective categorial judgments lies ultimately in the purposive teleology of language-use—the goal of successful communication. The information that I myself have about a thing at first hand is always personal and egocentric— based upon the contingencies of what I "happen to have experienced" about it and what I "happen to have gathered" about the experience of others. In making objective assertions about something it is thus critical that I *intend* to discuss "the thing itself" rather than "the thing just precisely as I conceive of it" relative to the body of information I have about it. Only the former is something that somebody else can also address himself to; the latter is not. We could never establish communicative contact about a common objective item of discussion if our discourse were geared to the things conceived as to correspond just exactly with our own specific information about them. Objective reference requires the transcendence of the data and of the conceptions we base upon those data. If our assertoric commitments did not go beyond our own data and our own conceptions we would never be able to "get in touch" with others about a shared objective world.

The quintessentially imputational move beyond the evidence in hand is called for by any step into the domain of the publicly accessible objects in whose absence interpersonal communication about a shared world becomes impossible. The teleology of communication about matters of objective fact provides the ulti- mate warrant for the imputational information-in-hand transcendence of our factual assertions. Without our imputational praxis of making evidence-in-hand-transcending assertions, all communication about an objective realm that we share in common would become impossible. The work of inductive *reason* is to enlarge the sphere of what we can communicate about (the range of the information we can convey); but the work of the imputational processes of inductive *judgment* is to put us into a position to communicate at all.

Such this-or-nothing argumentation, however, takes us no further than to establish the need for some information-in-hand transcending imputations. But what validates the particular linguistic mechanisms that constitute our vehicle for accomplishing this mission?

The evolutionary development of symbolic processes and conceptual schemes provides the key to rational validation here: *They are entrenched on Darwinian grounds and validated through pragmatic considerations.* The pragmatic aspect comes to the fore at this junction. The success of our inductive proceedings must be considered at least partly responsible for some of its accepted connections with our use of terms like "rational" and "justified." And perhaps the most dramatic and least understood success here relates to the practice of the objective discourse in whose terms we learn to link words to the world so as to communicate with others about our personal experiences within the setting of a community-wide, shared set of inductively based commitments concerning what kinds of things there are and how we are to speak of them. Our fact-oriented concepts evolve in the historical process of cognitive development with both aspects of meaning-content and use-appropriateness indissolubly fused by the pressure of the factual arrangements of this world.

A closer look at the precise character of the justification of our evidence-transcending imputations is in order. It was suggested above that this is simply a matter of this-or-nothing—that if we wish to achieve answers to our questions about the world and if we wish to communicate with one another about matters of objective fact, then we simply have no alternative but to undertake such evidence-transcending commitments. But this consideration that we *must* proceed in this way—the fact of *practical necessity* that there just is no alternative if our objective is to be reached—does not offer us any assurance that we actually will succeed in our endeavor if we do proceed in this way; it just has it that we won't if we don't. The issue of actual effectiveness remains untouched. And here we have no choice but to proceed experientially—by the simple strategem of "trying and seeing." Practical necessity remains a matter of *a priori* considerations. But efficacy—actual sufficiency—will be a matter of *a posteriori* experience; experience which shows that our praxis of inquiry and communication does actually work. The key fact here is that we can effectively and (by and large) successfully communicate with one another about a shared world, inquiry into and communication regarding whose nature and workings proceeds successfully as a communal project of investigation. This aspect of pragmatic efficacy is the ultimately crucial consideration that legitimates the evidence-transcending imputations built into the use-conditions of language.[7]

5. PARALOGISMS

The descriptive and taxonomic mechanisms of our language in whose terms we convey information are inherently "theory-laden"—they are as we have seen, predicated upon factual commitments as to how matters stand in the world. Meaning and theory (i.e., belief) are interdependent and develop in symbiotic coordination. And so, semantics, or the study of meaning-relationships, cannot be asceptically separated from natural science (i.e., the formation of beliefs as to how matters stand in the world). Throughout the descriptive and taxonomic sectors of our discourse, meaning and belief stand in inseparable interlinkage.

Suppose that I responsibly assert that the apparent color of a certain rose is red. This descriptive characterization encompasses, among other things, a commitment to (1) the claim of a characteristic *subjective* appearance of phenomenological color falling within a certain range, (2) the claim that by and large others would perceive the rose's color roughly as I do and would agree with its characterization as red, and (3) the claim that the rose has a certain sort of (otherwise not specific) physical constitution in view of which most of us perceive its color as red. Any descriptive or taxonomic concept operates similarly in its commitment to an extensive and complicated group of suppositions about how things work in the world. The coordination of use-conditions and truth-conditions means that our, and indeed *any* object-oriented discourse is geared to certain factual presumptions or presuppositions.

It follows that the strain that our concepts are able to bear under the pressure of hypothesis-assumption is seriously limited. A fact-laden concept is predicated on certain factual presuppositions and its applicability is compromised when these are abrogated or violated. We must not press such concepts beyond the binding-strength of the facts that make them viable as the concepts they are by fusing their logico-semantically disparate elements into a cohesive unit. I cannot be asked to assume that everybody else would (in standard conditions as to lighting, etc.) see that rose's color as I would see blue or that there is no significant physical uniformity between the surface of this red rose and that of yonder red rose. A hypothesis must not sever the bonds on which the very meaning of the terms operative in its own articulation is based. When the factual bonds that bind them together are cut, our concepts themselves fall apart.

The factual commitments of our language reflect presuppositions which we cannot abrogate in hypothesis without paradox and paralogism, because *such* a hypothesis would violate the suppositional basis upon which the range of language-use at issue is in fact predicated. Concepts cannot be pressed beyond their tensile capacity: abrogate facts by hypothesis and you thereby abrogate the basis of the viability of concepts. One cannot burst the factual bonds that bind the very language one is using and still claim to operate *within* the language framework.

Consider an example: "personal identity," at issue in our judgments that the individual we encounter on one occasion in one context is the same person as the individual we encounter on another occasion. This concept unites a plurality of factors, among which bodily continuity and sameness of personality are the outstanding members. These factors are held together in a harmonious symbiosis by the *factual* consideration that they ordinarily and standardly go together. Now suppose that, in the interests of eliminating the empirical element and obtaining semantical tidyness we put all of our conceptual eggs into one basket, and take one of these factors as essential, the other as accidental. Thus let us adopt bodily continuity as essential and relegate continuity of personality to the background. Immediately some clever doubter will pop up to construct a counter-example that cannot but make us uncomfortable with this choice. By mooting some fiendish electronic rewiring of their brain circuitry he will have Messrs. A and B exchange personality characteristics: knowledge and memory, performatory capabilities, talents, inclinations, dispositions, etc. Nothing is to remain the same except the lumps of material stuff. And now our objector protests: ''According to your thesis that bodily continuity is the determinating criterion, we should have no hesitancy in the case I have sketched about saying that we are dealing with the same person both before and after the personality exchange. But we unquestionably do feel a very considerable hesitancy. So the analysis that sees bodily continuity as decisive cannot be right.'' There seems to be much justification in this complaint. So let us try the opposite resolution, taking sameness of personality as determinative, and bodily continuity as incidental. At once another objector comes along with a different counterexample. He has one person so changed that all of his personality characteristics have altered over the course of a month or two, while someone else's personality has come to be far more like what his used to be. And then he protests ''According to your thesis that similarity of personality is the key criterion of personal identity, we should have no hesitancy about saying in such a case that the personality-altered individual is no longer the same person, and it would become moot to consider whether our subject individual has metamorphosed into his simulacrum. But we would actually hesitate very much about saying this sort of thing. So bodily continuity is in fact the decisive criterion.''

The implications of the two cases are diametrically opposed. And the crucial point is that quite evidently we are reluctant to live with the consequences of either resolution, because a ruling in favor of the primacy of any one of the fact-coordinated plurality of criteria does violence to our intuitive assessment of those cases where the other criteria come into prominence. The arguments for and against each resolution are evenly or substantially balanced; we can always construct pretty much equally good arguments either way. In short, we fall into a paralogism.

The general pattern is by now clear enough. Our empirical concepts, being standardly fact-coordinated, exhibit an inner semantical tension due to the plurality of their constituent components. This internal stress among logically divergent factors is standardly resolved by the favorable cooperation of empirical circumstance: the tension is unproblematic because the facts (as we see them) are duly cooperative. But once we give up our reliance on these facts in the interests of semantical neatness, the tension breaks out. For when we set the facts aside, the concept at issue itself disappears in a destructive fission. This disintegration manifests itself through opposing arguments—all seemingly equally good, but all in the final analysis equally unsatisfying. If we push matters too hard in framing our hypothesis, if we sever the carefully nutured links of meaning and belief that fuse truth-conditions and use-conditions into a viable symbiosis, then paralogisms are bound to result. They are the inevitable sign and symptom of an improper hypothesis that subjects the terms at issue to a stress they were never designed to bear in the process of cognitive development in which they have their place. (The traditional diplomats' aversion to "purely hypothetical" questions has some analogy in this domain.) In consequence, what appears on first view as conceptual tidyness in making an ordinary concept more precise, results in a paradox-generating clash with the initial concept as it actually works, based as it is upon a unification in which the other, now suppressed factors are actually no less prominent. The paralogisms that result are the inevitable indicators of this inner fission implicit in our fact-coordinated concepts.

From this standpoint, the fundamentally fact-dependent nature of our conceptual apparatus is a consideration of great relevance to the potential usefulness of hypothetical cases in concept-analysis. Our concepts can and generally do develop against the background of an understanding of "how things work" in the world (or better, "are taken by us to work"); they are tied to a view of the realities of nature and to the empirical detail of actually existing practices. If we introduce hypotheses to abrogate these "underlying realities," the foothold for our concepts dissolves and the relevant sector of our conceptual scheme simply goes up in smoke. It would go too far to say that no useful purpose whatsoever can be realized in this way. For example, a science-fiction hypothesis can effectively bring to light the significant fact *that* certain of our concepts are indeed fact-laden and rest on empirical presuppositions. But what this process cannot do is to serve as a basis for precisifying our *existing* concepts, because the supposedly more precise account that results in these circumstances will not and in the nature of the case cannot any longer qualify as a version of the concept with which we began.

Let us view this position in a Kantian perspective. Kant's basic thesis is that we cannot legitimately apply our concepts outside the limits of *possible experience,* and that when we do so we reach the intellectually unstable result of falling into antinomies. For Kant, the applicability of our concepts is validated through a categorical synthesis that renders them viable only when deployed *within* their area of valid employment: the domain of *possible* experience. Our own position is closely analogous, although critically different. We have made a crucial departure from Kant by replacing his *a priori* synthesis inherent in the faculty-structure of the human mind by a less ambitious but (I think) no less far-reaching reliance on the empirical synthesis built into a *Weltanschauung,* or some sector thereof. Accordingly, for us also, certain philosophically central concepts are seen as usable only within "the limits of possible experience." But *possible experience* now means *empirically* possible experience, relative to the factual commitments of a view of how things work in the world—that is, *actually* possible and not, as with Kant *transcendentally* possible. Our position, though Kantian in its fundamental structure, replaces his conceptual *a priori* necessity by a more modest empirical and *a posteriori* counterpart.

Of course conceptual change is possible—and indeed standardly happens. But this involves genuine innovation and calls for resolutions that cannot be rationally worked out in advance, because a course of genuine *invention* is required—of cognitive innovation in fact-oriented theorizing—and the direction in which this will take cannot (in the very nature of the case) be anticipated prior to the event. As we have seen, the use-conditions of a language involve commitments of a character closely akin to a commitment to laws of nature. Now we can certainly contemplate the prospect of changing our minds about these, abandoning them and putting something else in their place. But what we cannot say is what else would then stand in their place, or, at any rate, we cannot say this in advance of the event (and cannot even speculate about it intelligently short of knowing in full and precise detail the whole spectrum of considerations that create the cognitive pressures under whose impetus the changes at issue are being compelled).

6. PROBLEMS OF INTERPRETATION

A failure to distinguish properly between truth-conditions and use-conditions would yield serious consequences for epistemology. Of these, few are more serious than the fact that we are then cut off from any adequate account of understanding and interpretation across linguistic divides.

To understand and interpret the declarations of the speakers of another language, we must certainly presuppose that, in the various conditions and circumstances that arise, they by and large deploy their discourse *appropriately* relative to their own terms of reference. If we are to be in a position to penetrate their discourse at all, it must be the case that when an L-speaker uses P in a situation S, then generally and by and large S indeed satisfies L's use-conditions for P, so that u_L (S, P) obtains. This presumption of appropriateness is indispensable if people external to the linguistic community are to be in a position to acquire the language L (be it someone else's or that of one's own environing group).

Now if we did not distinguish carefully between use-conditions and truth-conditions, then adoption of the preceding principle of appropriateness would at once plunge us into grave difficulty. For we would then be led to the idea that when the L-speaker X actually asserts P in the situation S then, by and large, t_L (S, P) indeed obtains. The "principle of charity" that people by and large use language appropriately—the harmless Principle of Appropriateness that we must espouse if we are ever to understand the users of a different language—would at once commit us to a Principle of Truth. And this would be fatal. To understand and interpret the declarations of the speakers of another language we would now have to presuppose that they by and large speak *truly*. To understand evil-eye talk we would have to accept the evil-eye phenomenon. Only if we were prepared to grant that they by and large spoke truly—in the great bulk of situations—would we be entitled to claim that we understand their assertions.

This unhappy consequence of a conflation of use-conditions and truth-conditions is in fact a position into which some theorists have fallen. Donald Davidson, for example, writes:

> [For understanding another language] the only possibility at the start is to assume general agreement on beliefs. We get a first approximation to a finished theory [of interpretation] by assigning to sentences of a speaker conditions of truth that actually obtain (in our opinion) just when the speaker holds those sentences true. . . . Since charity is not an option, but a condition of having a workable theory, it is meaningless to suggest that we might fall into massive error by endorsing it. Unless we have successfully established a systemic correlation of sentences held true [by another] and sentences held true [by us], there are no mistakes to be made. Charity, is forced on us:—whether we like it or not, *if we want to understand others we must count them right in most matters.*[8]

On such a position, *understanding* would presuppose *agreement*.

But this position is surely untenable—indeed bizarre. It puts us in the position of an unworkable Hobson's choice. For it confronts us with the unpleasant dilemma that, as regards animism, astrology, Democritean atomism, or any abandoned theory-posture of the history of science, we have the choice between agreement and correctness-concession on the one hand, and rejection as unintelligible on the other. Our total rejection of (for example) phlogiston chemistry—or indeed any comparable instance of alterations wrought by cognitive dynamics—would mean that our view toward the theoretical stances at issue is not just that they are incorrect but that they are at bottom unintelligible.

Fortunately, however, this just is not how the matter actually stands. Given a rejected theory-posture *T*, our denial that $t_T(P, S)$

is ever so does not entail denying that u_T (P, S) is ever so. In rejecting *their* stance that u-satisfaction entails t-satisfaction we do not destroy the bridge of understanding. We need not deny that the people who spoke of animistic influences of the evil-eye bewitch-ments or phlogiston-effusions ever did so appropriately on their own linguistic terms of reference—perfectly *intelligibly*, though to be sure *incorrectly* as regards the facts of the matter.

The distinction between truth-conditions and use-conditions enables us to handle these issues in just the right sort of way. We would now say that the people whose linguistic stance espouses T are committed to viewing

$$u_T(S, P) \rightarrow t_T(S, P)$$

as a law of nature. And we ourselves would say that they are simply wrong in this regard: that their linguistic practices are based on factual suppositions as to how things go in the world that are simply incorrect. We are able to say what, in the circumstances, is just the right thing, namely that their ways of speaking are predicated on beliefs about the ways of the world in such a way that the incorrectness of the latter engenders the impropriety of the former—though not, to be sure, in such a way as to engender the *unintelligibility* of the language-employment at issue. Their talk remains perfectly accessible to anyone prepared to undertake the required suspension of disbelief. A. J. Ayer has written as follows:

> [T]here is a sense in which the concept of possession by evil spirits had empirical application. There were criteria for deciding when a person was so possessed; the malady had characteristic symptoms which differentiated it from any other: there was no doubt that these symptoms did occur. At a time when the belief in good and evil spirits was part of popular culture, to deny the possibility of demonic possession might have seemed to be flying in the face of common sense. Nevertheless we now find it perfectly easy to dissociate this concept from the phenomena to which it was taken to apply. We can dismiss the very notion of evil spirits as nonsensical, and still do justice to the facts which sustained it. We simply account for them in a very different sort of way.[9]

The only modification needed here is that where Ayer speaks of disassociating "the concept" from "the phenomena" we our-selves would speak of distinguishing "the truth-conditions" from "the use-conditions."

To be sure, when *we*, from the vantage point of our theoretical stance T* look at *their* commitment to the implication

$$u_T(S, P) \rightarrow t_T(S, P)$$

this principle plays the role of *a position of our own regarding their position. That is, we have*

$$t_{T^*}[u_T(S, P) \rightarrow t_T(S, P)]$$

which does not, of course, yield

$$u_{T^*}(S, P) \rightarrow t_{T^*}(S, P)$$

What is at issue (from our angle) is a *supposed* fact—viz, *their* picture of how things stand in the world. And this may quite unproblematically represent a clear contradiction to our own picture of "the real facts" (let alone the real facts themselves—whatever *they* may be). To repeat: understanding does *not* presuppose agreement. This is one of the lessons of the distinction between use-conditions and truth-conditions.

* * *

As these deliberations indicate, our empirical concepts in gen-eral stand correlative with beliefs, and our conceptual framework in the sphere of factual communication is part and parcel of the wider belief-structure that surrounds it. Accordingly, a concern with concepts and conceptual change and innovation leads un-avoidably into the larger theme of cognitive dynamics, the process of inquiry, and the progress of knowledge. Throughout the factual domain the topics of meaning and inquiry are inseparable.

II

Conceptual Schemes

SYNOPSIS

(1) The background of the idea of diverse conceptual schemes. (2) An exposition of the "Translation Argument" launched against the rationality of this idea. (3) Why this Translation Argument breaks down. (4) The alternativeness of alternative conceptual schemes does not hinge on *inter-translatability* but on their *functional equivalency*. (5) Alternative conceptual schemes involve variant factual (or, rather, fact-purporting) commitments. And, in particular, with cognitive change over time, one does not merely say things differently, but generally says altogether different things. (6) Different schemes need not assign a different determinate truth-status (*T* or *F*) to scheme-overlapping theses; the key to scheme-differentiation lies in the nonoverlap of theses—the fact that what can be said by one is simply outside the range of the other. (7) The untenability of the conception of a ubiquitous scheme-neutral imput that is simply handled differently by different conceptual schemes. (8) The untenability of the idea of form-content separability. The form-oriented issue of *how* people think cannot be hermetically separated from the content-oriented issue of *what* they think. However, the idea of a conceptual scheme is not committed to any such erroneous notions. (9) The difference of conceptual schemes basically resides in a multiplicity of concerns rather than a conflict of contentions: diversity not discord is the key. (10) Though conceptual schemes may be disjointed or incommensurable on the side of ideational meaning-content, they are comparable in regard to the range and effectiveness of the praxis they underwrite. (11) The superiority of our own scheme is by no means a foregone conclusion on this basis.

1. INTRODUCTION

Philosophers have often said things to the effect that people whose experience of the world is substantially different from our own are bound to conceive of it in very different terms. Sociologists, anthropologists, and linguists say much the same sort of things, and philosophers of science have recently also come to talk in this way. According to Thomas Kuhn, for example, scientists who work within different scientific traditions—and thus operate with different descriptive and explanatory "paradigms"—actually "live in different worlds."[1]

Supporting considerations for this position have been advanced from very different points of view. One example is a *Gedankenexperiment* suggested by Georg Simmel in the last century—that of envisaging an entirely different sort of cognitive being,[2] intelligent and actively inquiring creatures (animals, say, or beings from outer space) whose experiential modes are quite different from our own. Their senses respond rather differently to physical parameters—relatively insensitive, say, to heat and light, but substantially sensitized to various electromagnetic phenomena. Such intelligent creatures, Simmel held, could plausibly be supposed to operate within a largely different framework of empirical concepts and categories—the events and objects of the world of their experience might be very different from those of our own—their phenomenological predicates, for example, might have altogether variant descriptive domains. In a similar vein, William James wrote:

> Were we lobsters, or bees, it might be that our organization would have led to our using quite different modes from these [actual ones] of apprehending our experiences. It *might* be too (we cannot dogmatically deny this) that such categories, unimaginable by us to-day, would have proved on the whole as serviceable for handling our experiences mentally as those we actually use.[3]

Different cultures and different intellectual traditions, to say nothing of different sorts of creatures, will, so it has been widely contended, describe and explain their experience—their world as they conceive it—in terms of concepts and categories of understanding substantially different from ours. They may, accordingly, be said to operate with different conceptual schemes, with different conceptual tools used to "make sense" of experience—to characterize, describe, and explain the items that figure in the world as they view it. The taxonomic and explanatory mechanisms by means of which their cognitive business is transacted might differ so radically from ours that intellectual contact with them would be difficult or impossible. Accordingly, we are told such things as, for example, that one cannot secure an adequate grasp on the thought-world of an animistic society if one is unable or unwilling to enter into the thought-framework characteristic of such an approach, adopting what the Germans would call their *Denkmittel*—the conceptual instruments they employ in thought about the facts (or purported facts) of the world.

Recently, however, some philosophers have begun to question this doctrine of variant conceptual schemes. If the idea is conceived of in the standard way, as marking a potential contrast between distinct conceptual schemes—ours vs. theirs—then, so they argue, the whole notion of "alternative conceptual schemes" does not make sense, because the appropriate sort of alternativeness contrast cannot be developed.[4]

This position, however, cannot be taken without paying a substantial price. The notion of "alternative conceptual schemes" has its natural home primarily in four familiar disciplinary settings: (1) in descriptive sociology to contrast the mechanisms used by different societies in the categorization and explanation of human affairs and natural phenomena, (2) in intellectual history to contrast different perspectives of understanding, different *Weltanschauungen,* (3) in the history of the sciences to contrast the diverse explanatory frameworks encountered in different stages of scientific thought, for example, those of Galenic and modern bio-chemical medicine, and (4) in philosophical epistemology to contrast the fundamentally diverse approaches of diverse systems of thought to descriptive and explanatory issues. At any rate, the conception of a "conceptual scheme" that is to be at issue in the present deliberations is one that is geared to applications of this sort. To be in a position to deal realistically with conceptual change, conceptual innovation, and conceptual diversity, we must be in a position to utilize the idea of alternative conceptual parameters that vary in cognitively crucial respects. In brushing aside the idea of "different conceptual schemes," we would deprive ourselves of the means for doing justice to what those who invoke them to clarify such differences were getting at, incurring the risk of an impoverishment in our problem-horizons.

2. THE TRANSLATION ARGUMENT

One influential argument against the idea of alternative conceptual schemes is a line of reasoning, offered by Donald Davidson, which may be characterized as the Translation Argument.[5] The first step of this argument is the relatively unproblematic association of conceptual schemes with languages. A "concept," after all, is not a shadowy and problematic entity of some obscure sort. It is determined by the meanings of words, and stands correlative with the communicative tasks we assign to them in the operations of language. To speak of "concepts" is to do no more than indicate what is inherent in the operation of words—the mission or missions we assign to them as instruments of communication.

The next step is to supplement this association of conceptual schemes with languages by adopting linguistic intertranslatability as a criterion for the identity of these associated conceptual schemes. To quote Davidson:

> [S]peakers of different languages . . . share a conceptual scheme provided there is a way of translating one language into the other. Studying the criteria of translation is therefore a way of focusing on criteria of identity for conceptual schemes.[6]

This leads to the only mildly problematic idea that a failure of translatability is a necessary condition for a difference in conceptual scheme. (The idea is mildly problematic because speakers of one selfsame language could perhaps adopt radically different paradigms for understanding the world—say animism and atomism—and so might conceivably operate with different conceptual schemes despite speaking what would generally be viewed as "the same language.")

A further step in the argument is the rather more controversial contention that one is only entitled to call something a language if one is prepared to claim that one can translate its (putative) "assertions" into one's *own* language.

Davidson defends the position that language attribution requires the access of translatability in the following way:

> [To make sense of the idea of alternative conceptual schemes] we wanted to make sense of there being a language we could not translate at all. Or, to put the point differently, we were looking for a criterion of languagehood that did not depend on, or entail, translatability into a familiar idiom. . . . But whatever plurality we take experience to consist in—events like losing a button or stubbing a toe, having a sensation of warmth or hearing an oboe—we will have to individuate according to familiar principles. A language that organizes *such* entities must be a language very like our own.[7]

It is accordingly maintained that we can only know that something is a conceptual scheme if we can transpose its concepts and categories into those of *our* conceptual scheme. And then, of course, it is not really a radical alternative. The argumentation is now straightforward: intertranslatability establishes sameness of conceptual schemes; translatability into *our* lingo is the test criterion for something's being a language; ergo, one is never in a position, to hold that there are other, genuinely alternative conceptual schemes.

It emerges that the claim of "*alternative* conceptual schemes" involves a contradiction in terms—to establish that a conceptual scheme is present we must translate into our language, to establish alternativeness, the translation must break down, and clearly one cannot have it both ways! Since the idea of "*alternative* conceptual schemes" becomes unworkable, this whole notion of a conceptual scheme whose reason for being is, after all, to provide for a certain sort of *contrast,* comes apart at the seams. This, then, is the Translation Argument.

Note, moreover, that its bearing is even more drastic than might appear at first view. For someone who maintains that *total* intertranslatability between the "languages" associated with "conceptual schemes" is incompatible with alternativeness is now not in a position to concede that alternativeness can obtain in the face of *partial* intertranslatability. For a sequence of partial intertranslatabilities along mediating links can coexist with a total absence of intertranslatability between the mediated extremes. This is readily shown by considering the situation of three languages (A,B,C), each having two sectors. These are to be such that sector of #1 of A is intertranslatable (only) with #1 of B, and #2 of B is intertranslatable only with #2 of C. If alternativeness could be preserved by *partial* intertranslatability, then (given the obvious transitivity of this conception) we would have to regard A and C as alternatives *despite* the fact that there is no intertranslatability between them at all. So if a *total* lack of intertranslatability is to be incompatible with alternativeness—as Davidson and others insist—then we are seemingly constrained to admit that alternativeness cannot subsist on a basis of merely *partial* intertranslatability either.

One would thus arrive at the anomalous-seeming consequence that languages (or conceptual schemes) which merely have pockets that are translation-intractable from one another's standpoint cannot be looked upon as alternatives to one another. The circumstance that the camel terminology of classical Arabic and the automobile terminology of modern English yield mutually untranslatable contentions would be construed to mean that we are precluded from looking on these linguistic frameworks as reflecting distinct conceptual schemes. This upshot seems to leave no room at all for any useful application of the conception.

3. IS TRANSLATABILITY NECESSARY?

There is good reason, however, to think that this focus on actual *translation* is misguided. The key category in this area is surely not *translation* but *interpretation*. What counts for "their having a language" is not (necessarily) that we can literally *translate* what they say into our language, but that we be able to *interpret* at least some of their sayings—to make some sort of intelligible sense of them through paraphrase, "explanation," or the like. This, of course, is something we must do in our own language, but it certainly does not require the sort of transposition we standardly characterize as "translation"—a far looser sort of reinterpretative reconstruction will serve. And such "interpretation" may well involve a complex process of theory building, rather than anything as comparatively cut-and-dried as what is generally understood by "translation." Paraphrase, circumlocution, and all the other make-shifts of linguistic approximation can come into the picture. And often even such avenues to understanding seem too much to demand. It was clear that cuneiform inscriptions represented language-writing well before we had decoded them. As any cryptanalyst knows, one can tell *that* a language is being used, and even a good deal about *how* it is being used, well short of any ability to comprehend—let alone *translate*.

How do we know that the sounds or movements or "writings" being made by those creatures represent the use of a language at all? The rational imputation of language-use is not the result of intellectual inspiration or mystical insight, it is an item of theory building. The closer we can push towards translation, the better. But translation is a desideratum, not a necessity. Interpretative reconstruction can serve perfectly well. Language-attribution, like all empirical theorizing, is a matter of theoretical triangulation from observational data. And such theoretical systematization of the data can render attributions of language-use eminently reasonable.[8]

To establish that a purportedly "alternative language" is a genuine language there is certainly no need to claim intertranslatability with our own language (be it total or partial). This requirement would be much too stringent. We're home safe once we are able to report intelligently and informatively about what they're saying—to *interpret* it. Actual translation into the verbal resources of our language is certainly too much to ask for.

Observe however that once one makes this shift from *translation* to *interpretation,* the analogue of the scheme-countervailing contention "but where *translatability* obtains, there is no difference in the conceptual apparatus at issue" fails to hold. For interpretability is clearly not incompatible with scheme-differentiation. Some interpretative explanation will obviously always be possible no matter how diverse the scheme, seeing that devices like "a sort of *X*," "something rather like our *Y*," "their so-called *Z*'s or "what according to their lights is thus-wise'' and other such ways of establishing relations to our scheme without any actual embedding. Such explicit distancing devices of course do not establish an identity of schemes, but rather the very reverse. Of course, if we're going to understand their scheme then we've got to do it in conceptual terms that are accessible to us—that's both true and trivial. And this triviality certainly does not mean that their concept scheme may not be very massively different from ours—so different that even the somewhat desperate devices of paraphrase and circumlocution and interpretation may only give us a rather tenuous hold on their conceptual dealings. *Au contraire*, a constrained recourse to interpretation rather betokens than negates a difference in conceptual scheme.

An insistence on translatability into our language as test-criterion of the presence of a conceptual apparatus aborts any prospect of grasping how the differences between conceptual schemes actually work. There is and can be no literal translation where the descriptive, taxonomic or explanatory mechanisms— the whole empirically laden paraphernalia of empirical reportage —are substantially different. Linguistic/conceptual schemes differ precisely where, and just to the extent that the resources of paraphrase and circumlocution become necessary. "The congressman appealed to his constituents for understanding regarding his opposition to the economic policies of the administration." Think of translating this into classical Latin! Or of so translating a treatise on quantum electrodynamics. And the same sort of thing holds when the tables are turned. Consider the reverse process of "translation" of a passage into English in the case of the Melanesian utterance whose nearest literal English rendition runs (so we are told) as follows:

> We run front-wood ourselves; we paddle in place;
> we turn, we see behind their sea-arm Pilolu.[9]

It is obvious at a glance that there is no real *translation* going on here, but only a pseudo "translation"—an interpretative process that leaves various key terms inadequately accessible. Yet the matter of language use is never seriously in question.

The fact is that the Translation Argument against alternative conceptual schemes becomes entrapped in a dilemma: If "translation" is construed literally and narrowly, then it indeed follows that language-intertranslatability is incompatible with scheme-alternativeness, but it certainly does not then hold that only translation can establish the claim of another language to qualify as bearer of a conceptual scheme. If, on the other hand, "translation" is construed broadly (to include any sort of reconstrual or interpretation), then a demonstration of scheme-embodiment does indeed require such translatability, but *this* sort of "translation" no longer suffices to show that one selfsame conceptual scheme is at issue. (If merely "giving *some* idea of what's being talked about" is to be called for then we could indeed "translate" a modern chemistry text into the Ionic of Thales and Anaximander.) Either way, the argument comes to grief. And we need not, for present dialectical purposes, enter into the details of the difference between a literal "translation" and an approximate "interpretation" (with its proliferation of expressions of the type: "something like" or "somewhat analagous to"—its admitted lapses from exactitude). All that matters is assured by an informal understanding that a significant distinction is at issue here.

4. THE FUNCTIONAL EQUIVALENCY CONSTRUCTION OF ALTERNATIVE CONCEPTUAL SCHEMES

An analogy may help to clarify the issues. The *intertranslation* standard of "counting as a language" is akin to an *exchange* standard of "counting as money." On such an approach, it is only natural to take our own money as a basis of reference. What makes the German mark *money*—one would then hold—is just that it can be traded against ours at a certain "rate of exchange." If something couldn't be so exchanged, then it just wouldn't be money. This seems a plausible line, but it has serious deficiencies. Consider the Roman denarius. There is just no possibility of an exchange rate across the centuries.[10] As far as exchange rates go, modern dollars and cents and imperial Roman coinage are simply incommensurable units. But that surely does not preclude Roman "money" from qualifying as real *money*.

What qualifies the Roman "coin" to count as a *coin,* a genuine unit of money, is its *functional* role—the way it was used. Various Roman coins are the *functional* equivalent (given the *modus operandi* of Roman life) of our nickels and dimes, and it is this which establishes their claims to be real coins that serve as real money. Coins are what they are because of how they work.

A closely similar story holds for language-use in the contexts of "talk" or "writing" or the like. What makes such processes into uses of a language is their function in communicative transactions: coordinating action, eliciting responses, and so on. Not *translatability* as such, but *functional equivalency* is the determinant of language use: the issue is one as much of sociology as of semantics. What matters is that where certain tasks or objectives, certain areas or purposes are at issue, rather different mechanisms or processes can be used as alternative means toward achieving the same ends.

The teleological aspect is crucial here. Language is an information-processing vehicle, an inherently purposive resource. Ludwig Wittgenstein said somewhere that if lions could talk we could not understand them. But this is nonsense. Precisely because we are fellow mammals, the purposes relating to the acquisition of food and drink, of child care, of danger-detection, etc. are common to us in a way that gives us much insight into their telic situation and would afford us with some grasp on whatever "language" they might have. The operation of our linguistico-conceptual resources as instruments governed by environmentally embedded needs and aims, is a crucial key to their meaning, and *a fortiori,* to their meaningfulness.

To be sure, the following counterargument might be mooted:

> To assess the functional equivalency of *their* putative use of "language" with our unproblematic use of our own, we must know about their aims and purposes. To know this requires knowledge of their beliefs. But we now come up against vitiating circularity engendered by the seeming fact that "knowledge of beliefs comes only with the ability to interpret words."[11]

This objection does not stand. For it is clear that in suitable circumstances we can warrantedly ascribe beliefs as a matter of plausible theorizing on the basis of data regarding *non*-verbal action and behavior—or on the basis of an interpretation of linguistic behavior that stops well short of a capacity to achieve actual *translations*. However much it may be facilitated thereby, the ascription of beliefs does not demand a *prior* decoding of communicative data. (We may be sure that our opponents are signalling one another without recognizing just exactly how they are managing to do so.)

Other languages accordingly qualify as such not necessarily because what they *say* is invariably something that we can say in our own terms, but because what they *do*—their communicative job or function in conveying information and coordinating behavior—is something which is intelligible to us on sufficiently intimate analogy with our own language-using processes. What is at issue is a matter of different ways of going at a common job.[12] By now, some four thousand natural languages have evolved on the planet, and the remarkable thing about them is not so much that it is *difficult* for the speakers of one language to penetrate the thought-framework of another, but that it is *possible* to do so. And this is so, in the final analysis, not because their inherent conceptual schemes are identical, but because their users, endowed with a common biological heritage, face the same sorts of problems in making their way in the world.

To apply the idea of functional equivalency, we must, of course, have some conception of the functions at issue: some insight into the relevant structure of purpose and teleology. Now to be sure, the determination of the goals of other sorts of beings is a complex matter, but in general, the attribution of purposes calls for a substantial element of theorizing. The element of explanatory conjecture and of inductive imputation is at work when we attribute language use to others. And there is nothing anomalous about this. The same holds for the attribution of any talent, skill, or capacity, and indeed even for descriptive categorization (e.g., the claim that yonder tree is an elm). It should come as no surprise that language ascription across conceptual divides should involve an element of theorizing.

That attributions of language use are matters of theorizing—of basing empirical claims on potentially inconclusive data—is clear.

It would need no saying were it not that some philosophers seem to hanker here for a necessitarianism that they reject elsewhere. Thus Richard Rorty writes:

> I doubt that we can ever adumbrate general ways of answering questions like: Is it a conceptual framework very different from our own, or is it a mistake to think of it as a language at all? Is it a person with utterly different organs, responses and beliefs . . . or rather just a complexly behaving thing?[13]

This passage reflects a widespread reluctance to see the questions at issue as fundamentally *factual* questions that have to be resolved on the usual inductive basis of inference to the best explanation—the smoothest systematization of all the relevant facts we can lay our hands on.

On this account, then, it is the functional equilavency of the operations at issue that affords the needed principle of unification and renders diverse linguistic schemes as distinct instances of a common genus. Functional equivalency is the collecting principle that makes them congeners. What, then, renders them *distinct* as instances of this common type?

5. ALTERNATIVE CONCEPTUAL SCHEMES INVOLVE VARIANT FACTUAL COMMITMENTS

To become clear about what a conceptual scheme *is,* it is helpful to become clear as to what it does—how it *works*. A conceptual scheme is inherent in the employment of concepts, and concepts are themselves laden with empirical and factual commitments. For at this time of day it seems plausible to adopt the no longer novel idea—argued by all of the American Pragmatists against Kant— that the categories of human thought are empirical and not *a priori*. The fundamental concepts in terms of which we shape our view of nature—our taxonomic and explanatory mechanisms—are themselves the *a posteriori* products of inquiry.[14] And conceptual schemes differ in just exactly this regard—in undertaking different sorts of factual commitments about how things stand in the world. Our concepts and categories are permeated with a factual view of things, and these factual presuppositions demarcate limits of intelligibility in the conceptualization of experience. We conceptualize our experiences within the framework of a fact-oriented *Weltanschauung*. Different schemes involve different fact-purporting commitments; they embody different "theories" about how matters stand in the world. Such a conceptual scheme represents a Kant-reminiscent "form of understanding," but yet one that is *a posteriori* and empirical—it not only canalizes our view of the "facts of the world" but itself constitutes part and parcel of such a view.

On such a pragmatically oriented line of approach, it transpires that all of our concepts are factually committal—i.e., theory-laden —and that language is not a fact-neutral vehicle for making substantive commitments, but itself reflects such substantive commitments. This point emerges from the consideration that, to use the symbolism of the last chapter, any objectively oriented language is committed to the ampliative transition from use-conditions of its declarations to their truth-conditions—to the transition: $u_L\ (S,\ P) \rightarrow t_L\ (S,\ P)$. Such an "inference license," as we have seen, amounts to a factual commitment, a rudimentary law of nature. A conceptual scheme comes to be correlative with and embedded in a substantive position as to the "facts of the matter."

The history of a conceptual change illustrates clearly this symbiosis between language and beliefs. Consider, for example, what happened in the wake of a shift from, for example, the world view of contact-interaction theorists of the early 17th century to the electromagnetic conception of matter in the post-Maxwellian era. The issue here is not just one of new phenomena, but of new ways of looking at the old phenomena, of different modes of classification, description, explanation. Such innovation makes it possible to say things that could not be said before. It produces a broadening—or at any rate a *displacement* of the conceptual horizons, making it possible to deal with things simply not dreamt of in the old conceptual dispensation.

Innovation—the availability of assertions in one scheme that are simply unavailable in the other—thus affords an important key to understanding their difference. One conceptual scheme will envisage claims that have no even remote equivalents in the other framework. They lie beyond the reach of effective transposition exactly because of the different factual commitments and presuppositions which are involved. Given the change, it is not just that one says things differently, but that one says altogether different things.

6. SCHEME-DIFFERENTIATION AND THE TRUTH-STATUS OF THESES

If the conceptual scheme C' is to be thought of as an *alternative* to C along the lines we have in view, then one cannot think of C' as simply undertaking a comprehensively different assignment of truth values to the (key) propositions of C. One must avoid any temptation to view different conceptual schemes as distributing truth values differently across one selfsame range of propositions. The fact-ladenness of our concepts precludes this, and prevents us from taking the difference of schemes to lie in a pervasive disagreement as to the truth/falsity classification of one fixed body of theses or doctrines.

The difference between conceptual schemes is *not* a matter of treating the *same issues* discordantly, distributing the truth-value T and F differently over otherwise invariant propositions. Different conceptual schemes embody different theories, and not just different theories about "the same things" (so that divergence inevitably reflects disagreement as to the truth or falsity of propositions), but different theories about different things. To move from one conceptual scheme to another is not a matter of disagreeing about the same old issues, it is in some way to change the subject.

The key contrast here is that between saying something and saying nothing—not that between affirmation and counter-affirmation, but that between affirmation and silence. The difference between schemes does not lie in disagreement and conflict, it turns less on what they stand committed to saying than on what they do not and cannot say at all—on matters that simply *defy* any attempt at actual *translation* from the one scheme into the other, and call for the evasive tactics of paraphrase, circumlocution, and "explanation."

Donald Davidson maintains that the innovation involved in

going over from one conceptual scheme to another is based on a
change of mind about the truth-status of claims:

> We get a new out of an old scheme when the speakers of a language
> come to accept as true an important range of sentences they
> previously took to be false (and, of course, vice versa)[15]

But this does not get the matter aright. If one insists on describing
scheme-change in terms of a truth-value *redistribution,* then one
will need to resort to a three-valued framework of truth-values, one
that adds the neutral truth value *(N)* of interdeterminacy or
indefiniteness to the classical values of truth and falsity (*T* and *F*).
For the issue of scheme innovation at bottom turns not on
differences as to determinate truth-values, but on the having of no
truth-value at all, because the item in question lies outside the
boundaries of the conceptual horizon of a certain scheme. And the
key schematic changes are those from a definite (classical) truth-
status to *N* (i.e., from *T* or *F* to *N*) or those in the reverse direction
(i.e., from *N* to *T* or *F*). In the former case, the schematic frame of
reference of an old issue is rejected and it ceases to be meaningful;
in the latter, a new schematic frame of reference is introduced, and
gives meaning to a previously inaccessible issues. The "disagreement" of schemes does *not* turn on a varying truth-assignment to
overlapping theses but on differences as to conceivability (for-
mulatability) of these truths—the *nonoverlap* of theses—the fact
that what can be said by one is simply outside the range of the
other. A change of scheme is not a change of mind but at least in
part a change of subject. (Shades of Feyerabend and conceptual
incommensurability.) Accordingly, the difference of different conceptual frameworks lies not so much in *disagreement* (that #1 says
true where #2 says *false*) as in mutual *incomprehension,* in their
lack of mutual contact.

Thus different schemes are conceptually disjoint in substantial
degree. Certain key questions, theses, and issues of one scheme
are *unavailable* in the other—where one is eloquent, the other is
altogether silent. Various perfectly ordinary assertions from the
perspective of one scheme are altogether *ineffable* from that of the
other. Different schemes face one another across a gulf of

bafflement—total detachment from commitment. (At best #1 can speak of #2's so-called X's and purported Y's or draw on #2 for "loan-words.")

Galenic and Pasteurian medicine, for example, in *some* respects simply *change the subject* so as no longer "to talk about the same things," but rather to talk differently—each about things of which the other takes on cognizance at all. The differences as to "conceptual scheme" between modern and Galenic medicine is not that the modern physician has a different theory of the operation of the four humors from his Galenic counterpart, but that modern medicine has *abandoned* the four humors, and not that the Galenic physician says different things about bacteria and viruses, but that he has *nothing* to say about them—that they lie entirely beyond his conceptual horizon. (As was already noted, the connectability and mutual relevancy of these enterprises is not at bottom a semantical matter—one that turns on the meaning-content equivalency of their assertions—but a matter of their *functional* equivalency.)

The most characteristic and significant sort of difference between one conceptual scheme and another thus does *not* lie in the sphere of *disagreements* or *conflicts* of the sort arising when the one theoretical framework holds something to be *true* that the other holds to be *false*. Rather, it arises when the one scheme is committed to something the other does not envisage at all—something that lies outside the conceptual horizons of the other. The typical case is that of the stance of Cicero's thought-world with regard to questions of quantum electrodynamics. The Romans of classical antiquity did not hold *different* views on these issues; they held no views at all regarding them, because they lay outside their conceptual reach. This whole set of relevant considerations simply lay outside their conceptual repertoire. They did not assign the assertions in question a different truth status from the one we favor, but assigned them no truth values at all.

Different conceptual schemes take us into literally different spheres of thought. They are not incommensurate in the manner of geometric line segments—the side of a square say, and its diagonal—where, after all, very much the same sort of thing, namely *length*, that is involved. Rather, they go their separate ways in very much the same sort of way as different subject matter specialties that deal with altogether different sorts of issues, even when (as per the soldier, the farmer, and the geologist) they address themselves to something which appears as "the same thing" to a detached bystander (the same piece of terrain).

The difference between schemes is accordingly a matter of difference in *orientation* rather than one of disagreement in *doctrine*. It is less like that between the Christian heresies than like that between Christianity and Buddhism. To at least some extent, the denizens of different schemes live in different "thought worlds," as it were.[16] (What is at issue here is something relatively familiar in an era when the phenomena of cultural relativity are well known. In earlier times, when education in the classics was in vogue, one knew at first hand the contrast between the thought-world of classical antiquity and that of one's own day.)

Certainly the upshot of such a defense of conceptual schemes is not just the truism that there are different languages, nor yet the truism that different cultures and eras have different theories as to how things work in the world, important though these truisms are. Rather, the point is that in different cultural/linguistic settings one finds different conceptual mechanisms bound up with different world views in such a way as to make conceptual access difficult, complex, and perhaps even in some measure unattainable. At this juncture we are led back to the Wittgensteinean point that the limit's of one's language are the limits of one's world: that one's conceptual apparatus canalizes and delimits the range of facts one is in a position to entertain. (But of course to say that we cannot manage to "see" the world in the manner of a primitive, animistic society is very far from saying that we "cannot form a rough general idea" of their ways of talking, and that we cannot *interpret* their claims across the conceptual divide that separates us.)

7. THE MYTH OF A UBIQUITOUS, SCHEME-NEUTRAL INPUT

It will shed useful light upon conceptual schemes to consider certain misconceptions regarding them and to set aside errors sometimes imputed to their partisans—errors to which they in fact do not or need not stand committed to.

Conceptual schemes are sometimes objected to as based on a commitment to the view that there is one selfsame underlying substratum—one ubiquitously present, uniform, cognitive raw material of pure experience, bare sensation, elemental stimuli, or whatever—which different conceptual schemes (languages) proceed to process differently. Let us accordingly begin with the following objection:

> To adopt the idea of conceptual schemes is to commit oneself to the notion of a scheme-neutral epistemic basis—an ur-text, as it were, of raw (conceptually "uncooked") experience, sensation, or some such "given"—which different languages manipulate within their own conceptual idiom. The concept presupposes the model of *mediation* through language and concepts of a "thought-independent" givenness—an "an sich" world of preschematic representeds which we schematize into representations by means of concepts and language. The partisans of conceptual schemes must think of language as a way of depicting or encoding a (somehow) given, extralinguistic reality—of transforming one determinate structure into another. But (so the objection continues) any reality we can conceive of—any reality we can *say* anything about—is *already* linguistically and conceptually mediated. The idea of a "thought-independent reality" that is *prior* to the mechanisms of conceptualizing thought—a reality that lies "behind the curtain" of schematic conceptualization—is thus gravely misleading. The real is simply and solely "what we can really and truly say or think to be the case" and not an extra-conceptual substratum represented in our thought by the mediation of languages and conceptual schemes. The idea of conceptual schemes accordingly stands committed to an incorrect and improper model—that of a linguistic/conceptual processing of pre-schematic but yet determinate experiential inputs.

This objection views the conception of a conceptual scheme as predicated upon the model of a common, preexistent raw material input which is processed differently by different schemes. And this processing is to be thought of as subject to the idea of a single, invariant reality that is represented differently from the different "point of view" of various conceptual schemes[17] which themselves are so many distinct conventionalizations. Every scheme is to filter this shared reality through concepts in its own way, so that each filtering medium imposes its own characteristic imprint upon scheme-neutral reality—the way the world *really* is.[18]

The supposition of a diversity of conceptual schemes is accordingly objected to as based upon a mistaken form/content dualism in projecting the picture of invariant, universally shared, pre-schematic input which different conceptual schemes process differently. The idea of conceptual schemes, so it is held, is committed to the Myth of a Ubiquitous, Scheme-Neutral Input.[19] Donald Davidson has put the matter as follows:

> [R]etaining the idea of language as embodying a conceptual scheme . . . [means that] in place of the dualism of the analytic-synthetic we get the dualism of conceptual scheme and empirical content. . . . I want to urge that this second dualism of scheme and content, of organizing system and something waiting to be organized, cannot be made intelligible and defensible.[20]

It is only too clear that this whole model of the schematizing of a preschematic raw material is indeed objectionable. For it is always problematic to have explanatory recourse to something whose nature we cannot possibly describe (or can describe only as having no nature). And there just is no way of describing whatever "inputs" our cognitive processes may have, apart from the results to which these processes themselves lead us. (As Kant saw it, there is no positive descriptive information that can be offered regarding the *Ding an sich* which Sensibility is thought to deliver up to the cognitive processing of our Understanding.)

Even if one were to grant *in abstracto* the existence of a pre-schematically *given* over and over the schematically graspable, there is nothing one can *do* with this conception—there is no way of implementing this distinction, of *applying* it to something or other. Our cognition of the real is a matter of a *transaction* in which the respective contributions of thought and reality just cannot be separated off from one another.[21]

The decisive shortcoming of the idea of a pre-schematized "given" as an explanatory instrument of the theory of cognition is simply and *ex hypothesi* that one cannot possibly say anything about what this given is—that it inherently and necessarily lies beyond the reach of conceptualization. No intelligible content can be given to this idea. To invoke it is thus not to explain the obscure by the yet more obscure, it is to explain it by the impenetrable. As Richard Rorty has trenchantly put it, "the suggestion that our concepts shape neutral material no longer makes sense once there is nothing to serve as this material.[22] We must not become entranced by the metaphor of "seeing the same thing from different points of view" in a case where it is only too clear that there just is no earthly way of saying anything concrete about "the same thing" that is purportedly at issue. If "objects of thought" are always *constituted* relative to conceptual schemes (which, after all, represents the role and mission of such schemes), then there cannot—*ex hypothesi*—be any identifiable presystematic *something* for such schemes to schematize.

The issue is amusingly illustrated in an example of A. J. Ayer's, who writes that "[If] the members of a primitive tribe attribute every natural occurrence to the moods of Mumbo Jumbo, we may have no doubt that they are utterly deluded: nevertheless we do not want to deny their ability to detect that it is raining, even though they see the rain as the expression of Mumbo Jumbo's grief."[23] Where we think of rain as a matter of "drops of water falling *en masse* from oversaturated clouds in the sky", our natives *(ex hypothesi)* think of "Mumbo Jumbo weeping innumerable tears in the heavens." However, Ayer's reading of this situation is clearly problematic. For it would surely be a travesty to represent a natives' claim by stating, "They're saying that it's raining." Given the difference in approach it is hard to conceive of an honestly scheme-neutral formulation of "a common phenomenon" such that both they and we think of IT in our two distinctive ways. There simply is no specifiable scheme-neutrally invariant something that different schemes treat in their own several ways. To take such a stance would be to succumb once more to the Myth of the God's Eye View.

Let all this be granted, as it should and must be. All the same, the presently envisaged use of these considerations as a *point d'appui* for an objection to conceptual schemes as somehow improper and inappropriate. For this objection is based on the mistaken idea that the conception of diverse conceptual schemes rests on the presupposition of an incorrect and objectionable processing model according to which there is an invariant identifiable and thus describable raw material which is viewed differently from the perspective of different conceptual schemes. But this is quite wrong. This quasi-Kantian model of a difference-engendering schematic processing of a uniform pre-schematic raw material is nowise essential to the idea of different conceptual schemes. The idea of preexisting "thought-independent" and scheme-invariant reality that is seen differently from different perceptual perspectives just is not an inevitable presupposition here.

The partisan of different conceptual schemes, as this notion has been used in intellectual history and sociology, and as it can be used in philosophical epistemology, certainly need *not* espouse the thesis:

> (1) that there is a pre- or sub-linguistic cognitive substratum, and different languages afford us different ways to telling about IT (this preexisting substratum).

Rather, he only stands committed to what results when the difficulty-generating words of this proposition are deleted, to yield the contention

> (2) that different languages afford us different ways of talking—of saying different sorts of things, rather than saying "the same things" differently or making different claims about "the same thing."

Accordingly, in holding that there are different conceptual schemes one is not committed to the view that they must *disagree about the same thing*. To implement the notion that different conceptual schemes are at work we emphatically do not need to say that Aristotle, Newton, and Einstein "are making different claims about the same thing" in saying that the cosmos is spherical in the one case and that space-time is a four-dimensional and finite-but-boundless manifold in the other case. It is quite enough to hold that different schemes say different things "on the same theme" (*functionally* identified) rather than talking differently about the same object" (*substantively* identified). Both Galenic and Pasteurean medicine deal with classifying and explaining and treating maladies—though that does not render the respective entities they envisage capable of correlation nor make their characteristic *termina technica* inter-translatable. The correlation at issue can proceed via *functional* equivalency rather than via equivalency of designation. The view that failure of translatability shows the absence of language and of concepts founders on the fact that language-use never exists *in vacuo,* but always functions in a purposive context in which functional equivalency can fill the vacuum of conceptual inaccessibility.

If one holds—as only seems proper—that all individuation, all identification, and all description must proceed on the basis of a conceptual scheme, then it would clearly be inappropriate to say there is an identifiable something (reality, experience, *materia prima,* the manifold of sense-stimuli, or whatever) that is prior to and independent of any and all scheme based conceptualization. On such an approach, the notion of "scheme-independent reality" is not *constitutive,* not a substantive something that actually composes or constitutes the world—in contrast with the "mere appearances" present to our minds. Rather, this capital-R Reality represents a purely *regulative* idea whose function is to block the pretentions of any one single scheme to a monopoly on correctness or finality. The partisans of conceptual schemes take on a commitment to scheme-independent "things in themselves" which is not substantive, but represents a purely regulative contrast-device.[24]

Accordingly, the objection at issue does not invalidate a sensible approach to the idea of different conceptual schemes. For the erroneous conception of a common, identifiable, raw-material input is by no means an inherent and inevitable facet of the idea of conceptual schemes as such. As we have seen, in speaking of different conceptual schemes we need not say that different language communities "formulate *the same materials* (experience, sensation, or whatever) differently," but just that they employ different sorts of formulations in their fact-purporting discourse. We can say their descriptive practices differ without saying that they do so by way of offering different descriptions for *the same thing.*[25] Only a mistaken insistence on viewing scheme-differentiation in terms of a redistribution of classical truth values would constrain resort to such a mechanism to assure the community of focus needed to ground disagreement among schemes.

On a proper understanding of what conceptual schemes are and how they actually work, one can abandon entirely the myth of a uniform, shared, pre-schematic input without thereby being constrained to give up the idea of different conceptual schemes.

8. THE MYTH OF FORM-CONTENT SEPARABILITY

Kant taught that perception cannot be separated from conception—that in the domain of empirical fact, observation cannot be separated from descriptive characterization. Extending this line of thought, his latter-day Quinean successors stress that conception cannot be separated from judgment, that issues of *meaning* cannot be separated from issues of *fact* or purported fact, that "what we mean by words" in descriptive discourse and "what propositions we accept as true" are inseparably and inextricably commingled issues.

This position involves a crucial departure from Kant by replacing what he sees as an *a priori* synthesis inherent in the faculty-structure of the human mind by a less ambitious *empirical* synthesis built into an experentially based *Weltanschauung,* or some sector thereof. Once again, our concepts are seen as usable only within "the limits of possible experience," but *possible experience* now means *empirically* possible, that is, possible relative to the empirical commitments of a view of how things work in the world—and thus *actually* possible and not, as with Kant, *transcendentally* possible. Our position, though Kantian in its fundamental structure, replaces his *conceptual* necessity by a more modest factual counterpart (i.e., hypothetical necessity reliable to a foundation of experientially based commitments as to the ways of the world). There is an intimate, nay indissoluble interlinkage between the meanings of one's terms and the facts (or purported facts) one uses them to state: the meanings of words are shaped in terms of their user's beliefs about the issues. Meanings (concepts) are thus fact-correlative. They are at once the bearers *and also the creatures* of our factual beliefs, and are not only tools of inquiry, but also products thereof.

It is widely stressed nowadays that our conceptual schemes in the empirical domain are based upon views as to the facts or purported facts about the world; that empirical concepts are "theory permeated," to use Karl Popper's term: that they involve facts and are inconceivable without them. Our conceptual mechanisms evolve in an historical feed-back dialectic between cognitive projection on the one hand and experiential interaction with nature upon the other. They are globally *a posteriori* as products of past experience; they are only locally *a priori*, in that we bring them to the context of current experience and never operate with a conceptual *tabula rasa*.

In consequence of this interlinkage of meaning and belief it follows that "one will not be able to draw a clear distinction between the foreigner's using words different in meaning from any words in our language and the foreigner's having many false beliefs."[26] This general line of thought envisages a paradigm situation of the following type. Consider the case of someone whom we take (at first blush) to say about dogs exactly what we ourselves would say about cats (that they meow rather than bark, that they generally chase mice but not mailmen, etc.). As this circumstance emerges more fully, we ourselves would (very rightly) begin to wonder if we've got it right in thinking that they are talking about *dogs* but have very bizarre ideas about them, rather than that we've got it wrong and that they are really talking about *cats* after all (but using a somewhat odd nomenclature).

There is an inevitable tradeoff between the attribution of weird *beliefs* to others and the prospect of *misunderstanding* on our part—of error in our construction of their assertions. For that they really mean to talk about DOGS is in fact a *theory of ours* (with respect to a certain equivalency in translation or interpretation), and in framing such interpretative theories, we are governed by the precept: Adapt your interpretative hypotheses so as to maximize truth, to make as much as you can come out to be true. Interpretation *is*, after all, a matter of theory-building, and here the usual inductive standards of optimal systematization apply—of arranging our cognitive commitments with a view to the overall smoothness of their dovetailings.

It follows that one cannot handle meaning and truth *sequentially* as per the injunction: "Settle issues of meaning first, for only then can you profitably address yourself to issues of truth!" One cannot separate questions of the *meaning of terms* (how our concepts function in their linguistic setting) from questions of *truth-imputation* (views as to how matters go in the world). Meaning and truth—or, in large purview, semantics and science—emerge as interdependent and symbiotic throughout the factual domain. To grasp a language requires understanding the conceptual scheme it implements and thus requires knowing (at least in rough outline) what sort of world-view its users hold—their picture of the "laws of nature" (or some functional equivalent thereof).

Alternative *theories* always enter into alternative *concept-frameworks*. Quine's assault on dualism in this sphere stands valid: inquiry into meanings (word-use) and into purported facts (i.e., beliefs and opinions) must be handled as one holus-bolus enterprise within the overall system of which they are inseparable components.[27]

Now there is certainly a questionable and erroneous way of conceiving of a conceptual scheme—viz., as external to and detachedly "underlying" the *cognitive* scheme of its exponents (their *Weltanschauung*)—as dealing formally with the conceptual machinery of their thought quite independently of their materially substantive beliefs. This is surely wrong. Meaning-content and conceptual structure are interdependent issues. Clearly the form-oriented issue of *how* people think—of the categorial and taxonomic framework of their discourse—cannot be hermetically separated from the content-oriented issue of *what* they think, of the substantive materials of their beliefs.

But this incorrectness is nowise built into the idea of a conceptual scheme as such. There is—and this deserves great emphasis—*no need whatever* to subscribe to this view and to construe the idea of conceptual scheme as irrevocably committed to this rationalist notion of a neat form-content separability. There is no obstacle to construing conceptual schemes as part and parcel of a wider cognitive framework in which matters of concept-machinery and empirical substance stand in inextricable inter-linkage.

* * *

It would seem that the animus of various recent writers against the idea of conceptual schemes is largely due to their construing the notion as committed to the Myth of a Ubiquitous Scheme-Neutral Input (as per the deliverances of Kant's *sensibility*) and the Myth of Form-Content Separability (as per the schematizing labor of Kant's *understanding*). But this perspective unjustly visits upon conceptual schemes a construction geared too closely to the Kantian processing-faculty model, a construction from which this resource can certainly be extricated, and from which it is in fact free throughout most of its recent invocations.

The important point from this perspective is that the conception of a conceptual scheme as such is patently strong enough to survive the abandonment of such mistaken conceptions. The fact that conceptual schemes can be misconceived is no reason for invalidating the very idea at issue. (Mistaken conceptions can be had of virtually anything!) The notion of a conceptual scheme can survive the abandonment of such misconceptions about how conceptual schemes work as are at issue in the Myth of a Ubiquitous Scheme-Neutral Content or the Myth of Form-Content Separability.[28]

9. THE ALTERNATIVENESS OF CONCEPTUAL SCHEMES

In what sense can it be said that distinct conceptual schemes are *alternative* to one another? If it cannot be maintained that they process the same material differently—if they do not "make discordant claims about 'the same' facts" because their relationship is one of discontinuity and mutual incomprehension—how, then, can they conflict? The answer is that, strictly speaking, they do not disagree. They do not involve the sort of logical conflict that arises when one body of commitments claims one thing and another claims something incompatible about the very same item. The differences of diverse conceptual schemes basically rests in a multiplicity of concerns with a diversity of truths, rather than in a contradictory treatment of the same facts.

To be sure, if we ourselves are to make trans-scheme comparisons, this is, of course, something that we can and must do from the vantage point of *our own* scheme. Here our own stance is determinative: it is a *theory of ours* (an "equivalency hypothesis") that their *X* is our *Y*—their *canis* our *dog*. Trans-scheme comparisons must be effected by us from our own standpoint (we have no other!)[29] Does this not mean that "the same facts" must be at issue? Thus let *L* be our language scheme and let *L* 1 and *L* 2 be two other schemes under consideration. Note now that such use-condition coordination theses as $u_{L1}(S, P) \rightarrow t_{L1}(S, P)$ and $u_{L2}(S, Q) \rightarrow t_{L2}(S, Q)$ are in effect both theses of *our own* scheme *L*. Since *we* do the mediating, we do so on our terms: if *we* are to effect a comparison, then it must be effected in *our own* terms. Where we discern alternativeness, we do so in our own way. (Compare §6 of Chapter I.)

But such egocentric discernment is nowise a requisite for alternatives *per se*. Our evidence for the difference of schemes is one thing, the nature of such a difference itself is something else again. To be sure, if we are to discern the difference, we will do so from our own point of departure. But the difference can subsist without being mediated *ab extra* by us—or indeed by any third party. The fact of the matter is one thing and its being noted by us is something else. (We do doubtless deploy our own scheme in the course of taking note.)

We are told by Davidson that:

> Different points of view make sense, but only if there is a common coordinate system on which to place them; yet the existence of a common system belies their incomparability.[30]

But this is surely wrong—at any rate as long as we are not concerned with different points of view for viewing *the same things*. The domain of one novel, for instance, may be physically discontinuous with that of another: no common coordinate schemes unite the realms of the diverse approaches and disciplines—that of the impressionist and that of the contrast painter, for example. To insist on the coordination of a common system is once more to succumb to the Myth of the God's Eye View, as per Paul Feyerabend's problematic suggestion that schemes can be compared by "choosing a point of view outside the system or language," because behind all schemes and languages "there is still human experience as an actually existing process."[31] The alternativeness of schemes, just does not call for their alternative treatment of *the same* facts.

Yet if conceptual schemes do not actually conflict—if they do not disagree about the same things, then why not simply *conjoin* them, espousing one alongside the others? Several things must be said (somewhat telegraphically) in reply: (1) We do in fact to some extent do this, adjoining the scheme of science to that of ordinary life, for example. Or, again, think of the scholar's ability to move in the thought-worlds of different cultures or civilizations. (2) There are, however, weighty practical reasons why the extent to which we can do this is very limited: It is enormously demanding in learning and effort and attention. Even as very few people can master more than one language well enough to "pass for a native" in it, so only few can achieve a conceptual repertoire that makes them fully at home in significantly diverse conceptual frameworks. (3) In general, any fairly comprehensive conceptual scheme embodies a value-orientation in point of specifically *cognitive* values. It encorporates its own characteristic schedules of what sorts of things are important, interesting, puzzling, worthy of attention, etc. And this circumstance also produces limiting restrictions in that diverse desiderata, even if theoretically compatible, jostle one another off center stage. A concept-scheme is a demanding master: it is difficult to give allegiance to several. Most importantly, (4) different concept-schemes bear differentially upon praxis. The rules of chess do not conflict doctrinally with those of tennis. But few people can play chess and tennis at the same time. And a physician is unlikely to prescribe dual treatment in line with distinct medical systems.

As these considerations suggest, conceptual schemes do not conflict in the manner of mutually contradictory bodies of assertions. Rather they conflict in the manner of diverse instrumentalities—the manner in which we cannot make effective concurrent use of hammer and saw. It is this sort of *practical* incompatibility of diverse modes of operation—distinct functional resources—in the alternativeness of diverse conceptual schemes, rather than the *theoretical* incompatibility of mutual contradiction via conflicting theses.

10. THE APPRAISAL OF CONCEPTUAL SCHEMES

It is germane to consider briefly the question of the appraisal and evaluation of the relative merits of alternative conceptual schemes. If the situation were simply that the difference between schemes resided in a different distribution of the determinate truth-values T and F over fundamentally the same range of contentions, then the assessment of relative merits would be a rather simple process: we would simply ask ourselves which is right more often. And then, of course, we would have no alternative but to answer this question with reference to the truth-commitments that emanate from *our own* conceptual scheme. Scheme-assessment would have to be a matter of simply determining which scheme has a fuller grasp on the facts as we ourselves see them—of determining which is right about more things and wrong about fewer according to our own lights (the only one's we've got!). And, of necessity, it lies in the very nature of this process that our own scheme will always emerge victorious from such comparisons.

Again, something of the same sort would obtain if we were to compare schemes on the basis of subject-matter *coverage* (being ampler, richer, fuller, etc.). For *whose standards* as to what is a genuine enlargement and what is a pointless proliferation are going to be used here—which scheme can appropriately be used as the arbiter? Clearly, we would here be driven back once more to a reliance on the arbitrament of our own scheme. Any such consequence is surely unacceptable. There is, as we have seen, no proper justification for assigning a position of privacy to our own scheme. We are neither minded to nor justified in seeing ourselves as the center of the cognitive axis about which all else revolves.

Such considerations indicate the inappropriateness of a content-comparison approach to the issue of appraisal. They suggest—surely rightly—that comparative appraisal must be detached altogether from the sphere of *semantical* issues, and kept away from considerations of truthfulness, subject-matter coverage, or any other such consideration relating to a comparison of assertive content. For otherwise we would have little alternative but to advance our own scheme automatically into a position of standard of comparison, and so run afoul of that intellectual modesty which is not only seemly but wise in human affairs.

But how can linguistic frameworks and their correlative conceptual schemes possibly be compared on a linguistically neutral, meaning-abstractive basis? The answer here lies in recognizing that the appropriate basis of comparison is *pragmatic efficacy*. The traditional pragmatists have just put the key point well—C. I. Lewis, for example:

> There may be alternative conceptual systems, giving rise to alternative descriptions of experience, which are equally objective and equally valid, if there be not some purely logical defect in these categorial conceptions. When this is so, choice will be determined, consciously or unconsciously, on pragmatic grounds. New facts may cause a shifting of such grounds. When historically such change of interpretation takes place we shall genuinely have new truth, whose newness represents the creative power of human thought and the ruling consideration of human purpose. . . . [O]nce the categorial system, in terms of which it is to be interpreted, is fixed, and concepts have been assigned a denotation in terms of sensation and imagery, it is this given experience which determines the truths of nature. It is between these two, in the choice of conceptual system for application and in the assigning of sensuous denotation to the abstract concept, that there is a pragmatic element in truth and knowledge. In this middle ground of trial and error, of expanding experience and the continual shift and modification of conception in our effort to cope with it, the drama of human interpretation and the control of nature is forever being played.[32]

Even as scheme eligibility (i.e., *counting* as a conceptual scheme) is a teleological matter of *functional equivalency,* so scheme merit (i.e., counting as a *relatively good* conceptual scheme) is a matter of *functional efficacy.* The standard of judgment is that of the question: Which scheme underwrites more efficient and effective intervention in the course of events so as to conduct towards those desiderata for whose sake languages and their conceptual schemes are instituted as human resources in the context of communication and inquiry.

As pragmatists have rightly stressed (and some of the sceptics before them), languages and conceptual instrumentalities have been developed to facilitate effective action within our environing world. The pragmatic standard of successful praxis thus affords a natural and *semantically neutral* arbiter of our conceptual mechanisms. The efficacy of *their* scheme is not a matter of the extent to which it leads to results that agree with *ours,* but rather of the extent to which it facilitates their attainment of *their* purposes. Schemes may be disjoint or incommensurable on the side of issues of conceptual meaning-content, but they do indeed enter into mutual relevancy on the side of praxis. Their relative superiority or inferiority is emphatically *not* an issue of how much of the somehow scheme-neutral truth they manage to capture (how close they come to grasping the content of God's Mind), let alone of how much it brings them into agreement with us. Rather, it hinges on the practical issue of how effectively they enable us to find our way amidst the shoals and narrows of a difficult world.[33]

Schemes have often proved deficient (as per the animistic account of nature or the magical account of human interactions via such mechanisms as the evil eye). Yet such deficiency does not reside in any *theoretical* defect that would have been revealed by an arm-chair analysis of contents, but is the result of flaws—or, rather, comparative inferiorities—that ultimate manifested themselves on the pragmatic side. Here then we once again have a token of the primacy of practical over theoretical reason.[34]

It warrants stress that in this regard the question of the merits of our own scheme is by no means an academic one—its victory in the comparison process is by no means a foregone conclusion. Let us explore this issue.

11. THE QUESTION OF THE INHERENT SUPERIORITY OF OUR OWN CONCEPTUAL SCHEMES

Given that different linguistic-conceptual schemes can be evaluated along such lines as have been sketched (with conceptual disjointness superengrafted upon functional equivalency), what can in fact be said regarding the comparative merits of our own scheme? Seeing that it provides us with the paradigm standard in whose terms we ourselves do in fact take the measure of all else—a consideration that establishes its epistemic *priority* (for us, at any rate)—must we not concede to it a position of theoretical *primacy* as well? By no means! The present position does not entail the view that we ourselves constitute the center about which everything moves. We must resist all temptations to the egocentrism of putting ourselves and our parochial group at the center of all things.

To be sure, an objector might well attempt the following line:

> In chosing to transact your cognitive business within its framework, you surely commit yourself, at least implicitly, to a primacy claim. Do not your very actions betoken a preference for this scheme over others?

An emphatic denial is in order here. Our use of a scheme nowise involves us in claiming it as the best of all possible schemes. In adopting a scheme we simply "do what comes naturally." We simply use a tool that lies conveniently to hand. We actually have little overt choice here—we simply have to go on from where we are.

On first thought it might seem that we have to construe the idea of different conceptual schemes roughly as follows:

> The descriptive practices of Scheme #1 differ from those of Scheme #2 in that Scheme #1 treats such and such as issue A-wise, while Scheme #2 treats it B-wise.

Such a view immediately advances our own language/conceptual scheme into a controlling position. For it is going to be necessary to use *our* machinery to do the crucial work of (1) specifying the issue in question, and (2) describing the two different manners in which the schemes at issue treat this issue. It becomes a matter of transacting all the relevant comparisons and contrasts within the framework of our own conceptual scheme. Our own language/ scheme becomes the pivot point around which all else revolves.

But this just isn't how the matter actually stands. Neither on a cultural nor on a temporal comparison basis are we committed to the idea that the framework or our own thinking is inherently superior. Nothing stands in the way of a realization that ours is *not* inherently the best conceptual scheme—a kind of *ne plus ultra*.

Consider how cognitive progress happens. We can admit THAT the scientists of the future will have a better science, an ampler and more adequate understanding of the natural universe, and thus a better conceptual scheme—though, admittedly, we cannot anticipate just HOW this is to be so. We need not take the stance that our own conceptual scheme is somehow the last word. Our recognition *that* our scheme is imperfect, though correct and appropriate in the interests of realism, is, to be sure, of rather limited utility. A realization of the *en gros* deficiency of our conceptual machinery unhappily affords no help towards its emendation in matters of detail.

Nevertheless, this realization of the presumptive suboptimality of our own conceptual scheme plays a most useful role. It affords a *regulative* conception that preempts any claim to dogmatic finality, even if not a *constitutive* one that puts substantively informative data at our disposal. The presumption that there are other and perhaps better conceptual schemes than ours is eminently salutary in blocking the path to the deplorably egocentric view that we ourselves somehow stand at the cognitive center of things, occupying that pivotal position about which all else revolves.

Moreover this recognition of the prospect of superior alternative schemes is useful in another regard. The prospect of a real and possibly superior alternative forces us to come to grips with the issue of justification. (If there are no alternatives, it is simply a matter of this-or-nothing.) The concern for the provision of a justificatory rationale—a demonstration of valid applicability, a Kantian "deduction"—is pivotal, and can only be brought to a satisfactory resolution if we face a situation of alternativeness. And on the present approach the justificatory rationale at issue is seen as coming to rest ultimately not on the basis of the general principles of theoretical reason, but only on those of considerations of practical reason.

* * *

This chapter has been concerned to extend and consolidate its predecessor's insistence on the interlinkage of judgments and beliefs with meanings, theories, and concepts. These considerations are central to a proper grasp of the nature of inquiry.

For the conceptual terms of reference in which one frames problems and questions always emerge from and stand coordinate with an earlier state of knowledge. Concepts, questions, and theses (= answers) do not stand in a linear order of succession, but emerge in a cyclic dynamic of feedback and reciprocity of interrelation. This state of things becomes yet clearer when we turn to the theme of *categories* and examine the character of the terms of reference through which we formulate our questions about the nature of things.

III

Categories

SYNOPSIS

(1) Categories are correlative with questions; they are *the terms of reference* under whose aegis which we frame our questions about the world. The distinction between the *protocategories* that delineate our basic, starting-point questions regarding the ways of the world, and the sophisticated scientific categories that are ultimately developed in the course of grappling with these questions. (2) The traditional philosophical theory of categories is oriented towards the protocategories. (3) Categorial metaphysics is the systematic study of the relations obtaining among these traditional categories. (4) The nature of scientific categories. Their systematic ordering and rationalization is an important integral part of the scientific venture itself. (5) Historically, categorial metaphysicians have also striven to provide a theoretical rationale for the traditional categories. But this project of category-rationalization at the protolevel is a vain and Quixotic quest. (6) However, we cannot treat the protocategories as a ladder to be abandoned once we have climbed it. The protocategories are continually needed to establish the relevancy of our scientific discussions to the fundamental question-resolving mission of science. (7) Yet they are not immutable, but can themselves respond to scientific change, in that there is an eventual impact upon them through feed-back from the answers we give in the course of inquiry.

1. TWO TYPES OF CATEGORIES

The agenda of our cognitive business is set by our questions. And in the forefront here lies the key domain of our *factual* questions regarding "the nature of things," that is, about the furnishings of the world we live in and their modes of operation.

61

Categories are correlative with these factual questions. They delineate and canalize our efforts to secure information about the world. They provide the conceptual *frame of reference* in terms of which we pose our questions about the nature of things—the cognitive scaffolding we employ in erecting our view of the world, or some sector thereof. "To think is to order," said Thomas Aquinas, and the categories we use are our conceptual ordering tools, our devices for setting out on the task of collecting, gathering, and arranging our thoughts about how things stand. The theory of categories is accordingly the study of the means we use in structuring the agenda of the issues that we face in our thought about the facts (or purported facts) of the world.

Consider, for example, the issue of human actions. Here we are immediately confronted with a rather extensive catalogue of questions that can arise, as set out in Table 1.

Table 1

THE CHARACTERIZING ELEMENTS OF AN ACTION

(1) *Agent* (WHO did it?)
(2) *Act-type* (WHAT did he do?)
(3) *Modality of Action* (HOW did he do it?)
    a. Modality of manner (IN WHAT MANNER did he do it?)
    b. Modality of means (BY WHAT MEANS did he do it?)
(4) *Setting of Action* (IN WHAT CONTEXT did he do it?)
    a. Temporal aspect (WHEN did he do it?)
    b. Spatial aspect (WHERE did he do it?)
    c. Circumstantial aspect (UNDER WHAT CIRCUMSTANCES did he do it?)
(5) *Rationale of Action* (WHY did he do it?)
    a. Causality (WHAT CAUSED him to do it?)
    b. Finality (WITH WHAT AIM did he do it?)
(6) *Effects of Action* (What EFFECTS or PRODUCTS or CONSEQUENCES did the action have? What REACTIONS did it engender?)
(7) *Significance of Action* (What does it MEAN or SHOW or PORTEND?)

Such a thematic inventory of questions delineates the categories of the domain. These operative categories define the range of the issues, and set the terms of reference of our question-positing concerns.

Questions come in strata. There are the proto-questions with which inquiry begins, the elemental and elementary issues from which we start our cognitive explorations. These categories relate to questions which are "superficial", as it were, in lying near the surface of inquiry. But we are soon led to greater depths. The answers to our questions spawn yet further questions. And as we proceed along this question-and-answer route we come to increasingly sophisticated questions which arise out of our answers to earlier questions, and which themselves lead in turn to still more complex issues.

Categories thus arise at two levels. At one level we have the *protocategories* that delineate the "protoquestions" we face at the outset—the most basic and rudimentary questions that initially get the process of factual inquiry under way. Such questions are inventoried in Table 2, which summarizes the most elementary basic and fundamental sorts of issues to be raised about the furniture of the world. As this listing makes clear, categories delineate the various question-orientations, and categorial themes set the "frame of reference" for answering the sorts of questions at issue.

Protocategories accordingly delineate the terms of reference within which we frame our first-line answers to those rudimentary questions that initiate our journey towards ever more sophisticated questions. The protocategories define the conceptual issues that shape our initial, most basic efforts at posing our descriptive and explanatory questions about the world. The frame of reference of our first entry into the question/answer process is comparitively rudimentary because at this initial stage, we have not as yet exchanged the rough and ready resources of everyday life for the sophisticated precision of science. Nevertheless, even these rudimentary, starting-point questions have certain categorical orientations, because the very "meaning" of a question is bound up with the general *sort* of answer towards which it looks as a possible (admissible) response to the issue it sets out to raise. (At *every* level our questions are geared to a frame of reference that delineates the range of admissible answers.)

The protocategories thus contrast with the more sophisticated S-categories (*scientific* categories) that are correlative with the more developed questions we are eventually driven to in the pursuit of increasing adequacy. They relate to the way-stages and destinations rather than to the starting-points of our questionings.

Table 2

PROTOCATEGORIAL QUESTIONS

Categorial Process	*Paradigm Question*	*Categorial Themes*
I. identification	which one?	things or items
II. classification	of what kind?	types or species of items
III. description	of what properties? what manner?	characterizing qualities, features, attributes, characteristics
IV/1. affiliation	like what or which?	similarity comparisons
IV/2. subordination	to what or which? of what or which?	pertinence relations
IV/3. location	when? where? whence? whither?	the positioning of things in frameworks of placement
IV/4. composition	composed of what? how constituted?	the make-up and structuring of things
IV/5. quantification	of what size or magnitude (in this or that respect?)	the measurement of things
IV/6. process-characterization	in what way? by what means?	*modus operandi* (modes of manner and means of comportment)
V/1. function-specification	to what end? for what purpose? with what point?	purposes, aims, functions, teleological considerations
V/2. rationalization (or explanation)	why so? how to be explained? by what agency?	causal explanations

Note The numbering follows the sequence of the traditional category-schema: substance, kind, quality, relation, and rationale. Compare Table 4 on page 67 below.

It is useful to think here of the analogy of a question/answer game like Animal-Vegetable-Mineral, where we begin with this rudimentary (and, as it were, protocategorial) trichotomy, but are then driven to increasingly detailed and sophisticated taxonomic distinctions. Or again, consider the example of a medical disability. The inquiry may well begin with the question of the source of some overt symptom as described by the patient in the crude *lingua franca* of ordinary aches and pains. But this sort of question ("Why does my stomach hurt and what can I do about it?") is one which, at the physician's hands, eventually leads to others in the sphere of human biology, biochemistry, etc., ultimately giving rise to questions handled in very different and now genuinely scientific terms. While the protocategories relate to the questions that set the stage of inquiry, the subsequent scientific categories provide the more developed and sophisticated issues that emerge as products of the course of inquiry.

To be sure, to say that the protocategories are rudimentary and basic is by no means to say that they are *only* basic—that they operate *only* at the outset of inquiry. *Au contraire,* their fundamentality is further indicated by their pervasiveness. The fact that protocategorial questions arise at the prescientific level thus does not mean that questions of the same type cannot be posed at the scientific level as well. The issues they pose (classification, composition, description, etc.) can also quite properly be raised at the more developed levels—they are recurrent *Leitmotivs* throughout the unfolding of inquiry. Thus, all the various questions surveyed in Table 1 can also be asked (for example) about and molecules and the other creatures of the world of science. Our question-horizon enlarges rather than contracts with the accession of greater sophistication. But questions are now answered in very different terms. And so the protocategories yield priority to the more sophisticated S-categories of the scientific sphere.

As Table 3 indicates, the traditional protocategories of our ordinary (common-sense) scheme of things already exfoliate into the vast welter of distinctions and contrasts. From the very first, even before the more sophisticated conceptions of science come upon the scene, we make use of a varied complex of elemental distinctions in the cognitive structuring of our experience. Such distinctions, however, at first still remain at the protocategorial level. They relate to the frame of reference in which we set the problem-stage for our science, rather than to that in whose terms we formulate its solutions.

Table 3

SOME PROTOCATEGORIAL DISTINCTIONS

I. *Substance*

simple/composite	real/illusory (merely apparent)
existing/hypothetical (imaginary)	concrete/abstract

II. *Kind*

inert/living	instance/type
material/immaterial	

III. *Quality*

subject/object	substance/property

IV. *Relation*

past/present/future	particular/general
here/near/far	subjective/objective
timeless/temporal	normal/abnormal
changing/unchanging	

V. *Rationale*

natural/artificial	immediate/mediated
purposive/causal	means/end
random/lawful	instrument/goal
process/product	reason-governed/arational
cause/effect	

---

2. PHILOSOPHICAL CATEGORIES

The traditional philosophical categories—set out in Table 4—can, to all intents and purposes, be identified with what we have here characterized as protocategories. These traditional categories reflect an attempt to inventory our basic questions about the world.[1] Problem-oriented and not solution-oriented, they relate to the initial, rudimentary, presystematic stage of inquiry which precedes the availability of answers and solutions that themselves invite yet further, more sophisticated questions. Aristotle's categories are suggestive in this regard: the very names he gives them derive from the Greek interrogative pronouns that pose the various protoquestions.

Table 4

INVENTORY OF PROTOCATEGORIES

I. *Substance*
    —*things* or *items* (issues of identification and individuation)

II. *Kind*
    —*types* or *varieties* or *sorts* of things (issues of descriptive or classificatory taxonomy; e.g. material objects, animals, persons)

III. *Quality*
    —*properties* or *aspects* of things (issues of description: attitudes, features, characteristics, etc.)

IV. *Relation*
    —*modes of interrelationship* among things
    (1) in point of *resemblance* or *similarity* (affinity, affiliation, kinship),
    (2) in point of *possession,* going with, belonging to (subordination and coordination)
    (3) in point of *placement* or *position* (space, time, quality-spectra),
    (4) in point of part/whole orderings and their structure (complexes, congeries, aggregates, groupings),
    (5) in point of *size* (enumeration, measurement, qualification),
    (6) in point of *action* (action-reaction, causation, interaction, change)

V. *Rationale*
    —*explanations* or *rationalizations* (reasons, causes, hypotheses, theories, etc.); considerations of *purposes* (needs, wants, desires, strivings)

In affording the terms of reference in which we grapple with our fundamental protoquestions, the philosophical theory of categories represents an attempt to set out the fundamental items of the descriptive and explanatory machinery by means of which we initially formulate our view of the world, before the development of more sophisticated categorial issues to which we are led in scientific theorizing. Traditional category theory accordingly endeavors to detail the framework of basic concepts in whose terms we answer the most rudimentary questions that can be raised about the furnishings and doings of nature, and to reveal the what, when, how, why, etc., with respect to occurrences in the world about us. The task of the theory is to analyze and organize the conceptual instruments with which we begin the prospect of grappling with the basic questions we face in the attempt to "make sense" of our experience—to characterize, describe, and explain the items that figure in the world as best we can form a view of it in cognitive interaction.

The tabulated entries are, of course, adduced here only by way of example: an almost endlessly varied category-spectrum of increasing subtlety and complexity can be elaborated in these terms. Indeed, the prospect of their endless elaboration is implicit in the very nature of categories. The ideas at issue can always be applied iteratively to themselves as to give rise to further, derived categories. For example, we can take *kinds* of things as themselves things or items of a certain sort and then move on to:

kinds of (kinds of things)
qualities of (kinds of things)
relations of (kinds of things)
explanations of ([the existence of] kinds of things)

And the same can be done for qualities, relations, etc. Nor need one stop at such twofold combinations. One can move on to higher-order complications:

kinds of (kinds of (kinds of things))
qualities of (kinds of (relations among things))

and so on. The machinery of categorial characterization lends itself through recursive self-application to an exfoliative extension in many directions. The traditional categories are simply the basis of such more elaborate structures.

3. CATEGORIAL METAPHYSICS

Classical metaphysics from Aristotle to McTaggart was in significant measure devoted to the elaboration of categorial themes. In particular, much effort was dedicated to elucidating the relations of connection or exclusion among the traditional categories (i.e., the protocategories). Some examples of the resultant theses are:

1. Only concreta (things or complexes of things) can *act;* abstracta (features, kinds *qua* kinds, and interrelationships) do not exert agency. (*Ergo* only concreta have potentialities—abstracta do not.)
2. All agency and all casuality is governed by (takes place in accordance with) laws.
3. All agency and all causality has a product (which may, to be sure, only be "maintenance of the *status quo*").
4. Whatever has a place in space has a place in time, though not necessarily vice versa [e.g. worries].
5. Spatio-temporal placement is not applicable to abstracta, but only to concreta. (Relations, ideas, and explanations don't have a position in space-time.)
6. Qualities come in trichotomous groupings in line with the determinate/determinable/nondeterminable distinction (is blue, is non-blue, color doesn't apply [e.g., to abstracta]).

Such metaphysical principles express the various relationships which the traditional categories bear to one another or the standard construction of the issues involved.

We are not, of course, restricted to relating categories two at a time. A cross-correlation of categorial distinctions is also possible. In this regard, the particular cross-classification of Figure 1 is of interest because it reflects—in items (1)–(3), respectively—the categories that Charles Sanders Peirce designated as firstness, secondness, and thirdness. (Item (4) lay outside Peirce's scheme as reflecting—for him—matters of merely psychology rather than specifically ontological, world-descriptive interest.) Here again various categorial theses will result—e.g. that subjective particulars need not be taken to fall under the aegis of natural laws.

The idea of "category mistakes" is correlative with categorial theses of the aforementioned sort. Some categories stand in coordination, others just do not mix. Violations of the "conceptual logic" of categories can thus occur when (for example) one treats a quality or a relation like a physical object. (Again, it would be a category mistake to ascribe action to abstracta.) The categorial theses provide us with metaphysical guideposts—with a means for doing our intellectual bookkeeping.[2] In this way, the theory of categories plays a role roughly akin to that of dimension theory in natural science. It affords no solutions to any substantive problems, but merely sets out certain constraints which any adequate solution must satisfy.

Figure 1

A CROSS-CLASSIFICATION

	subjective	*objective*
specific (particular)	"that looks like an apple" (1) APPEARANCES	"that is an apple" (2) (PARTICULAR) FACTS
universal (general)	"apples might have pits (like peaches)" (4) [MERELY IMAGINARY] POSSIBILITIES	"apples have cores" (3) LAWS [OBJECTIVELY GROUNDED POTENTIALITIES]

4. SCIENTIFIC CATEGORIES

To this point, the discussion has focused upon the protoquestions of our ordinary, everyday, commonsense concerns and the traditional categories to which they give rise. Let us now shift to the language of science and the categorial scheme inherent in scientific discourse.

The single most crucial consideration here is that the scientific categories (S-categories) emerge from science itself. To be sure, some theoreticians (e.g., Immanuel Kant) have held that, while the *content* of our empirical knowledge is something *a posteriori* and experiential, the issue of its rational *form,* its taxonomic structure, is at bottom *a priori* and strictly theoretical. The prominence of distinctions like that between *statics* and *dynamics* in physics may on first thought lend credence to such a view. But the aura of apriority always vanishes on closer inspection. (As the discovery of the relativity of simultaneity in special relativity has shown, reference to the temporal element in the static/dynamic distinction leads to substantial enmeshment in factual/substantive issues.)

Chapter I has argued that our concepts (and the various categories into which they fall) are law-correlative—they embody and reflect a view of how things work in the world. This means that all our empirical concepts (descriptive, explanatory) are *theory-laden.* And so, in consequence, are the categories that coordinate them. The rational structure of our factual knowledge emerges from its content, and its systematic architectonic is as empirical an issue as that of the constituent theses: in the domain of cognitive systematics, *form is built into content, and conversely.* This circumstance has far-reaching implications for the structure of our scientific categories.

The scientific rationalization of its category-mechanisms is itself a major product of scientific progress. The organic connections that obtain among parts of empirical knowledge are a key aspect of the subject-matter of that knowledge. The apposite concepts, distinctions, and classifications, and even the appropriate questions for scientific inquiry, emerge from the process of inquiry itself, and the correlative categories emerge with them. Cognitive progress is progress not only with respect to the *volume* of information, but with respect to its *structure*—its mode of organization—as well. The long and short of it is that *our knowledge of the structural principles that underlie our taxonomy in cognitive systematization is a key aspect of factual knowledge itself.*

As even a casual glance at the history of natural science shows, the fundamental principles and concepts of any natural science change and alter in the course of its own development. The categories and classifications of science are subject to change—not only gradual modification, but even, occasionally, by way of

Concepts

abrupt and revolutionary transformation. And so while our prescientific protocategories are relatively stable, revolving about the
same ongoing sorts of questions and issues, the situation is rather
different in regards to the category-scheme of science. The S-
categories of science come to reflect the current—and thus ever-
changing—state of the cognitive art in this domain. Indeed, the
indications of scientific progress are no less striking on the side of
its organization, systematic structure than on that of substantive
content.

5. THE NON-RATIONALIZABILITY OF PROTOCATEGORIES

Traditionally one of the key tasks envisaged for the philosophical
theory of categories has been to devise a tidy theoretical rationale
capable of endowing the variety of categories with an elegant,
rationally systemic order. If categories were neatly rationalizable
as the logical development of a simple plan, then categorial
metaphysics could attain the status of a formal system, articulable
as a deductive science that unfolds in something like a Euclidean
manner.

Consider what would be at issue of our scheme of basic
categories could be represented as the simple unfolding of a
plausible, rational scheme. Suppose, for the sake of illustration,
that there were just two types of elemental entities, a-style and
δ-style (say concreta and abstracta), and two types of fundamental
generative relationships ① and ② (say, something like "pertaining
to" and "deriving from"). On this basis, we would then proceed to
the exfoliative elaboration of further categorial complexes:

$$
\begin{array}{ll}
\text{a ① a} & \text{a ② a} \\
\text{a ① δ} & \text{a ② δ} \\
\text{δ ① a} & \text{δ ② a} \\
\text{δ ① δ} & \text{δ ② δ}
\end{array}
$$

And we could then go on to develop still more sophisticated sorts
of complexes, such as

$$\text{(a ① δ) ② a}$$

Suppose now that the whole of our categorial scheme were to emerge from rational unfolding of a simple basis of this sort. Our categories—all duly derived in this manner—would then be endowed with an elegant rational systematic order.

For centuries philosophers have sought to reduce the welter of our categorial notions to such a rational order—an order sufficiently natural, symmetric, and simple in its overall structure to render manifest its own completeness and adequacy to the task. Many of the great names in philosophy (including Kant, Fichte, Hegel, Peirce) are prominently associated with this project of providing a natural *a priori* account of the taxonomy of the categories themselves. This general tendency of thought points towards the great Hegelian dream of a categorial "logic" that articulates the rational exfoliation of the categories through the sequential development of a rational dialectic. And so, philosophers have often hankered after this prospect of determining a small number of basic categorial elements whose natural exfoliation would generate the entire manifold of categories in a rational and logically compelling way.

Its powerful appeal to the rationalizing intellect notwithstanding, it has gradually emerged as an unwelcome fact, discernible only with the wisdom of hindsight, that such a "rationalization of the categories" cannot be achieved. Through repeated failure in the light of recalcitrant circumstances, it has become increasingly apparent that the project of category-systematization (subject to the usual parameters of cognitive systematicity: simplicity, economy, symmetry, elegance, and the rest) is futile and its object is unrealizable.

The fact is, that the framework of the protocategories of everyday life in which the philosophical categories are rooted simply *does not have a systematic rationale*. The philosophical categories lack systematic tidiness and exhibit no neat, rational groundplan. Their articulation is not a matter of logical development of theoretical principles but "catch as catch can." The protocategories that underly our ordinary (commonsense) conceptual scheme of things lack any "deep" grounding in the nature of things because they relate preeminently to the *goals* rather than to the *results* of inquiry. They are of course capable of *explanation* (they have a natural history, after all), but yet they are not capable of *rationalization*. That is, they do not have a neat (simple, orderly, logical) rational structure. In this regard, our "common sense" framework of categories differs crucially from that of natural science: the latter (as we have seen) is bound to emerge from science itself, but the former being inherently *prescientific*, is also in substantial measure *unscientific*.

The reason for this intractability is not far to seek. The philosophically decisive protocategories reflect the subjective and largely intuitive interests of a contingently constituted creature. Our question-schemata have developed pragmatically in response to the communicative needs of a particular sort of creature *(homo sapiens)*, geared to a visit and diversified host of practical concerns.

The descriptive and taxonomic schemata of everyday life subject the practical aims and purposes of a complex organism that has to make its evolutionary way in the world by its wits; their underlying rationale is practical, not theoretical, geared to action, not to cognition:

> Cherry trees will be differently grouped by woodworkers, orchardists, artists, scientists and merry-makers. To the execution of different purposes different ways of acting and reacting on the part of trees are important. Each classification may be equally sound when the difference of ends is borne in mind.[3]

Their very origin and reason for being explains the recalcitrance of our categorial framework to elegant rational systematization with reference to "deep" theoretical principles.

There is accordingly a relatively straightforward reason for the recalciliance of the categories towards the imposition of a simple systematic rationalization. This reason lies in their very nature as cognitive *instruments* developed through historical evolution under the governing aegis of the purpose of understanding the course of natural events and communicating with one another about it. Take instruments of any other sort—woodworking instruments, for example, or musical instruments, or medical instruments, or gardening tools. Nowhere in such cases do we find a tidy inherent order that is articulable through the logical exfoliation of a simple rational plan. What may be characterized as the rational amorphousness of the categories derives from the pragmatic aspect; it is simply part and parcel of the rational untidiness and systemic complexity that one encounters with tools and instrumentalities in general. It is only reasonable to expect that the taxonomy of our everyday *conceptual* tools should exhibit the same sort of inherent complexity, diversity, and rational intractability that is found in the case of instrumentalities in general (be they artificial or natural). Given the diversity and complexity of the task at issue in human cognition and communication, one should not expect that the conceptual tools for its accomplishment should exhibit a simpler and more "logical" systematic structure than those of other sectors of the instrumental sphere. The scientific categories, on the other hand, are by their very nature systematic, seeing their very science and origin is a matter of cognitive systematization.[4] It is because of their fundamentally pragmatic rather than theoretical nature that there is no neat architectonic rationalization of the philosophical categories such as Kant and his idealistic successors dreamt of.

6. THE SCIENTIFIC CATEGORIES VS. THE TRADITIONAL CATEGORIES

We must confront the interesting question of whether the scientific categories can—and, if so, *should*—be taken to *replace* the protocategories of ordinary life. Why should the standard concept-framework of our everyday language not simply be abandoned, allowing the sophisticated categories of science to supplant their cruder cousins of the *lingua franca* of our workaday dealings and affairs?

The answer here is that any such idea of abandonment must be rejected because science does not *eliminate,* but rather *implements* the protocategorial framework. The questions of science grow out of questions which grow out of questions, etc.—until we ultimately return to the prescientific or subscientific protoquestions of ordinary life. We are led back to the very reason for being of the scientific project. Science is what it is because of its exfoliative source in those conceptions and issues operative in our basic questions regarding the world about us.

And these protoquestions are primordial not only in the historical order, but in the conceptual order as well. We always begin with such rudimentary prescientific questions as "Why and how do rainstorms or rainbows or eclipses occur?" And it is in the interest of obtaining optimally tenable answers to such elemental questions that we build up that impressive structure of meteorological and hydrographic and optical and astronomical (etc.) machinery. The answers to our elemental questions themselves generate further questions, and with the resulting process—with *science,* in short—we embark on an ongoing pursuit of increasing sophistication, generality, and detail. But those initial issues are always with us. It is in *their* interest that the whole structure is devised, and this structure rather implements than abrogates them.

Science gets its *point*—indeed its *mission*—from the protoquestions or ordinary life, which literally provide the ancestral starting-point without which the deliberations of science would have no bearing. Consider an example. No matter how complex and sophisticated medicine (for example) may become, its starting-point is with issues of the type "Why does my stomach hurt and what can I do about it?" These starting-point issues are everpresent and ineliminable. And those deliberations which are not connectible with such issues as how people feel and fare in the ordinary course of life can have no place in medicine as we understand it.

The pre- or sub-scientific scheme affords our cognitive hold on the world into which we are born, the world of which we learn at mother's knee, the world in which we live and play and interact with our fellows—until the stern régime of the schoolroom re-orients our thinking. No matter how elaborately and extensively we develop the scientific scheme, it is still those rudimentary questions at the level of ordinary common-sense that we are trying to answer—indeed they provide the very reason for being on which the whole scientific enterprise pivots. New questions are elaborated; new distinctions come on the scene; but the old issues are never abolished because it is in the interest of resolving them that these innovations are introduced.

The commonsense protocategories are thus fundamental (or ultimate) for inquiry then, because they furnish the frame of reference in whose terms of which we "set the problem". They get the process of inquiry started. In due course, to be sure, they give way to the more sophisticated in determining its *relevance*.

The protocategories of the common sense scheme are thus basic—*not* in the sense that they are all-sufficient and need no supplementation and elaboration (quite the reverse!), but only in the sense that they provide the starting-point: they pose the issues for the sake of whose resolution the whole elaborately sophisticated business of inquiry gets under way.

Suppose that matters within an area of science stood in such a condition that no connection at all could be established to link its questions to issues statable in the commonplace language of everyday life. No chain of means-ends exfoliation connected the "scientific" questions with any prescientific ones. Then such deliberations would have no place in science as we understand it—they would stand in utter isolation from "our world," the one and only realm in whose interests the project of scientific inquiry has come to be instituted.

The categorial scheme of science accordingly *supplements and implements* that of ordinary life—i.e., extends it in the direction of precision, informativeness, etc. But, rather than *abolishing* the protocategorial scheme of our ordinary-life questions, it leads towards more adequate (general, systematic, deep, etc.) answers to—ultimately—the same old issues with which we grappled from the very outset.

Accordingly, science does not come to destroy, but to fulfill. It does not abandon or abolish our crude, everyday starting-point questions regarding the nature of the world, but offers us the means of obtaining more sophisticated (exact, etc.) and more useful answers to them.[5]

7. THE MUTABILITY OF CATEGORIES

To what extent (if any) are categories subject to mutation and change? With regard to S-categories the answer is simple: they are changeable and indeed change constantly with the progress of science itself. It is clear on even cursory inspection that—for example—the categories in whose terms Galenic medicine depicts diseases differ drastically from those in whose terms Pasteurian medicine does so. With our scientific categories, it is strikingly clear that they are not merely the tools but also the products of scientific inquiry. The descriptive and taxonomic mechanisms of science unfold from the theories of science itself, with the result that our S-categories are strongly geared to the changing cognitive state-of-the-art.

But what about the protocategories of our unsophisticated pre- or sub-scientific picture of things?

Here the situation is somewhat complicated. Although it does seem at first view that the all too evident mutability of our S-categories distinguishes them sharply from the stability of our pre- of sub-scientific protocategories, it emerges on closer inspection that this difference is only one of degree, and not of kind. For our protocategories too are mutable. As the course of our inquiries unfolds, we eventually come to take a different perspective on things even at the level of the rough-and-ready issues that were our starting point. The feedback cycle that is at issue here is, of course, a very big one indeed, and the revisions that arise are bound to be slow and relatively minor at any particular stage. When we begin the process of inquiry with a protocategorial question our conceptions are so indefinite, and our expectations as to the nature of apposite answers so minimal, that this initial predisposition is not prone to be much affected by what ensues—no matter how things eventually turn out. Accordingly, the S-categories of science pay for their advantage over the prescientific categories of everyday life in increased vulnerability—in greater fragility and changeability. Their very strength of having a superior rational basis constitutes a weakness in point of vulnerability.

Thus while there are indeed changes even with respect to protocategories, they are extremely glacial, slow, and always marginal, as it were, in making only minor readjustments. Yet even glacial change is still change, and like water gradually wearing away stone, will eventually produce massive alterations. (The transition from an animistic to a naturalistic world-view affords one paradigm example, and the gradual demise of the concept of final causation and purposiveness in nature affords another.) There will always be protocategories, but they will certainly not always be just the same.

The main upshot of these deliberations is thus their indication of a distinctly non-Kantian (because *empirical* and *a posteriori*) conception of categories, one that reckons with the nowadays no longer novel point—particularly emphasized throughout the tradition of American pragmatism—that the concepts we deploy in grapping with our factual questions are themselves the products of our empirical inquiries and factual commitments. A vast change was wrought in the Kantian theory of categories by the American pragmatists. Kant saw the categorial structure of reality—i.e. of *our* cognized reality—as inherent in the very structure of the human mind, as an integral necessary part of its very constitution. The pragmatists rightly saw it as a contingent historical development—a product of *cultural* rather than *biological* evolution. As William James wrote:

> [B]etween categories fulminated before nature began, and categories gradually forming themselves in nature's presence, the whole chasm between rationalism and empiricism yawns. To the genuine ''Kantianer'' . . . [the pragmatist] will always be to Kant as a satyr to Hyperion.[6]

In summary, two facts stand out:

(1) There always are *some* protocategories: a pre- or sub-scientific level of thought is always there. We have to make our intellectual entry into science from without. The process of man's introduction to his world must inevitably begin at a point where the sophistication of science lies in the distant offing.

(2) But while there are always *some* protocategories they are not always exactly *the same* ones. Change and mutation does take place. With the ongoing development of inquiry there is eventually some feedback upon the initial starting-point: We no longer conceive of classification (say) or of measurement in just the way the Romans did.

And so protocategories, though everpresent are not immutable. They serve to get inquiry started, but yet are not immune from its outcome. They form part of a great cyclic spiral in which the products of inquiry eventually revise our view of what the starting-point is—or ought to be.

PART TWO
Knowledge

IV

Cognitive Dynamics

SYNOPSIS

(1) The idea of membership in a "body of knowledge." (2) Our knowledge, that is to say, our *putative* knowledge, has an ineliminably historical dimension; one cannot but recognize the reality of cognitive change and its correlativity with a transient "states of knowledge." (3) An analysis of the structure of cognitive dynamics and of the modes of change in the perceived truth-status of particular propositions. (4) The "growth" of knowledge: its lack of continuity and cumulativity. (5) Cognitive Copernicanism: our present "state of knowledge" as simply one stage among others that are in principle on all fours with it. (6) Cognitive Relativism: All we achieve is a changing sequence of historic state-of-the-art stages in scientific inquiry. In science, we have no access to a "position of reason" outside the ever-changing succession of historical positions.

1. THE IDEA OF A BODY OF KNOWLEDGE

The preceding chapters have stressed that the concepts we use in thinking about the world and the categories in terms of which we frame our questions about it reflects a state of knowledge and belief that is transitory in principle and transient in practice. We shall now undertake a closer study of cognitive change and its wider implications for a proper understanding of the process of inquiry.

Standardly, the terminology at issue so operates that in flatly saying that "X *knows* that p" one not only gives a report about X's cognitive posture, but also *endorses* the proposition P that is at issue. To disengage oneself from this commitment one must say something like, "X thinks (or is convinced) that he knows that *p*." In the present discussion, however, it will be just this latter sort of thing—apparent or purported knowledge—that is under consideration.

Knowledge claims can be regarded from two points of view, viz. *internally and committally*, subject to an acceptance thereof as correct and authentic, and *externally and detachedly*, viewed from an "epistemic distance" without the commitment of actual acceptance, and seen as merely representing *purported* knowledge. We shall here adopt this second perspective, viewing knowledge in an externalized way, so that we shall be dealing with *ostensible* knowledge rather than certifiedly *authentic* knowledge. Our concern is with the merely *putative* knowledge of fallible, flesh-and-blood humans and not the capital-K Knowledge of an omniscient being.

It is useful to look, in this light, at the thesis that membership in a "body of knowledge" entails truth, symbolically: $p \in K \rightarrow p$. To be sure, someone who stakes or concedes the claim that *p* is an authentic item of knowledge thereby stands committed to claiming the truth of *p*. It is a contradiction in terms to say: "X knows that *p*, but *p* is not (or even 'is perhaps not') the case." But if $p \in K$ is viewed detachedly and commitment-externally—as stating merely that *p* is part of someone's purported knowledge—then it by no means follows that *p* must be the case. (It makes perfectly good sense to say, "X purports to know that *p*, but *p* is not the case.") Accordingly, in placing a certain proposition within a body of knowledge *K* we proceed committment-externally, and shall not presuppose that it is actually true—that it is real rather than apparent knowledge. We thus reject the aforementioned implication principle.

But while our concern here is with merely purported knowledge—with what people *think* they know—still it is directed at knowledge claimed in a way that is not wholly frivolous and idiosyncratic, but espoused responsibly on a basis deemed adequate by the standards of the community. Our business is with epistemology (with a responsible adherence to rational standards), and not with psychology (with whatever may actually be thought, no matter how weird). This discussion addresses itself to what people justifiedly and responsibly take themselves to know—the cognitive "state-of-the-art" so to speak.

The historical realities force us to recognize that what people—ourselves presumably included—see as the putative truth is shot through with error. It is plausible—nay unavoidable—to recognize that "our knowledge" as it stands is subject to two modes of error, being not only incomplete, with errors of omission, but also being replete with (specifically unidentifiable) falsehoods, with errors of commission.

Nevertheless, given that K_n is *(ex hypothesi)* our own current body of (putative) knowledge—the body of knowledge K_t with $t = n$ for "now"—we ourselves unquestionably do stand committed to the inference schema:

$$p \in K_n \rightarrow p$$

At the level of specific claims, we have no alternative but to look upon *our* knowledge as real knowledge—a thesis p wouldn't be part of "*our* truth" if we didn't take it to form part of "*the* truth." The "knowledge" at issue is to be knowledge according to our own lights—the only ones we've got. Nevertheless, despite our committment to this inference principle at the level of particular claims, we certainly do not stand committed to

$$(\forall p)(p \in K_n \supset p)$$

as a general thesis. *Au contraire,* we realize full well that its negation may also hold—nay, almost certainly does so. We occupy the position of the so-called Preface Paradox, accepting p_1, and p_2, and p_3, etc., but also $(\exists n) \sim (p_1 \& p_2 \& p_3 \& \ldots \& p_n)$. Our body of knowledge is thus unabashedly meta-inconsistent, and no violation of the "principles of rationality" is involved in this inconsistency.[1]

Subscription to the inference-schema $p \in K_n \rightarrow p$ is thus not a matter of what holds at the level of theoretical general principles, but simply a matter of the practical politics of the epistemic domain—a consequence of our committment to K_n. It reflects the fact that our "*purported* knowledge" is always "purported *knowledge*"—that in claiming to know that p we commit ourselves to maintaining the truth of *p*. The implication is one of *practical* and not of *theoretical* reason. The truth of *p* certainly does not follow from its inclusion as K_n. But this remains an *in abstracto* realization that we are unwilling and unable to apply *in concreto*.

It seems appropriate to dwell briefly on the idea of membership in a body of knowledge. It should be stressed from the very outset that epistemic theory cannot profitably orient itself to the "formal logic" of *occurrent* knowledge—with what people transiently heed within their range of active and explicit attention—because such a concept is too subjective and idiosyncratic to underwrite the drawing of any useful conclusions. Nor can epistemic theory deal helpfully with people's dispositions to give assent. For this mode of "knowledge" leaves too much room for person-relative and psychological idiosyncrasies, and engenders something too variable and volatile to support a framework of inference. Accordingly, in speaking of a "body of knowledge," we shall have to envisage a certain element of *latency* or potentiality. In saying that something belongs to the cognitive corpus of a group, we don't mean to say that there is somebody in the group who does actually then and there actively realize this. Rather, we mean that it is something that could be extracted by actually and realistically available methods from what is latently accepted by many or most group members. In speaking of a "body of knowledge" or a "state of knowledge" at a certain time we shall thus suppose both a certain element of *consensus* and a certain element of *potentiality*. What we have in view is what *most of the (duly rational) people of the group would ultimately come to accept if they addressed themselves to the matter by the then-established ideas and methods*.

This issue of latent extractibility is closely connected with a certain *systematicity* of knowledge, a systematicity implicit in such principles (among others) as the following:

$$(p \in K \ \& \ q \in K) \to (p \& q) \in K \qquad \text{[Conjunctivity]}$$
$$(p \in K \ \& \ [p \to q] \in K) \to q \in K \qquad \text{[Implicational Closure]}$$

Both implement the usual notion of rational competency. They have it that the knowers in view are able to put two and two together, as it were. We must presuppose that the individuals at issue can safely be assumed to make at least the most basic and rudimentary inferences from their knowledge.

Put together, the two preceding principles yield:

$$(p_1 \in K \ \& \ p_2 \in K \ \& \ \ldots \ \& \ p_i \in K \ \& \ [(p_1 \ \& \ p_2 \ \& \ \ldots \ \& \ p_i) \to q]$$
$$\in K) \to q \in K$$

This thesis indicates that our ''body of knowledge'' is construed to be deductively self-contained; and so articulates a further aspect of the latency at issue in stipulating that whatever follows by known inferential principles from known facts is to be taken as known. This latency entitles us to suppose that a body of knowledge is closed with respect to those deductive inferences, at any rate, that are themselves part of one's knowledge.

On the other hand—and by way of useful contrast—it is certainly *not* the case that:

$$(p \in K \ \& \ [p \to q]) \to q \in K$$

This unacceptable thesis of course makes a much stronger claim than its *K*-relativized predecessors in its commitment to the idea that all the implicit consequences of known theses are *eo ipso* known: that if we know the axioms we thereby know the theorems as well. No such logical omniscience can be assumed. We must construe a ''body of knowledge'' not as comprising what is *logically* implicit in our overt commitments, but what is *manifestly* contained in them. To be sure, if the ''knowledge'' at issue in our discussion were *wholly virtual* knowledge, if it dealt with what *can in theory* be deduced (by anybody) from what a person accepts, then the principle at issue would indeed obtain. But the *latent* knowledge that presently concerns us does not meet this extreme condition. It deals with what people can realistically and plausibly be expected to extract from their stock of knowledge given the cognitive ''state of the art'' that is *available* to them, and not with what ''can in *theory*'' be extracted therefrom by an omniscient being.[2]

2. THE STATUS OF THESES WITHIN A BODY OF KNOWLEDGE

Let us now turn to the theme of knowledge-acquisition. The developmental aspect of knowledge makes it needful to consider more closely the temporalized and historicized idea of the state of knowledge obtaining at a particular time t. A bit of further notational machinery is useful to this end. As indicated above, K_t will represent the "state of 'knowledge' at the time t." This is to be understood as the "body of scientific knowledge" as generally accepted as t—the cognitive corpus comprising the commitments of the broad consensus of the scientific community of the day, the set of propositions embraced within the then-current systematization of scientific information. Since it is to be *putative* knowledge that is at issue, it must be stressed that $p \in K_t$ does not guarantee that $p \in K_{t'}$ for any t' more than trivially distant from t; indeed the former has no inferential bearing whatsoever upon the latter.

The ambiguity of $p \notin K_t$ should be noted. This could mean either (1) at t people simply don't yet know about p, their state of information, or, rather, of ignorance is such that the whole issue of p vs. not-p has not yet arisen, or (2) at t people do indeed consider the issue of the p vs. not-p, but are simply unable to settle it: they simply do not know whether p or not-p, or (3) p is actually blocked from K_t because its contradictory is in fact known; we have $\sim p \in K_t$ the question of p vs. not-p is a live issue, and has been resolved in favor of not-p.

It emerges on this perspective that the K-relative status of propositions engenders the following many-valued scheme of epistemic truth-values, using the notation $/p/_k$ to represent the epistemic truth-status of the proposition p relative to the body of knowledge K.

$/p/_K$ = T   iff p is cognitively determined as true: $p \in K$ & $\sim p \notin K$

$/p/_K$ = F   iff p is cognitively determined as false: $p \notin K$ & $\sim p \in K$. [Case (3) above]

$/p/_K$ = I   iff p is a K-relatively meaningful (truth-determinate) thesis whose truth-status determination cannot be settled. [Case (2) above]

$/p/_K$ = U   iff p is undefined (meaningless, unformulable) relatively to K. [Case (1) above.]

The third contingency arises under the condition of inadequacy of *information:* the information of K cannot provide for a decision as between p and not-p. The fourth contingency arises under the condition of a *conceptual* inadequacy resulting when p involves issues that—for one reason or another—are simply not envisageable within K. In these four cases at issue, we shall speak, respectively, of K-truth, K-falsity, K-indeterminacy, and K-inexpressibility.

The last of these circumstances—that of K inexpressibility or indefinition—is particularly interesting from an epistemological point of view. The evolution of knowledge brings changes not only in what is *said* (maintained-to-be-true) but in what is *sayable* (thinkable or imaginable). For example, otherwise available concepts might be combined in ways that K does not countenance as meaningful—the "frame of reference" is inhospitable in disallowing the conceptual combinations at issue (as Newtonian physics does not provide for psychokinesis). Most interestingly, the propositions at issue might involve concepts that have not yet been invented. The 19th-century English scientist George Gore offers some illustrations:

> That which is inconceivable by one man, or in one age, is not necessarily so by another man, or in another period. . . . Ideas which at one period are beyond reason, do in many cases, by the progress of knowledge, come within its domain. . . . Some discoveries which are unattainable in one age or stage of knowledge become attainable in another; for instance, the laws of electro-magnetism or of electro-chemical action could not have been discovered in an age when electro-currents were unknown, nor could the principle of conservation of matter and of energy have been arrived at when science was in its infancy.[3]

It's not just that Caesar didn't *know* what the half-life of californium is, but that he couldn't have *understood* this fact if someone had told it to him: it simply lay beyond—or, to put it less prejudicially, outside—his cognitive range. Development of the relevant concepts still lay in the future. The language of emergence can perhaps be deployed profitably to describe this situation. What is at issue is not an *emergence of the features of things,* but an

Knowledge

emergence in our *knowledge* about them. The blood circulated in the human body well before Harvey; uranium-containing substances were radioactive before Becquerel. The emergence at issue here relates to our cognitive mechanisms of conceptualization, not to the objects of our conceptualization in and of themselves.

3. COGNITIVE DYNAMICS

The topic of "cognitive dynamics" relates to changes in the body of (putative) knowledge over the course of time, the cognitive consequences encountered in the transition from K_t to $K_{t'}$, where $t \angle t'$.

In this context it is helpful to begin with a survey of changes in the epistemic truth-values of propositions, with $/p/_{Kt}$, or more simply $/p/_t$ as the status-index of the proposition p relative to the body of knowledge K_t. The situation is summarized in Table 1, which envisages five main types of changes:

(1) *Truth-status Determination*
   $/p/$ changes from I to T or F.

Here we discover—or learn, so to speak—what is the truth-condition of a previously indeterminate proposition.

(2) *Issue Aquisition*
   $/p/$ changes from U to T or F or I

Here we develop the new concepts needed to formulate a contention that could not previously be entertained at all. We have the accession of a new issue: the old body of knowledge K did not even allow the issue of p vs not-p to arise, but it now does so.

(3) *Truth-status Revision*
   $/p/$ changes from T to F or from F to T

Here we simply change our mind as to truth status of a thesis in light of "new information." The old body of knowledge K included not-p, and now that we have accepted p, we must replace K by a K'

which includes *p,* excludes not-*p,* and makes whatever other revisions of *K* are necessary and appropriate to effect this change of mind.[4]

(4) *Reopening*
/*p*/ changes from T or F to I

Here new information leads us to become unsure of the truth-status of a proposition we had previously classed as true or false. The issue of the truth-status of the proposition at issue is, as it were, reopened.

(5) *Issue Dissolution*
/*p*/ changes from T or F or I to U

Here we discover that a thesis heretofore regarded as meaningful is not conceptually viable. (For example, the current epistemic status of positive contentions regarding Galen's humors or Priestley's phlogiston.)

Table 1

MODES OF COGNITIVE CHANGE BY WAY OF
BEFORE—VS.—AFTER TRANSITIONS

Status After (at $t' > t$)

	/*p*/$_{t'}$ → /*p*/$_t$ ↓	T	F	I	U
	T	X	(3)	(4)	(5)
Status Before (at *t*)	F	(3)	X	(4)	(5)
	I	(1)	(1)	X	(5)
	U	(2)	(2)	(2)	X

These five items inventory all of the various ways in which the epistemic status of propositions can change with changes in the cognitive "state of the art."

As these deliberations suggest, the salient fact about knowledge—or, at any rate, about *purported* knowledge—is its changeability, its historical mutability and cultural relativity—its correlativity with the "state of the cognitive art" of the *time* and/or the *culture* at issue.

This idea of a cognitive "state of the art" is crucial. It serves to bring out the transitoriness and the circumstance-dependency of what we take ourselves to know. And this, of course, holds not only for the contents of our "body of 'knowledge'," but also for the methods and standards operative in its constituting.

This state of affairs has two characteristic aspects: (1) From the epistemic truth-condition of p at t—*any* t, including $t = n$ (for *now*)—one can make no inference regarding the (absolute) truth-condition of p. Nothing decisive follows from the character of $/p/_t$ regarding $/p/$ itself, not even if t is "now" or "a long time hence." (2) From the truth-condition imputed to p at t nothing follows regarding its condition at t' (for $t' \neq t$); any fixing of $/p/_t$ leaves open the prospect of *any other* fixing for $/p/_{t'}$, as long as $t' \neq t$. A condition of radical independence obtains here.

The facts which one era or school of thought takes as established and evident may be rejected by another—or indeed may be entirely outside its ken. No adequate theory of knowledge can fail to reckon appropriately with this dynamical and circumstantial character of (purported) knowledge.

4. COGNITIVE ESCHATOLOGY

Since it is *putative* or *purported* "knowledge" that is at issue throughout our discussion—knowledge as it is claimed by imperfect men, and not the capital-K Knowledge set down in the book of some infallible recording angel—we shall not have a

> *Law of the Conservation of Knowledge*
> What is once "known" always remains "known":
> $$(\forall t)(\forall t')(\forall p)([t \angle t' \ \& \ p \epsilon K_t] \supset p \epsilon K_{t'})$$

Such a "law" fails for two reasons: (1) "knowledge" can be forgotten, as in fact much of Greek astronomy was lost in the

"Dark Ages"; and (2) "knowledge" can be abandoned: the scientific community may no longer accept a once-accepted thesis, and indeed such a thesis may even be replaced by its contradictory (as parts of Newtonian physics are actually inconsistent with Einsteinian physics). Scientific knowledge is not cumulative; the progress of science not only exhibits *additions* but *subtractions* as well. (As we have already noted, membership of K_t has no inferential bearing whatsoever upon membership of $K_{t'}$, for $t' \neq t$.)

This circumstance that one cannot simply conjoin or *aggregate* putative knowledge renders it attractive to contemplate the idea of a body of knowledge that is not, indeed, total and all-comprehensive, but does manage, at any rate, to be final or ultimate. Let us explore this prospect.

Might it perhaps be that the realm of potential discovery is one of ultimately limited proportions? A position of just this sort was maintained by Charles Sanders Peirce (1839–1914). Peirce, in effect, saw the history of science as progressing through two stages: an initial or preliminary phase of groping for the general structure of the *qualitative* relations among scientific parameters, and a secondary phase of *quantitative* refinement—of filling in with increasing precision the exact values of parameters that figure in equations whose general configuration is determined in the initial phase. Once the first phase has been gotten over with—as Peirce believed to be the case in his own day, at any rate with regard to the physical sciences—ongoing scientific progress is just a matter of increasing detail and exactness, of determining the ever more minute decimal-place values of quantities whose approximate value is already well-established.[5]

We have here a metaphysical view of cognitive evolution according to which science will finally reach a condition of ultimate cumulativity—that science is evolving along a winding and circuitous route into a condition of eventual stability in point of "knowledge"-retention:

Thesis of the Ultimate Conservation of Knowledge
A time (t^ω) will be reached after which anything that becomes known will always remain known:
$$(\forall t)(\forall t')(\forall p)([t_w \angle t \angle t' \ \& \ p\epsilon K_t] \supset p\epsilon K_{t'})$$

In this circumstance, science will *ultimately* reach—at some otherwise indefinite juncture—a conservationist condition of things in which whatever subsequently becomes "known" will ever-after remain "known," so that a point of *eventual* preservativism is ultimately reached, everything then "known" always surviving, unaffected by whatever further additions or supplementations may yet appear.

This line of thought suggests the further more particularized idea of a

> *Thesis of the Finalization of Knowledge* (at *t*)
> Everything known at *t* will remain known ever-after:
> $$(\forall t')(\forall p)([t \angle t' \ \& \ p \epsilon K_t] \supset p \epsilon K_{t'})$$

In such a circumstance, a position will be reached where everything "known" will ever remain so, unaffected by whatever further discoveries may come along.

A somewhat cognate but actually very different idea of knowledge-completion is that of knowledge-termination (at *t*) arrived at by forming the *converse* of the preceding thesis. This envisages a circumstance where everything ever "known" is then "known":

> *Thesis of the Termination of Knowledge* (at *t*)
> Everything ever to be known is known at *t*:
> $$(\forall t')(\forall p)([t \angle t' \ \& \ p \epsilon K_{t'}] \supset p \epsilon K_t)$$

In such a circumstance, knowledge is completed in the sense of its development coming to an end—reaching a condition where no further augmentations are forthcoming.

The combination of the ideas of knowledge-conservation and knowledge-termination may be characterised as knowledge-*ossification*. Its definitive principle may be formulated as follows:

> *Thesis of the Ossification of Knowledge*
> A time will be reached after which there are neither gains nor losses in knowledge:
> $$(\exists t)(\forall t')(\forall p)(t \angle t' \supset [p \epsilon K_t \equiv p \epsilon K_{t'}])$$

This principal envisages the eventual arrival of a condition of cognitive stability: the evolution of science towards a totally fixed and unchanging cognitive posture. Such a theory looks to a final completion of the scientific enterprise.

All positions of this general sort run into grave difficulty, as our subsequent discussion will argue in substantial detail. (See Chapters VIII and IX.) They are all untenable because they envisage a course of cognitive evolution in the scientific domain that does violence to the fundamental processes actually at work here.

5. COGNITIVE COPERNICANISM

There is no alternative but to adopt, in all due realism and humility, a cognitive *Copernicanism* that rejects the claim that we ourselves occupy a pivotal position in the epistemic dispensation. With respect to "the real truth" of things, we must recognize that there is nothing inherently sacrosanct about our own present cognitive posture *vis-à-vis* that of other historical junctures. (K_t with $t=n = now$ is nowise in a position that is priviledged in comparison to $K_{t'}$ with $t' \neq n$.) There is no reason to think that *our* view of things—be it of individual things (the moon, the great wall of China) or of types thereof (the domestic cat, the common cold)—is any more definite and final than that taken by our predecessors in the cognitive enterprise. As one acute observer has written:

> The ephemeral nature of scientific theories takes the man of the world by surprise. Their brief period of prosperity ended, he sees them abandoned one after another; he sees ruins piled upon ruins; he predicts that the themes in fashion today will in a short time be succeeded in their turn. . . .[6]

The original Copernican revolution made the point that there is nothing *ontologically* privileged about our own position in space. The doctrine now at issue effectively holds that there is nothing *cognitively* privileged about our own position in time.

Unlike a Peircean convergentism which sees K_t tending in a fixed and discernible direction with the increase of t, Cognitive Copernicanism sees all the K_t as essentially on a par in point of definitiveness or finality. To be sure, in point of evidential *warrant,* as contradistinguished from substantive *accuracy,* the later stages of science "have more to be said for them" than the earlier ones, but this content-external, epistemological fact must not be construed *ontologically*—it does not mean that the world-picture of later science is somehow "nearer to the truth". Later science may be better science, but it is nowise more final or definitive. (We shall return to this issue in the next section).

The classical, pre-Kantian view of epistemology embodies a particular approach to things through the contrast between how they appear to us (in terms of our present knowledge or purported knowledge about them) and how they are absolutistically and *an sich* (in terms, say, of God's knowledge about them). The approach taken here exchanges this perspective for one based on the contrast between the *present* view of things and the prospect of an "improved" *future* view of them. It *historicizes* the issue into a sequence of temporal stages in our knowledge (i.e., purported knowledge) of things. This perspective urges that *there is nothing epistemically privileged about the present*—ANY present, our own prominently included. These considerations point towards the humbling view that just as we think our predecessors of 100 years ago had a fundamentally inadequate grasp on the future of the world, so our successors of 100 years hence will take the same view of *our* knowledge (or purported knowledge) of things.

Such a Cognitive Copernicanism cannot—i.e., *should* not— daunt us in our pursuit of the cognitive enterprise. It does *not* underwrite a scepticism that annihilates any and all entitlement to claim knowledge. Tentativity and fallibilism notwithstanding, we must admit that our scientific beliefs represent the very best we can do to resolve our questions as to how things stand in the world, that they can unashamedly be put forward as representing the best estimate of the truth that can be made in the present state of the cognitive art. Admitting that our "scientific knowledge" is no more than *putative* and potentially defeasible knowledge—for how could it possibly be more?!—we can quite appropriately regard it as consisting of our best estimates of the truth. The validation of knowledge claims does not—and, within the bounds of reason, cannot—ask that we should do more than the very best we can do in the epistemic circumstances under which we do and must labor.[7]

6. COGNITIVE RELATIVISM

It is certainly not an implication of our Cognitive Copernicism that there is no such thing as cognitive progress. Quite the contrary is the case. But the sort of progress there is is not a matter of the substantive content of our scientific theories but of the character of their evidential support. Every cognitive state-of-the-art K_t, regardless of t, is evidentially superior to its predecessors and will prove to be inferior to its successors. But this transpires in such a way that there is no basis for speaking of a "convergence" or "approximation" of any sort at the level of theory-content. Different stages of science yield theoretical world pictures so different that there are no trends within this changing sequence itself. Rather progress in science is evidenced by greater applicative adequacy: it is a matter, not of the monotonic accretion of more information, or even of better information in a content-oriented sense of "better", but in superior performance in point of prediction and control over nature. It is betokened by the better *grounding* of our claims, and not by some feature of their *content*.[8] Later theories do not give a "better picture" of things.

The fact remains that what constitutes "scientific knowledge"—the *content* of science—is a matter of historical relativization. We cannot speak of "scientific knowledge" *per se*, but only of "scientific knowledge as seen by the ancient Greeks" or "by our own contemporaries," or "by our successors two millennia hence." There is no priviledged time t for which K_t is "science perfected," and certainly the present, $t = n$, will not do the trick. And even if *(per impossibile)* "ideal science" were to exist, we have no way to get there from here. Not only *can any one* of our scientific theories turn out to be unacceptable, but *most of them will* eventually turn out to be so. Our claims to knowledge must always be tempered by the fallibilistic realization that the current state of knowledge is simply one among others that are in principle on all fours with it in point of vulnerability.

We thus arrive at the view that no scientific account grasps the nature of "the real" definitively and directly, finally and absolutely. A scientific account always affords information that is relative to the historical state of the art within which it arises, and reflects the conditioning impetus of the historical circumstances in

Knowledge

which it comes to realization.[9] In this regard the concept of *knowledge* stands on a footing very different from that of *truth*. The idea of an absolute truth-status, of "being true" *simpliciter,* makes perfectly good sense (even though we can only *know* about it in a state-of-the-art relativized manner). But the idea of an absolute knowledge-status ("being known" *simpliciter)* clearly does not. There is nothing we can do with the conception of capital-K, God's eye view Knowledge: we can only deal with the knowledge-claims of particular people at particular times.

Once it is recognized that purported "knowledge" is relativized to a time (or culture, etc.), it no longer makes sense to abstract from this relativization and to speak of knowledge simply as such—in an unrelativized and absolutistic way. And in particular, it makes no sense to speak collectively and indiscriminately of "all knowledge" as with an aggregative formula like

$$K = {}_{df} \bigcup_{t} K_t$$

so that $p \in K$ iff $(\exists t) \ p \in K_t$. Given the variation and divergence within the K_t such a merely formal unification would be senseless. To repeat: we cannot simply conjoin putative knowledge across different eras. No compilation into one single, aggregate body is possible here; to attempt it is to embark on an inappropriate hypostatization.

Rationalization can be given to this sort of circumstance through the following general principle:

> Where each element is relativized in being functionally (parametrically) conditioned, one cannot in general aggregate meaningfully to an unconditional whole.[10]

As each English-speaking group has its mode of pronunciation, so each era has its (putative) knowledge. And it makes as little sense to contemplate a knowledge-in-general as it does to contemplate a spoken-English-in-general. A violation of this principle represents the sort of illicit aggregation already condemned by Hume and Kant.

In line with these ideas, however, someone might well offer the following objection to our present proceedings:

> You proscribe our speaking of knowledge absolutistically outside the relativizing confines of some K_t-framework. Yet you yourself make cross-framework comparisons when you speak of one self-same and thesis p as belonging to distinct frameworks when $p \in K_t$ and $p \in K_{t'}$. How can one make these cross-scheme comparisons save from the vantage point of a "higher", scheme-external position outside the manifold of particular schemes. How—for example— can you reidentify theses across cognitive schemes, except from that God's eye scheme-transcending viewpoint which you yourself disavow?

The answer to this objection is straightforward. There is indeed no scheme-external standpoint for trans-scheme comparisons. That a thesis of scheme #1 is the same thesis as one of scheme #2 is a contention of ours—a thesis of *our own* scheme insofar as it relates to these two. When we discuss conceptual schemes *ab extra,* we of course do not do so from a God's-eye view, but from our own standpoint—the only one that is accessible to us. That schemes stand in a certain relationship is, after all a theory of ours, a facet of our systematizing, a creature of inference to the best explanation.[11]

We arrive then, at a position of cognitive relativism. The temporal relativization of a cognitive "state of the art" K_t in scientific inquiry is ineliminable. In factual inquiry, there is no way of getting outside the K_t-series and somehow reaching a privileged K^*, distinct from the K_t themselves, with which these imperfect K_t-stages can be compared and contrasted. If we insist on projecting the conception of an idealized superknowledge K^* we must realize that this is at best a contrast-conception of which we can make no concrete application. There is no getting rid of the relativized (subscripted) character of K_t. The great dream of rationalist philosophers cannot be implemented: we have no way of reaching a vantage point outside history—a transcendental position in the cognitive domain. We can attain no intellectual *locus standi* outside the course of human history: there is no resting place for the Archimedean lever of transcendental knowledge, no "position of reason" outside the ever-changing succession of historical positions with respect to scientific issues.

We must accept with respect to natural science a rough functional equivalent of the "historicist" position urged by Wilhelm Dilthey and others with respect to history. Science is a cultural artefact whose status is alien to that of the rest in *point* of change and transience. We can attain no "position of reason itself" outside of contradistinguished from the fallible and imperfect positions that constitute the changing sequence of historical stages. Such progress as the development of science affords—and substantial it is—is not a matter of discernible evolution toward some transcendental, history-external position, but a matter of exchanging for one imperfect and ephemeral position yet another position that nevertheless has some significant point of advantage over its predecessor in point of its substantiating warrant.[12]

V

Communication,
The Progress of Knowledge,
and the Nature of "Things"

SYNOPSIS

(1) The chapter considers how our ineliminably *subjective* experience can provide a cognitive basis for interpersonal communication about an *objective* world-order. Our cognitive grasp of things is inherently limited: real things always have experience-transcending features. (2) Any real thing whatever is cognitively inexhaustible: inquiry cannot get to the bottom of it. (3) As our inquiry into a thing progresses, we do not merely *add* to our knowledge of it, but generally *change our mind* about it in important ways. The idea of cognitive progress is oriented towards a realm of things and circumstances that are themselves conceived of as relatively stable and unchanging vis-à-vis our changeable conceptions of them. (4) Further aspects of the cognitive inexhaustibility of things. (5) Our *conception* of a thing is thus always corrigible: we always hold it tentatively and provisionally, subject to the realization that it is possibly, nay even presumably, both incomplete and incorrect. (6) The principle of communicative parallax—the circumstance that although throughout one's discourse one only manages to put forward facets of one's own conception of a thing, one always *intends* to convey information about "the actual thing itself." (7) This fundamental intention of objectification—of, say, discussing "the moon itself" (the *real* moon), regardless of how untenable one's ideas about it may ultimately prove to be—is a basic precondition of the very possibility of communication. (8) This intention overrides our commitment to our own conceptions and renders them communicatively irrelevant.

This chapter will address itself to the Kant-reminiscent question: How is interpersonal communication about an intersubjective, common world possible? Given that experience is particular, personal (egocentric), and episodic, how can we project a cognitive bridge from this restricted realm of appearances to the shared, impersonal, and objective order in which alone communication about "the real world" can be realized? It will be argued here that this is possible only by means of certain *imputations*—certain postulated working presuppositions or procedural presumptions whose epistemic bearing does not emerge from experience, but rather affords the basis on which alone the data of experience can be exploited to communicate about an objective factual realm. On this perspective, it emerges as necessary to accord a relatively low weight to our own particular conceptions of communally accessible things in the interests of communicating about them with others.

Let us begin by exploring some basic features of our everyday concept of a *thing* and, in particular, those of its special features that indicate the inherent imperfection—the *inadequacy*—of our knowledge of things.[1] To begin with, it is clear that, as we ordinarily think about things in the conceptual framework of everyday thought and discourse, *any* real thing has more facets than it will ever actually manifest in experience. For every objective property of a real thing has consequences of a dispositional character and these are never surveyable *in toto,* because the dispositions which particular concrete things inevitably have endow them with an infinitistic aspect that cannot be comprehended within experience.[2] This desk, for example, has a limitless manifold of phenomenal features of the form "having such-and-such an appearance from such-and-such a point of view." It is perfectly clear that most of these will never be actualized in experience. Moreover, a thing *is* what it *does:* thing and law are correlates—a good Kantian point. No entity without identity (as Quine has taught us), and world-emplaced things have no identity without nomic comportment. And where there is law, there is an element of universality and nomic necessity that outruns the reach of any finite, actually obtainable evidence. This fact that objectivity demands lawfulness means that the finitude of experience precludes any prospect of the *exhaustive* manifestation of the descriptive facets of any real thing.[3]

Not only do things have more properties than they *ever* will overtly manifest, they have more than they *possibly can* actually manifest. This is so because the dispositional properties of things always involve what might be characterized as *mutually preemptive* conditions of realization. This cube of sugar, for example, has the dispositional property of reacting in such-and-such a way if subjected to a temperature of 10,000° C and of reacting in such-and-such a way if emplaced for 100 hours in a large, turbulent body of water. But if either of these conditions is realized, we destroy the lump of sugar as a lump of sugar, and thus block the prospect of *its* ever bringing the other property to manifestation. The perfectly possible realization of various dispositions may fail to be mutually *compossible,* and so the dispositional properties of a thing cannot ever be manifested completely—not just in practice, but in principle.

The concepts at issue (viz. "experience" and "manifestation") are such that we can only ever *experience* those features of a thing which it actually *manifests*. But the preceding considerations show that real things always have more experientially manifest*able* properties than they can ever actually manifest in experience. The experienced portion of a thing is like the part of the iceberg that shows above water. All real things are—as such—necessarily thought of as having hidden depths.

It is important to realize that the existence of this latent (hidden, occult) sector is a crucial feature of our concept of a thing. Neither in fact nor in thought can we ever simply put it away. To say of the apple that its only features are those it actually manifests is to run afoul of our very conception of an apple. To deny—or even merely to refuse to be committed to the claim—that it *would* manifest such-and-such features *if* such-and-such conditions came about (for example, that it would have such and such a taste if eaten) is to be driven to withdrawing the claim that it is an apple. The process of corroborating the implicit contents of objective factual statements is in principle endless, and such judgments are thus "nonterminating" in C. I. Lewis' sense.[4]

A real thing is always conceptualized as having experience-transcending features. All discourse about objective things involves an element of *experience-transcending imputation*—of commitment to claims that go beyond the experientially acquirable information, but yet claims whose rejection would mean our having to withdraw the thing-characterization at issue. To say of something that it is an apple or a stone or a tree is to become committed to claims about it that go beyond the data we have—and even beyond those which we can, in the nature of things, ever actually acquire. Any claim about the objective features of real things carries us beyond the limits of actual experience.

2. THE COGNITIVE INEXHAUSTIBILITY OF THINGS

The preceding paragraphs have argued that our concept of a thing is such that there is always more to a thing than we can ever actually *experience* of it. We come now to the more radical consideration that this concept is such that there is always more to a thing than one can ever possibly *know* of it.

One basic point must be made at the very outset. The "knowledge" at issue in this discussion is knowledge-that, i.e. that something or other is the case—the sort of knowledge that can be communicated and conveyed by language (rather than by demonstration, as with how-to knowledge of the type at issue in how to hit a forehand at tennis). It is the sort of knowledge that can be formulated and codified, transmitted and received, recorded and stored—language-articulated knowledge, in short.

The number of true descriptive remarks that can be made about a thing—*any* thing—is theoretically inexhaustible. Take a stone. Consider simply its physical features—its shape, its surface texture, its chemistry, etc. And then consider its causal background: its historical genesis and evolution. And then consider its functional aspects as relevant to its uses by the stonemason, the architect, the landscape decorator, etc. There is in principle no theoretical limit to the different lines of consideration available to yield descriptive truths about a thing, so that the totality of facts about a real thing—about anything whatever—is inexhaustible.

Given this circumstance, it follows that we cannot ever feel confident of the capacity of language to afford us the means for coping with the real world. For once it is admitted that there can be nondenumerably many distinct independent facts about an object, then we can no longer suppose our (inherently recursive) descriptive resources to be adequate to the range of objects with which we may have to deal.

The recursive aspect of language means that the most it can ever do is to put a denumerable number of object-descriptors (F_{ij}) at our disposal. Now let it be assumed that the following scheme represents a complete inventory of object-descriptions as articuled in terms of our descriptive resources:

OBJECT CHARACTERIZATIONS IN TERMS OF
INDEPENDENT PRIMITIVE DESCRIPTIVE PARAMETERS

OBJECTS	Parameter 1	Parameter 2		Parameter j
o_i	F_{i1}	F_{i2}		F_{ij}

The "descriptive parameters" at issue here should—given the conditions of the argument—be supposed to represent distinct (independent) primitive descriptive features.

Clearly, it will now be possible to project the hypothesis of an object whose description differs in point of parameter 1 from F_{11}, and in point of parameter 2 from F_{22}, and in general in point of parameter *i* from F_{ii}. And *such* an object—i.e. one answering to *this* description—can nowhere occur within the framework of whatever enumeration the recursive resources of our language has been put at our disposal, though it is certainly not inherently impossible. As a matter of demonstrable necessity, the prospect that there may well be objects that elude our descriptive net cannot be eliminated.

Accordingly, the supposition that our (inherently recursive) descriptive mechanisms can possibly be adequate to the characterization of objects is no longer tenable once the range of (distinct and independent) descriptive facts about an object is admitted to be potentially infinite. Our descriptive resources must now be presumed inadequate to the characterization of objects, and we can no longer count on our ability to get at the whole domain of real-world things by means of the conceptualizing machinery that language affords us.

It is helpful to introduce a distinction at this stage. By a "truth", one should understand a *linguistic* entity—the formulation of a fact in some actual language. Any correct statement in some (actual) language formulates a truth. (And the converse obtains as well: a truth must be embodied in a statement, and cannot exist as a disembodied ghost.) A "fact" on the other hand is *not* a linguistic entity, but an actual circumstance or state of affairs. Anything that is correctly statable in some *possible* language is a fact.[5]

There are *prima facie* more facts than truths. Every truth must state a fact, but it is in principle possible that there will be facts that are never statable in any available language. Facts are *potential* truths whose actualization as such hinges on the availability of appropriate linguistic apparatus for their formulation. Accordingly, it must be presumed that there are facts which will never be captured as truths—though it will obviously be impossible to adduce any concrete instances of this phenomenon.[6]

Truths involve a one-parameter possibilization—they embrace whatever *can* be stated truly in some *actual* language. Facts, on the other hand, involve a two-parameter possibilization—they embrace whatever *can* be stated truly in some *possible* language. Truths are *actualistically* language-correlative, while facts are *possibilistically* language-correlative.[7]

Now knowledge—or at any rate knowledge of the sort that concerns us here, viz., linguistically formulable knowledge-that—is always a recognition of *truths* as such. We thus have no alternative to supposing that the realm of fact regarding things is larger than that of the body of knowledge about them we can possibly ever really possess.

The number of truths (or purported truths) that can be *articulated* about a thing is always (at any historical juncture) finite and remains denumerably infinite even over the theoretical long run. But our concept of the real world is such that there will always be nondenumerably many facts about a thing. And so we cannot articulate—and thus come to know explicitly—"the whole truth" about a thing. The domain of fact transcends the limits of our capacity to *express* it, and a fortiori those of our capacity to know it in overt detail. There are always bound to be more facts than we are able to capture in our linguistic nets.

Yet surely—it might be said—we could have latent or implicit knowledge of an infinite domain. After all, a general truth will always encompass many particular ones—even infinitely many of them. The finite set of axioms of a system will yield infinitely many theorems. And so when we make the shift from overt or explicit to implicit or tacit knowledge, we have the prospect of capturing an infinitely diverse knowledge-content within a finite propositional basis by recourse to deductive systematization.

The matter is not, however, quite so convenient. The totality of the deductive consequences that can be obtained from any finite set of axioms is always denumerable. The most we can ever hope to encompass by any sort of *deductively* implicit containment within a finite basis of truths is a *denumerably infinite* manifold of truths. And thus as long as implicit containment remains a recursive process, it too can never hope to transcend the range of the denumerable, and so cannot hope to encompass the whole of the transdenumerable range of descriptive facts about a thing. (Moreover, even within the denumerable realm, our attempt at deductive systematization runs into difficulties: as we know from Gödel's work, one cannot even hope to systematize—by any recursive, axiomatic process—all of the inherently denumerable truths of arithmetic.)

To be sure, the following objection may still be attempted:

A single suitably general truth can encompass infinitely many descriptive facts—even a transdenumerable infinity of them. If I say of a particular spring that it obeys Hook's law (over a certain range)—assigning it the infinitely rich disposition to displace proportionally with imposed weights—I have implicitly provided for a transdenumerable infinity of descriptive consequences by means of the continuous parameter at issue. Accordingly, while it is true that the actual deductions which one can carry out from an axiomatic

Knowledge

basis are denumerable, they can certainly manage to "cover"—at a
certain level of implicitness—a transdenumerable range of descriptive fact.

The reply here lies in observing that the envisaged process allows
for only one very limited sort of infinitism: the positing of a
determinate value at a certain point of one and the same infinitistic
range of determination—the fixing of particular cases within a
prespecified spectrum. The objection is thus transcended when
one recalls our earlier point that there is in principle no theoretical
limit to the lines of consideration available to provide descriptive
perspectives upon a thing—that the range of descriptive spectra
can always, in principle, be extended. But, to meet the objection at
a still deeper level, let us shift the discussion onto a different
ground and consider some ramifications of the fact that human
inquiry into the nature of things proceeds in an *historical*
framework.

3. EMERGENCE IN THE COGNITIVE SPHERE

The preceding considerations relate to the limits of the knowledge
that can be rationalized on a *fixed and given* conceptual basis. But
in real life a conceptual basis is never "fixed and given." Our
conceptions of things always present a *moving* rather than a *fixed*
object of scrutiny, and this historical dimension must also be
reckoned with.

Any adequate theory of inquiry must recognize that the ongoing
process of science is a process of *conceptual* innovation that
always leaves certain theses wholly outside the cognitive range of
the inquirers of any particular period. This means that there will
always be facts (or plausible candidate-facts) about a thing that we
do not *know* because we cannot even *conceive* of them. For to
grasp such a fact means taking a perspective of consideration that
we simply do not have, since the state of knowledge (or purported
knowledge) is not yet advanced to a point at which its entertain-
ment is feasible. In bringing conceptual innovation about, cognitive progress makes it possible to consider new possibilities that
were heretofore conceptually inaccessible.

The language of emergence can perhaps be deployed profitably
to make the point. But what is at issue is not an emergence of *the*

features of things, but an emergence in our *knowledge* about them. The blood circulated in the human body well before Harvey; uranium-containing substances were radioactive before Becquerel. The emergence at issue relates to our cognitive mechanisms of conceptualization, not to the *objects* of our consideration in and of themselves. Real-world objects are conceived of as antecedent to any cognitive interaction—as being there right along, "pregiven" as Edmund Husserl puts it. Any cognitive changes or innovations are to be conceptualized as something that occurs on our side of the cognitive transaction, and not on the side of the objects with which we deal.[8]

And the prospect of change can never be dismissed in this domain. The properties of a thing are literally open-ended: We can always discover more of them. Even if we view the world as inherently finitistic, and espouse a Principle of Limited Variety which has it that nature can be portrayed descriptively with the materials of a finite taxonomic scheme, there can be no *a priori* guarantee that the progress of science will not lead *ad indefinitum* to changes of mind regarding this finite register of descriptive materials. And this conforms exactly to our expectation in these matters. For where the real things of the world are concerned, we not only expect to learn more about them in the course of scientific inquiry, *we expect to have to change our mind about their nature and mode of comportment.* Be they elm trees, or volcanoes, or quarks, we have every expectation that in the course of future scientific progress people will come to think differently about them in days to come than we ourselves do at this juncture.

Cognitive inexhaustibility thus emerges as a definitive feature of our conception of a real thing. In claiming knowledge about such things, we are always aware that the object transcends what we know about it—that yet further and different facts concerning it can always come to light, and that all that we *do* say about it does not exhaust all that *can* be said about it.

Things are cognitively opaque—we cannot see to the bottom of them. Knowledge can become more *extensive* without thereby becoming more *complete.* And this view of the situation is rather supported than impeded if we abandon a cumulativist/preservationist view of knowledge or purported knowledge for the view that new discoveries need not *supplement* but can *displace* old ones. We realize full well that people will come to think differently about things from the way we ourselves do—even when thoroughly familiar things are at issue.

The concept of a thing so functions in our conceptual scheme that things are thought of as having an identity, a nature, and a mode of comportment wholly indifferent to the cognitive state-of-the-art regarding them, and presumably very different from our conceptions of the matter. But this is something we presume or postulate; it is certainly not something we have discovered—or ever could discover. We are not—and will never be—in a position to evade or abolish the contrast between "things as we think them to be" and "things as they actually and truly are." Their susceptibility to further elaborative detail—and to changes of mind regarding this further detail—is built into our very conception of a "real thing." To be a real thing is to be something regarding which we can always in principle acquire more information.

And much the same story holds when our concern is not with things, but with *types* of things. To say that something is copper (or is magnetic) is to say more than that it has the properties we think copper or magnetic things to have, and indeed to say more than that it meets our test-conditions for being copper (or being magnetic). It is to say that this thing *is* copper (or magnetic). And this is an issue regarding which we are prepared at least to contemplate the prospect that we've got it wrong.

This factor of cognitive inexhaustibility is closely linked to the discussion (in Chapter II above) of the epistemic gap which always separates the evidence from the content of our objective factual claims. Not by *closing*, but only by *leaping across* this gap—a move rendered possible by the distinction between use-conditions and truth-conditions—do we manage to attain objectivity. The tolerant acceptance of this gap is the price we must pay for the attainment of objectivity in the face of the cognitive inexhaustibility of things.

4. IMPLICATIONS OF COGNITIVE INEXHAUSTIBILITY

In view of the cognitive inexhaustibility of things, we must never pretend to a cognitive monopoly or cognitive finality. This recognition is inherent in our conception of a "real thing." For, as we have seen, it is a crucial facet of our epistemic stance towards the real world to recognize that every part and parcel of it has features lying beyond our present cognitive reach—at *any* "present" whatsoever.

In this regard real things differ in an interesting and important way from their fictional counterparts. To make this difference plain, it is useful to distinguish between two types of information about a thing, namely that which is *generic* and that which is not. Generic information tells about those features of the thing which it has in common with everything else of its kind or type. For example, a particular snowflake will share with all others certain facts about its structure, its chemical composition, its melting-point, etc. On the other hand, it will also have various properties which it does not share with other members of its own infimum species—its particular shape, for example, or the angular momentum of its descent. These are its nongeneric features.

Now a key fact about *fictional* particulars is that they are of finite cognitive depth. A point will always be reached with regard to them when one cannot say anything characteristically new about them—presenting non-generic information that is not inferentially implicit in what has already been said. (New *generic* information can of course always be forthcoming through the progress of science. When we learn more about coal-in-general we learn more about the coal in Sherlock Holmes' grate.) The *finiteness* of their cognitive depth means that the presentation of ampliatively novel non-generic information must in the very nature of the case come to a stop where fictional things are at issue.

With *real* things, on the other hand, there is no reason of principle why this process need ever terminate. *Au contraire,* we have every reason to presume them to be cognitively inexhaustible. And any adequate metaphysico-epistemological world-view must recognize that the ongoing progress of science is a process of *conceptual* innovation that always leaves some facts about things wholly outside the cognitive range of the inquirers of any particular period.

It is of course imaginable that natural science will come to a stop, and do so not in the trivial sense of a cessation of intelligent life, but in Charles Sanders Peirce's more interesting sense of eventually reaching a condition after which even indefinitely ongoing inquiry will not—and indeed actually *cannot*—produce any significant change. Such a position is in theory possible. But we can never *know*—be it in practice or in principle—that it is actual. We can never establish that science has attained such an ω-condition of final completion: the possibility of further change lying "just around the corner" can never be ruled out finally and decisively. We thus have no alternative to *presuming* that our science is still imperfect and incomplete.

A further line of consideration is important here. Man's material resources are limited. And these limits inexorably circumscribe our cognitive access to the real world. There are interactions with nature of so massive a scale (as measured in such parameters as energy, pressure, temperature, particle-velocities, etc.) that their realization would require the deployment of resources so great that we can never achieve them. But if there are interactions to which we have no access, then there are (presumably) phenomena which we cannot discern. It would be unreasonable to expect nature to confine the distribution of phenomena of potential cognitive significance to those ranges that lie within the horizons of our vision. Where there are inaccessible phenomena, there must be cognitive incompleteness. To this extent, at any rate, the empiricists were surely right. Only the most hidebound of rationalists could uphold the capacity of sheer intellect to compensate for lack of data. Where there are unobserved phenomena we must reckon with the prospect that our theoretical systematizations may well be (nay, presumably are) incomplete. And so, if certain phenomena are inaccessible (even if only for the "merely practical" reasons mooted here), then we have no alternative but to presume our scientific knowledge of nature to be imperfect.[9]

It thus emerges that fundamental features inherent in the very structure of man's inquiry into the ways of the world comspire to assure the incompleteness of the knowledge we can attain in this sphere. We are led back to the thesis of the great Idealist philosophers (Spinoza, Hegel, Bradley, Royce) that human knowledge inevitably falls short of "perfected science" (the Idea, the Absolute), and must be presumed deficient both in its completeness and its correctness.

5. THE CORRIGIBILITY OF CONCEPTIONS

To be sure, these deliberations regarding cognitive inadequacy are less concerned with the correctness of our particular *claims* about things than with our very *conceptions* of them. And in this connection it deserves stress that there is a significant and substantial difference between a true or correct *statement* or *contention* on the one hand, and a true or correct *conception* on the other. To make a true contention about a thing we need merely get *some one particular fact* about it straight. To have a true conception of the thing, on the other hand, we must get *all of the important facts* about it straight. (It is clear that this involves a certain *normative* element—namely what the "important" or "essential" facets of something are.) With a correct contention (statement) about a thing, all is well if we get the single relevant aspect of it right, but with a correct conception of it *we must get the essentials right—we must have the correct overall picture.*[10]

To assure the correctness of our conception of a thing we would have to be sure—as we very seldom are—that nothing further can possibly come along to upset our view of just what its important features are and just what their character is. The qualifying-conditions for true conceptions are thus far more demanding than those for true claims. No doubt, in the 5th Century, B.C., Anaximander of Miletus may have made many correct contentions about the sun—for example, that it is not a mass of burning stuff pulled about on its circuit by a deity with a chariot drawn by a winged horse. But Anaximander's *conception* of the sun (as the flaming spoke of a great wheel of fire encircling the earth) was seriously wrong.

At this stage the discussion will enter upon a crucial transition. So far it has been concerned to stress the *incompleteness* of our knowledge of things. But now we must recognize its presumptive *incorrectness* as well. For our conception of any real particular is always held tentatively, subject to a mental reservation of sorts—a full recognition that it may ultimately prove to be mistaken. We view conceptions as inherently defeasible. Since having a correct conception of something as the object it is requires that we have all the important facts about it right, and since the prospect of discovering further important facts can never be eliminated, the possibility can never be eliminated that matters may so eventuate that we may ultimately (with the wisdom of hindsight) acknowledge the impropriety of our earlier conceptions.

With *conceptions*—unlike propositions or *contentions*—incompleteness means incorrectness, or at any rate *presumptive* incorrectness. A conception which is based on incomplete data must be assumed to be at least partially incorrect. If we can decipher only half the inscription, our conception of its over-all content must be largely conjectural—and thus must be *presumed* to contain an admixture of error. When our information about something is incomplete, obtaining an overall picture of the thing at issue becomes a matter of theorizing, or guesswork, however sophisticatedly executed. And then we have no alternative but to suppose that this over-all picture falls short of being wholly correct in various (unspecifiable) ways. With conceptions, falsity can thus emerge from errors of *omission* as well as those of *commission,* resulting from the circumstance that the information at our disposal is merely incomplete, rather than actually false (as will have to be the case with contentions).

It is important to be clear about just what point is at issue here. It is certainly not being denied that people do indeed know many truths about things, for example, that Caesar did correctly know many things about his sword. Rather, what is being maintained is not only that there were many things he did not know about it (for example, that it contained tungsten), but also that his over-all conception of it was in many ways inadequate and in some ways incorrect.

In his *Cartesian Meditations,* Edmund Husserl develops the interesting idea of a *horizon* in perceptual knowledge, a phenomenon that roots in the fact that our awareness always pertains to a mere *aspect or part* of the object that we actually perceive, and never the whole thing. It follows that some element of indeterminacy is present throughout perceptual knowledge, because the percipient is never separated from a recognition that, for all he knows, the unperceived aspects of the object may be quite different from what he *thinks* them to be. Our present discussion in effect shifts this discussion from the sphere of *perception* to that of *conception.* The point is that our conceptualized knowledge of things is always limited by a horizon across which we cannot "see" and beyond which matters are so situated that the impressions we have based upon incomplete information may well become falsified.

An inadequate or incomplete description of anything is not thereby false—the statements we make about it may be perfectly true as far as they go. But an inadequate or incomplete conception of a thing is *eo ipso* one that we have no choice but to presume to be *incorrect* as well,[11] seeing that where there is incompleteness we cannot justifiably take the stance that it relates only to inconsequential matters and touches nothing important. Accordingly, our conceptions of particular things are always to be viewed not just as cognitively *open-ended,* but as *corrigible* as well.

The concept of a *thing* that underlies our discourse about the things of this world is thus based on a certain sort of tentativity and fallibilism—the implicit recognition that our own personal or even communal conception of things may well be wrong, and is in any case inadequate. At the bottom of our thought about things there is always a certain wary scepticism that recognizes the possibility of error.

6. COMMUNICATIVE PARALLAX

The fact that real things have hidden depths—that they are cognitively opaque—has important ramifications that reach to the very heart of the theory of communication.

Any particular thing—the moon, for example—is such that two related but critically different versions of it can be contemplated:

    (1) the moon, the actual moon as it "really" is

and

    (2) the moon as somebody (you or I or the Babylonians)
        conceives of it.

The crucial fact to note in this connection is that it is virtually always the former item—the thing itself—that we INTEND to communicate or think (= self-communicate) about, the thing *as it is,* and not the thing *as somebody conceives of it.* Yet we cannot but recognize the justice of Kant's teaching that the "I think" (I maintain, assert, etc.) is an everpresent implicit accompaniment of every claim or contention that we make. This factor of attributability dogs our every assertion and opens up the unavoidable prospect of "getting it wrong."

Ambitious intentions or pretentions to the contrary notwithstanding, all that one can ever actually manage to bring off in one's purportedly fact-assertive discourse is to deliver information about item (2)—to convey what one thinks or conceives to be so. I can readily distinguish the features of (what I take to be) "the real moon" from those of "the moon as *you* conceive of it," but I cannot distinguish them from those of "the moon as *I* conceive of it." And when *I* maintain "The moon is roughly spherical" all that I have successfully managed to deliver to you by way of actual information is "Rescher maintains that the moon is roughly spherical." And there is nothing that can be done to alter this circumstance—it doesn't matter how loudly I bang on the table. If you bind me by the injunction, "Tell me something about the Eiffel Tower, but please don't put before me your beliefs or convictions regarding it; just give me facts about the thing itself, rather than presenting any parts of your conception of it!", you condemn me to the silence of the Lockean *je ne sais quoi.*

Let us employ the phrase *communicative parallax* to signalize this circumstance that throughout one's discourse about things one always INTENDS to convey information about "the actual thing itself" but only MANAGES to disclose facets of one's *conception* of the thing. With optical parallax, *where* you see something to be depends on *where you stand* in regard to it. With communicative parallax *how* you see something to be depends on *how you stand* in regard to it. This parallax reflects an inevitable slippage between intention and accomplishment in all fact-stating or fact-purporting discourse.

Now it is important to realize that it is *not* the case that two *different things* are at issue where we talk of "parallax." It would be a grave mistake of illicit hypostatization to reify "the *X* as we see it" into a *thing* distinct from the real *X*. "Harry as I picture him" may be very unlike, and quite different from, "the real Harry," but it is still the real Harry that is the *intended object* of my conception, however little it may do him justice. The world is not populated by many Harrys—the real one, and mine, and yours, etc., each answering to our respective (distinct) conceptions of him. "Harry as I conceive of him" may well not exist *as such* but this does not block my conception from having Harry—the *real* Harry—as its object. The star we take ourselves to see (the star "as we see it") is not a different *entity*—a thing distinct from "the real star." It *is* the real star, but seen as somehow displaced from its true position in the scheme of things. And much the same holds where communicative parallax is at issue. Here "the thing itself" that contrasts with "the thing as we conceive of it" is not a *different* thing: it is the very selfsame thing which our conception *intends* to capture. The *distinction* between our moon, say, and that of the Babylonians represents no *difference* in object. We have to espouse the view that only one thing—the moon itself—is at issue, which is, as it were, "seen differently" by different discussants. To bring it on the stage of discussion is not to multiply entities by invoking the membership of a cognitively inaccessible transcendental realm, but simply to employ a distinguishing contrast to give convenient expression to the crucial fact of the potential inadequacy of our conceptions.

To speak of parallax is misleading in one way. For we know what allowances to make for astronomical parallax. We do not—and in the nature of the thing *cannot*—know what allowances to make for *communicative* parallax. We are never in a position to realize *how* our conception of a thing is inadequate—we can only realize *that* it may well be so.[12]

7. THE INTENTIONALITY OF INTERPERSONAL COMMUNICATION

There is nothing unfortunate or regrettable about the fact of communicative parallax. Quite the reverse, it serves an important and positive function. For it is crucial to the achievement of intersubjective objectivity in discourse.

After all, the teleology of language is nothing mysterious and occult. Language is primarily a purposive instrument whose cardinal aim is the transmission of information for the sake of implementation in action. Language is designed to afford us resources for information storage and mechanisms for the inter-personal exchange of information needed for the coherent pursuit of individual goals and the coordination of effort in the pursuit of common goals. And only the accomplishment-transcending IN-TENTION to discuss "the thing itself" makes communication possible. If my discourse were directed at *my* moon-conception and yours directed at *your* moon-conception, we could never lock communicative horns. Two different objects would be at issue. The prospect of agreement and disagreement would vanish and the prospect of interpersonal communication about a common object would vanish with it. Moreover, any trans-historical comparability of objects would go by the board. The sun and moon of the Babylonian priest-astrologers would be as disjoint from ours as are our respective deities. Communicative parallax would be over-come, but at an awesome price—communicative anarchy. The exact configuration of information that I myself have about a thing at first hand is always something personal and idiosyncratic—based upon the contingencies of what I "happen to have experi-enced" about it and what I "happen to have gathered" about the experience of others. In making objective assertions about some-thing, it is thus crucial that I intend to discuss "the thing itself" rather than "the thing just precisely as I conceive of it" relative to the body of information I have about it. Only the former is something that somebody else can get hold of; the latter certainly is not. The imputational move beyond the data at hand is indispens-ably demanded by that step into the domain of the publicly accessible objects in whose absence interpersonal communication about a shared world becomes impossible.

This fundamental intention of objectification, the intention to discuss "the moon itself" (the real moon) regardless of how untenable one's own *ideas* about it may eventually prove to be is a basic precondition of the very possibility of communication. It is crucial to the communicative enterprise to take the egocentrism-avoiding stance of an epistemological Copernicanism that rejects all claims to a privileged status for *our own* conception of things.

The workings of communicative parallax root in the fact that we are prepared to "discount any misconceptions" (our own included) about things over a very wide range indeed—that we are committed to the stance that factual disagreements as to the character of things are communicatively irrelevant within enormously broad limits. The incorrectness of conceptions is venial.

We are able to say something about the (real) Sphinx because of our submission to a fundamental communicative convention or "social contract" to the effect that we *intend* ("mean") to talk about it—the very thing itself as it "really" is—our own private conception of it notwithstanding. We arrive at the standard policy that prevails with respect to all communicative discourse of letting "the language we use," rather than whatever specific informative aims we may actually "have in mind" on particular occasions, be the decisive factor with regard to the things at issue in our discourse. When I speak about the Sphinx—even though I do so on the basis of my own conception of what is involved here—I will nevertheless be taken to be discussing "the *real* Sphinx" in virtue of the basic conventionalized intention at issue with regard to the operation of referring terms.

Communication requires not only common *concepts* but common *topics*—shared items of discussion, a common world of selfsubsistently real "an sich" objects basic to shared experience. The factor of objectivity reflects our basic commitment of a shared world as the common property of communicators. Such a commitment involves more than merely *de facto* intersubjective agreement. For such agreement is a matter of a *posteriori* discovery, while our view of the nature of things puts "the real world" on a necessary and *a priori* basis. This stance roots in the fundamental convention of a shared social insistence on communicating—the commitment to an objective world of real things as affording the crucially requisite common focus needed for any genuine communication.

Someone might object:

> How can recourse to "the thing itself" possibly facilitate communication? My interlocutor cannot lay hold of this any more than I can,

> seeing that it has features transcending anyone's conception of it. So how can it serve to establish contact between us.

This objection misses the point. We do indeed "lay hold of" the thing itself—not by way of information, by inquiry or investigation, but *by fiat or postulation*. What links my discourse with that of my interlocutor is our common subscription to the *a priori* presumption (a defeasible presumption, to be sure) that we are talking in common about a shared thing, our own possible misconceptions of it notwithstanding. Communicative parallax assures us of being in touch with one another from the very outset. And it means that no matter how much we change our mind about the *nature* of a thing (the moon) or type of thing (the whale), we are still dealing with exactly the same thing or sort of thing. It assures reidentification across theories and belief-systems.

Again someone might object:

> But surely we can get by on the basis of personal conceptions alone, without invoking the notion of "a thing itself." My conception of a thing is something I can convey to you, given enough time. Cannot communication proceed by correlating and matching personal conceptions, without appeal to the intermediation of "the thing itself."

But think here of the concrete practicalities. What is "enough time"? When is the match "sufficient" to underwrite out right identification? The cash value of our commitment to the thing itself is that it enables us to make this identification straight away by imputation, by fiat on the basis of modest indicators, rather than on the basis of an appeal to the inductive weight of a body of evidence that is always bound to be problematic. Communication is something we *set out* to do, not something we ultimately discern, with the wisdom of eventual hindsight, to have accomplished retrospectively.

Nevertheless, these objections make a useful contribution. They engender recognition that "the thing itself" operative in this discussion is not a peculiar sort of *thing*—a new ontological category—but rather a shorthand formula for a certain policy of communicative presumption or impulation, namely that of an *a priori* commitment to the idea of a commonality of objective focus that is to be allowed to stand unless and until circumstances arise to render this untenable.

The objectifying imputation at issue here lies at the very basis of our cognitive stance that we live and operate in a world of real and objective things. This commitment to the idea of a shared real world is crucial for communication. Its status is *a priori:* its existence is not something we learn of through experience. As Kant clearly saw, objective experience is possible only if the existence of such a real, objective world is *presupposed* at the onset rather than seen as a matter of *ex post facto* discovery about the nature of things.

What is at issue here is thus not a matter of *discovery*, but one of *imputation*. The element of community, of identity of focus is not a matter of *ex post facto* learning from experience, but of an *a priori* predetermination inherent in our approach to language-use. We do not *infer* things as being real and objective from our phenomenal data, but establish our perception as authentic perception OF genuine objects through the fact that these objects are given—or rather, *taken*—as real and objectively existing things from the first.[13] Objectivity is not deduced but imputed.

A closer look at the precise character of the justification of our evidence-transcending imputations is in order. The authorizing warrant for the imputational thrust of our objective categorial judgment ultimately resides in the purposive teleology of language-use—the desire for successful communication. It was suggested above that this is simply a matter of this-or-nothing— that if we wish to achieve answers to our questions about the world and if we wish to communicate with one another about matters of objective fact, then we simply have no alternative but to undertake such evidence-transcending commitments. But we now see that this focus on this-or-nothing considerations is by no means the whole story. For the consideration that we *must* proceed in this way—the fact of *practical necessity* that there just is no alternative if our objective is to be reached—stops well short of achieving full adequacy in its justificatory force. It does not offer us any assurance that we actually will succeed in our endeavor if we do proceed in this way; it just has it that we won't if we don't. The issue of actual effectiveness remains untouched. And here we have no choice but to proceed experientially—by the simple strategem of "trying and seeing." Practical necessity remains a matter of *a priori* considerations, but efficacy—actual sufficiency—will be a matter of *a posteriori* experience. The justification of claims of efficacy emerges through pragmatic retrojustication—a retrospective revalidation in the light of experience. The pragmatic consideration that our praxis of inquiry and communication does actually work—that we can effectively and (by and large) successfully communicate with one another about a shared world, inquiry into whose nature and workings proceeds successfully as a communal project of investigation—is the ultimately crucial consideration that legitimates the evidence-transcending imputations built into the praxis-governing use-conditions of language.

In answering the question of what justifies our recourse to the evidence-transcending imputations we thus proceed at two levels. On the negative side we confront the realization that we *must* accept them; it is this or nothing, given the goals of the enterprise. On the positive side, we involve a pragmatic retrojustification based on the fact that our proceeding in this way underwrites an actually effective praxis.[14]

8. THE COMMUNICATIVE IRRELEVANCE OF CONCEPTIONS

The objectivity at issue in our communicative discourse is a matter of its status rather than its content. It is not (necessarily) the substantive content of the work that tells us whether it is factual or fictional, but something we determine from the context (e.g., the introduction or even the dust jacket) before we take up the work itself. It is a matter of the frame, not of the canvas. The fact-oriented basis of our exchanges is a matter of a conventionalized intention, fixed *a priori,* to talk about "the real world."

This intention to take real objects to be at issue, objects as they are in themselves, our potentially idiosyncratic conceptions of them quite aside, is fundamental because it is overriding—that is, it overrides all of our other intentions when we enter upon the communicative venture. Without this conventionalized intention we should not be able to convey information—or misinformation—to one another about a shared "objective" world. We could never establish communicative contact about a common objective item of discussion if our discourse were geared to the things as conceived of in terms of our own specific information about them.

Any pretensions to the predominance, let alone the correctness of our own conceptions regarding the furniture of this realm must be put aside in the context of communication. The fundamental intention to deal with the objective order of this "real world" is crucial. If our assertoric commitments did not transcend the information we ourselves have on hand, we would never be able to "get in touch" with others about a shared objective world. No claim is made for the *primacy* of our conceptions, or for the *correctness* of our conceptions, or even for the mere *agreement* of our conceptions with those of others. The fundamental intention to discuss "the thing itself" predominates and overrides any mere dealing with the thing as we ourselves conceive of it.

This ever-operative contrast between "the thing itself" and "the thing as we ourselves take it to be" means that we are never in a position to claim definitive finality for our conception of a thing. We are never entitled to claim to have exhausted it *au fond* in cognitive regards—that we have managed to bring it wholly within our epistemic grasp. For to make this claim would, in effect, be to *identify* "the thing itself" in terms of "our own conception of it," an identification which would effectively remove the former item (the thing itself) from the stage of consideration as an independent entity in its own right by endowing our conception with decisively determinative force. And this would lead straightaway to the unpleasant result of a cognitive solipsism that would preclude reference to intersubjectively identifiable particulars, and would thus block the possibility of interpersonal communication.

Seen in *this* light, the key point may be put as follows: It is indeed a presupposition of effective communicative discourse about a thing that we purport (claim and intend) to make true statements about it. But it is *not* required for such discourse that we purport to have a true or even adequate conception of the thing at issue. On the contrary, we must deliberately abstain from any claim that our own conception is definitive if we are to engage successfully in discourse. We deliberately put the whole matter of conception aside—abstracting from the question of the agreement of my conception with yours, and all the more from the issue of which of us has the right conception.[15]

If we were to set up our own conception as somehow definitive and decisive, we would at once erect a grave impediment to the prospect of successful communication with one another. Communication could then only proceed retrospectively with the wisdom of the hindsight. It would be realized only in the implausible case that extensive exchange indicates that there has been an *identity* of conceptions all along. We would then learn only by experience—at the end of a long process of wholly tentative and provisional exchange. And we would always stand on very shaky ground. For no matter how far we push our inquiry into the issue of an identity of conceptions, the prospect of a divergence lying just around the corner—waiting to be discovered if only we pursued the matter just a bit further—can never be precluded. One could never advance the issue of the identity of focus past the status of a more or less well-grounded *assumption*. And then any so-called communication is no longer an exchange of information but a tissue of frail conjectures. The communicative enterprise would become a vast inductive project—a complex exercise in theory-building, leading tentatively and provisionally toward something which, in fact, the imputational groundwork of our language enables us to presuppose from the very outset.[16]

The fact that we need not agree on our conceptions of things means, *a fortiori*, that we need not be correct in our conceptions of things to communicate successfully about them. This points, in part, to the trivial fact that I need not agree with what you are saying to understand you. But it points also, more importantly, to the consideration that my having a conception of a thing massively different from yours will not prevent me from taking you to be talking about the same thing that I have in mind. Objectivity and referential commonality of focus are matters of initial presumption or presupposition. The issue here is not with what *is* understood, but with what *is to be* understood (by anybody) in terms of a certain generalized and communicative intentions. (The issue here is not one of *meaning* but only of *meaningfulness*.)

Our concept of a *real thing* is accordingly such that a thing is a fixed point, a stable center around which communication revolves, the invariant focus of potentially diverse conceptions. What is to be determinative, decisive, definitive, (etc.) of the things at issue in my discourse is not my conception, or yours, or indeed anyone's conception at all. The conventionalized intention discussed above means that: a coordination of conceptions is not decisive for the possibility of communication. Your statements about a thing will convey something to me even if my conception of it is altogether different from yours. To communicate we need not take ourselves to share views of the word, but only to take the stance that we share the world being discussed.

In communication regarding things we must be able to exchange information about them with our contemporaries and to transmit information about them to our successors. And we must be in a position to do this in the face of the presumption that *their* conceptions of things are not only radically different from *ours*, but conceivably also rightly different. What is at issue here is not the commonplace that we do not know *everything* about anything. Rather, the key consideration is the more interesting thesis that it is a crucial precondition of the possibility of successful communication about things that we must avoid laying any claim either *to the completeness or even to the ultimate correctness of our own conceptions* of any of the things at issue.

It is crucial that the mechanisms of human communication should lie within the domain of human power. Now with respect to the *meanings of words* this condition is satisfied, because this is something that we ourselves fix by custom or by fiat. But *the correctness of conceptions* is not simply a matter of human discretion—it is something that lies outside the sphere of our effective control. For a "correct conception" is akin to Spinoza's *true idea* of which he stipulates that it must "agree with its object"[17]—in circumstances where this issue of agreement may well elude us. (Man proposes but does not dispose with respect to this matter of idea/actuality coordination.) We do, no doubt, *purport* our conceptions to be correct, but whether this is indeed so is something we cannot tell with assurance until "all the returns are in"—that is, never. This fact renders it critically important *that* (and understandable *why*) conceptions are communicatively irrelevant. Our discourse *reflects* our conceptions and perhaps *conveys* them, but it is not substantive *about* them.

The conception of a thing may be the vehicle of thought, but it is never the determinant of reference. By their very nature, conceptions are too personal—and thus potentially too idiosyncratic—for our communicative needs. For communication, interpersonal and public instrumentalities are indispensably requisite. And language affords this desideratum. It provides the apparatus by which the *identity* of the referents of our discourse becomes fixed, however imperfectly we ourselves perceive their nature. (The specifications of things as enshrined in language are Kripkean "rigid designators" in an *epistemic* manner: our indicators for real-things-in-the-world are *designed* in both senses, constructed and intended to perform—insofar as possible—an invariant identificatory job across the diversified spectrum of epistemic worlds.)

How do we really know that Anaximander was talking about *our* sun? He isn't here to tell us. He didn't leave elaborate discussion about his aims and purposes. How can we be so confident of what he meant to talk about? The answer is straightforward. That he is *to be taken* to talk about *our* sun is, in something that turns, the final analysis, on two very general issues in which Anaximander himself plays little if any role at all: (1) our subscription to certain generalized principles of interpretation with respect to the Greek language, and (2) the conventionalized subscription by us and ascription to other language-users in general of certain fundamental communicative policies and intentions. In the face of appropriate functional equivalences we allow neither a difference in language nor a difference or "thought-worlds" to block an identity of reference.[18]

The pivotal INTENTION to communicate about a common object—resigning any and all claims to regard our own conceptions of it as definitive (decisive)—is the indispensable foundation of all communication. And this intention is not something personal and idiosyncratic—a biographical aspect of certain particular minds—it is a shared feature of "social mind," built into the use of language as a publicly available communicative resource. The wider social perspective is crucial. In subscribing to the conventionalized intention at issue, we sink ''our own point of view'' in the interests of entering into the wider community of fellow communicators. Only by admitting the potential distortion of one's own conceptions of things through ''communicative parallax'' can one manage to reach across the gulf of divergent conceptions so as to get into communicative touch with one another. In this context, the pretention-humbling stance of a cognitive Copernicanism is not only a matter of virtue, but one of necessity as well. It is the price we pay for keeping the channels of communication open.

The commitment to *objectivity* is basic to our discourse with one another about a shared world of ''real things'' to which none of us is in a position to claim privileged access. This commitment establishes a need to ''distance'' ourselves from things—i.e., to recognize the prospect of a discrepancy between our (potentially idiosyncratic) conceptions of things and the true character of these things as they exist objectively in ''the real world.'' The everpresent contrast between ''the thing as we view it'' and ''the thing as it is'' is the mechanism by which this crucially important distancing is accomplished.

The information that we may have about a thing—be it real or presumptive information—is always just that, viz. information that WE lay claim to. We cannot but recognize that it is person-relative and in general person-differentiated. Our attempts at communication and inquiry are thus undergirded by an information-transcending stance—the stance that we communally inhabit a shared world of objectively existing things—a world of ''real things'' amongst which we live and into which we inquire but about which we do and must presume ourselves to have only imperfect information at any and every particular stage of the cognitive venture. This is not something we learn. The ''facts of experience'' can never reveal it to us. It is something we postulate or presuppose. Its epistemic status is not that of an empirical discovery, but that of a presupposition that is a product of a transcendental argument for the very possibility of communication or inquiry as we standardly conceive of them.

We thus arrive at the key idea which these lines of thought contribute to the present deliberations. True enough, cognitive change carries conceptual change in its wake. But nevertheless—

and this point is crucial—we have an ongoing commitment to a manifold of objective *things* that are themselves impervious to conceptual and cognitive change. This committment is built into the very ground-rules that govern our use of language and embody our determination to maintain the picture of a relatively stable world amidst the ever-changing panorama of cognitive world-pictures. The continuing succession of the different states of science are all linked to a pre- or sub-scientific view of an ongoing "real world" in which we live and work, a world portrayed rather more stably in the *lingua franca* of everyday-life communication and populated by shared things whose stability amidst cognitive change is something rather *postulated* than learned. This postulation reflects the realistic stance that the things we encounter in experience are the *subject* and not the *product* of our inquiry.

PART THREE
Questions and Inquiry

VI

The Epistemology of Factual Questions and Inquiry

SYNOPSIS

(1) Preliminary observations regarding questions. The idea of an explicit answer. An analysis of issues involved in the *presuppositions* of questions. (2) A survey of various modes of illegitimacy of questions. (3) How an erotetic agenda stands correlative with a *cognitive* "state of the art." (4) Questions can not only be *answered,* they can also become *dissolved.* (5) The state of questioning is a transitory phenomenon dynamically geared to an everchanging body of knowledge. (6) How questions can prove to be unavailable. (7) Kant's Principle of Question Propagation and the role of new questions in providing an ever-renewed impetus to inquiry.

1. INTRODUCTION

Before turning to the *epistemology* of questions and inquiry, it is useful to review some preliminary issues regarding the *logic and semantics* of questions.[1]

The idea of an information-eliciting question is correlative with that of answers endeavoring to provide the information asked for. When an answer is offered, the questioner need not, of course, be in a position to recognize whether or not this answer is *correct.* But the questioner should certainly be in a position to recognize that the proffered answer is an *admissible* one that is apposite to the question at issue. One has not posed a well-defined question if one is not in a position to recognize a *possible* answer to it as such—if one does not even know what is to count as an answer. A question is only posed cogently when one has in view a range of admissible (*possible* or *feasible* or *appropriate* answers)—statements that afford *ostensible,* but not necessarily *true or correct* answers. Such a range of possible alternative answers may be either finite ("Was he present—yes or no?") or infinite ("What is the length of yonder bridge?" or "What's an example of a calculus problem?"). Indeed, in principle this range can be all-inclusive and wholly boundaryless ("What's Henry thinking about right now?").

An *explicit* (ostensible) answer to a question is one that repeats the substance of the question itself, so that it is determinable from the answer itself that is is an answer to the question at issue (inter alia). ("What's an example of a color?"—"Red is an example of a color.") Not every (ostensible) answer to a question is an explicit one (the reply to the preceding question might simply have been "red"), but every question has such explicit answers. To be sure, a given proposition may explicitly answer very different questions, for example "Henry is the tallest person in the room" will answer "What's distinctive about Henry?" or "Who is the tallest person in the room?" But an explicit answer is one that is so formulated as to make evident that it could serve as an answer to a particular question. (The somewhat stilted response, "Henry is the person who is the tallest person in the room" affords an example for the preceding case.) An explicit answer wears its question on its sleeve, and is such that it counts as completely, but just completely answering the question.[2]

When actually different albeit verbally same-seeming questions are at issue, their explicit answers will bring this fact to light. Thus "Why do owls hoot?" may mean "Why do *owls* hoot (while sparrows, for example, chirp)" or else "Why do owls *hoot* (rather than, say, bark)?" In specifying the range of full (ostensible) answers, a questioner disambiguates the issue, and bring to light the exact question he has in view. This is particularly clear with questions like "When did X occur?" or "How long is Z?" which in fact cover a whole spectrum of distinct questions: "When (to the nearest second, or day or year, etc.) did X occur?" or "How long (to the nearest centimeter, or inch, or mile) is Z?" Such questions remain ill-defined until a degree of precision is specified. They invite a counter-question rather than an answer.

A *presupposition* of a question is a thesis (or proposition) that is entailed by each and every one of its admissible explicit answers. Its presuppositions enter into the very way in which the question is formulated. Thus the question "Have you stopped beating your wife?" has two ostensible answers: "(Yes,) I have stopped beating my wife" and "(No,) I have not stopped beating my wife." Both of these alternatives, "Yes" and "No" alike, share the supposition that I have a wife, which, accordingly, is a presupposition of the question, as is (among others) "I can beat my wife." Again, "Who murdered Sir George?" has a range of ostensible answers: "The butler murdered Sir George," "The chauffeur murdered Sir George," etc., all of which imply "Someone murdered Sir George" (i.e., "Sir George has been murdered"), which, accordingly, emerges as a presupposition of the question. The presuppositions of our questions reflect *precommitments*—they constitute what we bring to the very posing of our questions, rather than something we take away as a result of answering them. A question whose presuppositions are not satisfied simply "does not arise." If Sir George is alive and well, or if he died of old age peacefully in his sleep, the question of who murdered him is totally inappropriate.

A few further examples of question/presupposition relationship may help to clarify the issue:

Question	Presupposition
"Is it—or is it not—the case that p?"	"p is a meaningful thesis"
"Why is it the case that p?"	"p is a true thesis"
"When is it the case (i.e., does it happen) that p?"	"It does sometimes happen that p"
"With what did X kill Y?"	"X killed Y with something"
"Is the present king of France here?"	"There is a present king of France."
"Can anything move faster than the velocity of light?"	"There is such a thing as the (fixed) velocity of light."

The bearing of the first of these examples is particularly far-reaching: every question presupposes the meanings and, *a fortiori*, the meaningfulness of the concepts in terms of which it is posed.

All questions have various presuppositions.[3] For example, every question presupposes that it has some true answer or other. For *any* proposition p that is an explicit answer to a question Q will entail "There is some (true) proposition that is an admissible explicit answer to Q." To be sure, a question can be *virtually presupposition-free* in the sense of having only trivial presuppositions—those that are logico-conceptual truths. An example of such a question is: "Is it the case that p?" which has no presuppositions apart from those entailed by its meaningfulness as a question—an issue which turns on p's meaningfulness as a proposition. Again, "Are there any truths?" is another example. Accordingly, various questions can have only minimal presuppositions. But by the time we remove *all* of its presuppositions, we have nothing left by way of a meaningful question.[4]

In particular, every *factual* question presupposes that it itself arises and is moot. For example, "Are there unicorns?" presupposes that it makes sense to look for unicorns, so that "There might be unicorns" is a presupposition of this question. (A negative answer would have to be construed as "No, as a matter of fact, there are no unicorns in the world, though there very well *might be*.") In *this* regard questions in the *factual* domain differ from formal ones. ("Are there any round squares?" does not presuppose that there might be.)

The presuppositions of a question generally engender yet further presuppositions lying "further down the implicational road" as it were. Thus "Smith has a wife" entails "Smith is a person," "Smith is of age," "Smith is male," etc. Whatever a presupposition of a question entails or requires is itself one of that question's presuppositions. Seeing that (as we have defined the term) every logical consequence of a presupposition is itself a presupposition, it transpires that every question has infinitely many presuppositions. It is hardly to be expected, however, that a questioner would entertain all of them explicitly.

All the same, to pose or otherwise endorse a question is to

undertake an at least tacit commitment to all of its presuppositions. As one recent analysis helpfully observes:

> To ask a question with a substantive presupposition is, in ordinary circumstances, to hold oneself responsible for the truth of the question's presupposition and, thus, implicitly to make a statement. Putting a question conveys information, and we do not mean "meta-information." One can learn something "about the world" by being asked for the proportions of sodium to chlorine in common table salt, or for the name of the man who was seen with one's wife. Lawyers are for this reason not supposed to ask questions which presuppose debatable claims not yet established, for in this way they could communicate information to the jury in illegitimate ways.[5]

Presuppositions are especially important in science, where the technical terminology used in the formulation of a question is laden with prejudgments regarding the *sort* of answer that is possible.

It will aid in clarifying the ideas at issue to introduce a bit of formal machinery. Thus let $Q, Q', Q''. \ldots$ represent *questions*. And let the set of a question consist of (all) its correlative (full) answers:

$\alpha(Q) =$ the set of all possible (feasible, ostensible, theoretically admissible) explicit answers to the question Q.

Moreover, to indicate that the question Q has the presupposition p we shall write: $Q \ni p$. This can now be defined as follows:

$$Q \ni p \text{ iff } (\forall q) [q \in \alpha(Q) \supset (q \to p)].$$

A presupposition of a question is accordingly a thesis (proposition) that is assured by *all* its explicit answers, following from each and every one of them. Note that the mode of implication ($\to$) at issue in this definition must be a strong one, lest things go awry. For example, if it were material implication, every question would presuppose *every true proposition*.

The aforementioned circumstance that every question presupposes that it has some correct answer or other can be seen from the fact that a truism results when the 'p' of the right-hand side of the preceding definition is replaced by:

$$(\exists \, r) \, [r \, \& \, r \, \epsilon \, \alpha(Q)].$$

Adopting the notation $p@Q$ for "p *(correctly) answers Q*" via the definition

$$p@Q \text{ iff } p \, \& \, p \, \epsilon \, \alpha(Q),$$

we can formulate the just-stated finding in terms of the thesis:

$$(\forall \, Q)[Q \ni (\exists \, p) \, p@Q]$$

Note that the preceding definition of presupposition could be reformulated as

$$Q \ni p \text{ iff } (\forall \, q)[q@Q \supset p], \text{ or, equivalently } (\exists \, q) \, q@Q \supset p.$$

A proposition is thus a presupposition of a question Q iff it is a consequence of the mere fact that the question is answerable (i.e., has some true answer or other).[6]

One question may be said to *preempt* another when they have mutually incompatible presuppositions. Thus "When did Henry commit suicide?" and "Why did John murder Henry?" are at odds with one another in this manner. Conflicting bodies of assertions will always engender mutually preemptive questions—namely questions that presuppose the contradictions at issue.

2. ISSUES REGARDING THE LEGITIMACY OF QUESTIONS

A question can manage to be *trivial* in the sense that its very presuppositions afford an answer to it: "Are there meaningful questions?" for example, or "Does this question have an answer?" The answer to such a question is a forgone conclusion.

The Roman poet Publilius Syrus long ago proffered the dictum that "It is not every question that deserves an answer." A *proper* (or *appropriate*) question will be one whose presuppositions are all (known to be) true: *prop* (Q) iff $(\forall p)[(Q \in p) \supset p]$, or else, knowledge-relatively, $\text{prop}_K Q$ iff $(\forall p)\ [(Q \ni p) \supset (p \in K)]$.

"Why is the moon made of green cheese?" is an improper and illegitimate question. Unless the presuppositions of a question are satisfied, the question simply "does not arise"—*cadit quaestio* as the Roman jurisconsults were wont to put it.

Questions having presuppositions whose truth-status is unknown or indeterminate—but none that are actually (known to be) false—might be characterized as *problematic*. To raise such a question at the present epistemic juncture is inappropriate because this would be *premature* in that the whole question could well become undone by the discovery of the falsity of such a presupposition. For example, the question "Why is there anything at all?" if construed specifically as "What is the reason or the cause for the existence of the world?" presupposes the viability of an answer of the form "X is the reason for the existence of the world." That is, it presupposes the existence of a single monolithic cause or reason for the existence of the (or a) world. But there is no assurance of this in the present state of our knowledge—seeing that existence could be the collaborative result of a plurality of distinct and independent causes—and so the question at issue is problematic. Such problematic questions are, however, perfectly "proper" ones—both informally and on our present technical construction of the term.

Questions that have *false* presuppositions are inappropriate in an even stronger sense. Such questions cannot be asked correctly or properly: *every* one of their (full) ostensible answers is false, so that we encounter falsity whichever way we turn, with every possible answer. From the very start there is no hope of finding an acceptable answer to such a question. This is the case, in particular, with *indefinite* questions like "How long is a novel?" Any straightforward answer—"A novel has length L" is going to be false. We can either respond to the question with another question "Which novel?" and, so remove the indefiniteness; or, alternatively, we can reconstruct the question à la "What is the *range of length* of novels?" or "What is the *average length* of novels?", so as to obtain a well-defined question. To be sure, some questions can be based on false presuppositions that are (*pro tem*) *assumed* to be true. Such hypothetical questions ("Suppose Napoleon had won at Waterloo: Would he have invaded England?") will not concern us in the present discussion.[7]

Questions can go wrong in other ways as well. For example, a question is *absurd* when it has no viable answers at all because every one of its (full) ostensible answers is *self-inconsistent:*

$$\text{abs } (Q) \text{ iff } (\forall p) [p \in \alpha(Q) \supset (p \rightarrow \sim p)]$$

"Why is that tree inorganic?" is an example. If it is indeed a *tree* that is at issue, then it *cannot* be inorganic. A question can also be self-contradictory in involving a *conflict* of presuppositions—i.e., by having a presupposition that is untenable given the other presuppositions of the question. An example in such a question is: "Is 'No' the correct answer to this (very) question?" (Or alternatively: "Is it correct to answer this (very) question in the negative?") Such questions are simply foolish, to use the terminology of Belnap and Steel, and fall subject to their *Hauptsatz: Ask a foolish question and you get a foolish answer.*[8] Such absurdity is something stronger than mere impropriety. With an absurd question, every one of its ostensible (full) answers is actually incoherent in that it leads to inconsistency or paradox. The mere assumption that the question has an answer leads *ad absurdum.*

If one body of assertions, S_1, includes the thesis p among its entailments, while another S_2, fails to include p, then we can ask the rationale-demanding question "Why is it that p is the case?" with respect to S_1, where the presupposition that p is the case is met, but not with respect to S_2 where this presupposition fails. Discordant bodies of (putative) knowledge engender distinct, mutually divergent bodies of questions because they provide the material for distinct sets of background presuppositions.

This fact—that different bodies of knowledge provide for different questions in affording diverse bodies of available presuppositions—of itself blocks the cumulationist view of scientific progress. Some theorists have maintained that science progresses cumulatively because its later theories both (1) answer (and answer better) the questions answered by the earlier theories and (2) answer more questions besides. This view has been severely criticized for failing to depict factually the way in which science has in fact progressed.[9] The present line of thought also indicates that this position has grave theoretical shortcomings.

3. THE KNOWLEDGE-RELATIVITY OF QUESTIONS

A "state of knowledge" K is always correlative with a body of questions $Q(K)$ that can be posed on its basis, that is, whose presuppositions it is able to assure. Accordingly, a question belongs to $Q(K)$ if all of its presuppositions are forthcoming from K, that is, if the question is K-relatively appropriate:

$$Q \in Q(K) \text{ iff } (\forall p) [(Q \ni p) \supset p \in K]$$

The question-set $Q(K)$ thus represents the *erotetic agenda* of a body of knowledge K the entire manifold of questions spawned by this body of knowledge.

The questions of $Q(K)$ are appropriately formulable relative to K-available concepts and K-available theses; each of these questions is such that its concepts are meaningful relative to K, and all of its other presuppositions are K-true, so that it can be mooted relative to K-available presuppositions.

The key fact is that the question-set $Q(K)$ of a body of knowledge K suffices uniquely to determine this body. Indeed all the following schemes are readily established on the basis of these preceding definitions:

(T1) $K = K'$ iff $Q(K) = Q(K')$
(T2) If $K \subset K'$, then $Q(K) \subset Q(K')$
(T3) If K and K' are mutually incompatible, then there will be questions in $Q(K)$ that K' does not even allow to be posed.

Thus consider (T1). The direction from left to right is easy. Let us then go from $K \neq K'$ on the left to $Q(K) \neq Q(K')$ on the right. By hypothesis one of K or K' will contain a thesis P not contained in the other. But then any question for which this thesis is a presupposition—for example "Why is p the case?"—will belong to the question-agenda of the one but not the other. Q.E.D.

Analogous arguments can be constructed for the remaining theses.

An interesting and not altogether obvious relationship holds between the posability and the answerability of questions. A body of knowledge K views a question Q as "answerable in principle" whenever it takes the stance that an answer to this question indeed exists: $(\exists p)(p@Q) \epsilon K$. A relatively straightforward argument can be developed to show that such answerability stands correlative with the knowledge-correlative posability of questions at issue in $Q \epsilon Q(K)$. This result is the substance of the *Fundamental Theorem of Question Posability:*

$Q \epsilon Q(K)$ iff $(\exists p)(p@Q) \epsilon K$

PROOF

Stage 1

   (1) Suppose: $Q \epsilon Q(K)$
   (2) $(\forall p)[(Q \ni p) \supset (p \epsilon K)]$ from (1)
   (3) $Q \ni (\exists p)(p@Q)$ a general fact (see p. 134 above)
   (4) $(\exists p)(p@Q) \epsilon K$ from (2), (3)

Stage 2

   (1) Suppose: $(\exists p)(p@Q) \epsilon K$
   (2) $Q \ni q$ hypothesis (for a suitable q)
   (3) $(\exists p)(p@Q) \supset q$ from (2) by a general fact (see p. 136 above)
   (4) $q \epsilon K$ from (1), (3)[10]
   (5) $Q \ni q \supset q \epsilon K$ from (2)–(4)
   (6) $(\forall p)[(Q \ni p \supset p \epsilon K)]$ from (2)–(5)
   (7) $Q \epsilon Q(K)$ from (6)

Accordingly, a body of knowledge admits a question as legitimately posable iff it takes the stance that this question actually *has* an answer—though not necessarily one which it can itself provide.

To see a question as answered is, of course, to see it as answerable. And it is, in fact, easily shown that $(\exists p)(p@Q) \epsilon K$ follows at once from $(\exists p)(p@Q \epsilon K)$:

(1) $(\exists p)(p@Q \epsilon K)$ by assumption
(2) $p_1@Q \epsilon K$ by (1), for a suitable p_1
(3) $p_1@Q \supset (\exists p)p@Q$ by quantificational logic
(4) $(\exists p)(p@Q) \epsilon K$ from (2), (3)[11]

But, of course, the converse relationship does not hold. To pose a question is, in general, a far cry from being able to claim a solution for it. A body of knowledge can have it that a question is answerable without itself providing the answer. The thesis $(\exists p)(p@Q) \epsilon K$ simply asserts that, according to K, Q *has* an answer (is "answerable in principle")—that Q is K-posable, in that K sees all of its presuppositions as satisfied. But $(\exists p)(p@Q \epsilon K)$ has it that K actually offers an answer to Q—that there is some K-relatively true proposition which (according to K) offers an answer to Q. We must beware of the quantifier-scope confusion of conflating these two very different contentions.

Let us define

$K@Q$ iff $(\exists p)(p@Q \epsilon K)$
    and so iff $(\exists p)(p \epsilon K \,\&\, [p \epsilon \alpha(Q)] \epsilon K)$

On this definition, K affords an answer to Q (or, at any rate, *purports* to do so) if there is some statement that K recognizes as correctly affording an explicit answer to Q. This, of course, is a rather special circumstance; in general, we may well stand in a position of K-relative ignorance with regard to a question.

Questions are always projected on the basis of the cognitive "state of the art," relative to an existing body of putative knowledge. The fact that it is an illicit hypostatization to speak absolutistically of "*the* body of scientific knowledge" (without adding something like "of the late 19th century" or "of the present day"), means that it also makes no sense to speak of "the body of scientific questions." And this means that we must be very careful about our all-statements: we had better make sure of our category-limitations when embarking on declarations beginning with "all scientific questions. . . ." Such caution is particularly germane when we realize that the "scientific knowledge" of different eras can contain mutually incompatible contentions, so that their questions can be mutually preemptive in having incompatible presuppositions.

4. QUESTION DISSOLUTION

One way a body of knowledge K can deal with a question is, of course, by *answering* it. Yet another, importantly different way in which it can deal with a question Q is by *disallowing* it. This circumstance may be defined as follows:

$$K\delta Q \text{ iff } Q \notin Q(K), \text{ or equivalently, } (\exists p)[(Q \ni p)\&(p \notin K)].$$

That is, K disallows Q if there is some presupposition of Q that K does not countenance (either by way of outright denial or else by way of simple noninclusion). A question can accordingly fail to fall within $Q(K)$ when it has a presupposition that is unavailable for one of three reasons: K-falsity (K-relative F status), K indeterminacy (K-relative I status) and K-inexpressibility (K-relative U status). We arrive at three modes of question-disallowing: (K-relative U status). We arrive at three modes of question-disallowing:

(1) *impropriety* which arises when a question has a K-relatively *false* (F-status) presupposition, (We may say in this case that K *blocks* the question at issue.)
(2) *problematicity* which arises when a question has a K-relatively *indeterminate* (I-status) presupposition.
(3) *ineffability* which arises when a question has a K-relatively conceptually inaccessible (U-status) presupposition. (In these two latter cases we may say that K *omits* the question at issue.)

A question that is disallowed by a body of knowledge (in any one of the three ways at issue) may be said to be *illegitimate* with respect to it. It is convenient for terminological reasons to adopt the nomenclature that a body of knowledge K *resolves* a question Q when K either answers or disallows Q: $K@Q \lor K\delta Q$. (This circumstance is not trivial; a glance at the definitions involved shows that the prospect of unresolved questions is a perfectly real one.)

Consider some examples. Given relativity theory, all questions about the behavior of physical systems having components moving faster than the speed of light are blocked being rendered improper by the purported infeasibility of transluminar velocities.[12] Again, given the present state of our knowledge, questions about the learning processes of extra-terrestrial inhabitants of our galaxy will be problematic. On the other hand, ineffable questions can only be instanced through historical examples of issues that were ineffable prior to certain developments.

Immanuel Kant's *Critique of Pure Reason* is dedicated to the proposition that certain issues (viz. those of traditional metaphysics) cannot be legitimately posed at all—i.e., are *absolutely* illegitimate—because they overstep *the limits of POSSIBLE experience.*[13] The present deliberations pose the more mundane but yet interesting prospect that certain questions cannot be legitimately posed on a *particular cognitive basis*—i.e., are *circumstantially* illegitimate—because they transcend *the limits of ACTUAL experience,* in that certain presuppositions of these questions run afoul of the body of knowledge on hand, which dissolves them in one or another of the preceding ways.

Some questions, to be sure, do not so much rest on our background knowledge as undertake deliberate departures from it. These are explicitly hypothetical questions of the form "What would happen if p?" in circumstances where we know that not-p. Such hypothetical questions, based on a suppositional transformation of K into K', raise special problems of their own, and their interest for the theory of inquiry is by no means insignificant, though their study leads in directions we cannot pursue here.[14] It suffices to stress that deliberations regarding question-illegitimacy must not be construed to impugn such hypothetical questions based as they are on a transformation rather than exploitation of the body of knowledge at issue.

The failure of a certain question Q to arise within a K-relative question framework $Q(K)$ may conceivably not be a defect of K, but an advantage of it—a point of strength. It is an important consideration here than any scientific framework for the systematization of our factual knowledge is entitled to establish certain sorts of questions as improper—as "just not arising at all."

Thus when a certain form of motion (be it in Aristotle's circles or in Galileo's straight lines) is characterized as "natural," then we are precluded from asking why—in the absence of imposed forces—objects move in this particular manner. Or again, considering that the half-life of a certain species of californium is 235 years, we must not ask—given modern quantum theory—just why a certain particular atom of this substance decayed after only 100 years. Such questions have presuppositions that are at odds with commitments of the body of knowledge at issue. When a cognitive corpus actually *dissolves* certain questions in this way, we cannot automatically regard its failure to reckon with them as counting to its discredit.

5. THE DYNAMICS OF EROTETIC CHANGE

Epistemic change over the course of time thus relates not only to what is "known" but also to what can be *asked*. The accession of "new truths"—new T-status propositions—will engender the opening up of new questions. And when the epistemic status of a presupposition changes away from T—we have not so much the opening of new questions as the disappearance of various old ones through dissolution. Questions regarding the *modus operandi* of phlogiston, the behavior of caloric fluid, the structure of the luminiferous aether, the character of faster-than-light transmissions, or those as to why certain radioactive disintegration occurred just when they did, are all examples of questions that have become lost to modern science because they involve presuppositions that have been abandoned. The phenomenon of presupposition means that our questions are tied to the state of knowledge (i.e., *putative* knowledge) of the day.

Where different presuppositions are available, different bodies of questions can be raised. The state-of-the-art regarding questions is inseparably geared to the state-of-the-art regarding knowledge. When the membership of K changes, so of course does that of its erotetic agenda, $Q(K)$, the corpus of questions that can be appropriately asked on the basis of K.

This idea cries out for temporalization. It is accordingly profitable to consider more closely the temporalized or historicized "state of questioning" at the time t. Taking $Q(K_t)$ to be the set of questions or problems appropriately posable on the basis of the "state of knowledge" obtaining at t—the problem-field as it stands at the historical juncture t, comprising all the questions explicit or implicit in the committments of the scientific community of the time. On this basis let us consider the following

Thesis of the Conservation of Questions
Once posable, a question forever remains so:
$$(\forall Q)(\forall t)(\forall t')([t \angle t' \ \& \ Q \in Q(K_t)] \supset Q \in Q(K_{t'})$$

Note that the failure of what we characterized earlier on as the *Thesis of the Conservation of Knowledge* (pp. 93–4) ensures the failure of this present thesis as well. For a presupposition of Q that is available at t from K_t may fail to be available at t' from $K_{t'}$. Not only is it possible for answers to questions to be forgotten, but, as we have seen, questions may not only be *solved* but also *dissolved* in the course of scientific evolution, when the scientific community comes to abandon their presuppositions.

The coming to be and passing away of questions is a phenomenon that can be mooted on this basis. A question *arises* (i.e., can meaningfully be posed) at the time t iff all its presuppositions are then known or at any rate taken to be true. And a question *dissolves* at t iff one or another of its previously accepted presuppositions is now no longer accepted. More generally:

If previously	whereas now	then Q
Some presupposition of Q was classed as $\neq$ T	all presuppositions of Q are classed as T	now arises as a new Q
All presuppositions of Q were classed as T	some presupposition of Q is classed as $\neq$ T	has been dissolved

Questions should thus be regarded as entitles that exist in an *historical* setting. They arise at some junctures and not at others; they can come into being and pass away.

The idea of questions that *cannot* be answered also deserves scrutiny. To begin with, some questions are not just *answerable* but actually *unaskable* because—in the given state of knowledge—they cannot even be posed on grounds of conceptual inaccessibility. Caesar could not have wondered whether plutonium is radioactive. It is not just that he did not know what the correct answer to the question happens to be—the very question not only *did* not, but actually *could* not have occurred to him, because the cognitive framework of the then-existing state of knowledge did not afford the conceptual instruments with which alone this question can be posed. Conceptual innovation means that certain issues cannot even be contemplated at a particular juncture of the cognitive state of the art. The history of science is replete with cases of this sort. (Compare the discussion of K-indefinition at pp. 88–89 above.) In the main, today's scientific problems could not even have arisen a generation or two ago: their presuppositions were cognitively unavailable.

In line with the distinction between merely unanswerable questions and actually unaskable ones, ignorance—the inability to resolve questions—falls into two very different types. It prevails at a surface level of mere incapacity when we can grasp a question but, under the prevailing circumstances, are unable to answer it. (Think of the status of speculations in 1850 about mountains on the far side of the moon.) Ignorance prevails at a deeper level of actual inaccessibility when we would not even pose the question—and indeed could not even *understand* an answer should one be vouchsafed us by a benevolent oracle—because U-status presuppositions are involved in such a way that the whole issue lies beyond the conceptual horizons of the day. (Think of the status that questions about radium would have had in the days of Newton.) It is not difficult to envisage present-day questions that exhibit surface ignorance—any practicing scientist can readily give examples of this kind from the domain of his own research. On the other hand, inaccessibility-ignorance cannot be illustrated, except in retrospect. Nevertheless, the fact that certain *current* ideas went unrealized at *all earlier* historical stages is readily amplified to the speculative prospect that some intrinsically feasible ideas may go unrealized at *all* historic stages whatsoever. For it is perfectly conceivable that a proposition *p* should be true but never recognized as such, so that $(\exists p)\,[p\ \&\ (\forall t)(p \notin K_t)]$. (Indeed, we must accept this thesis if we are not prepared to endorse the inherently implausible idea that every truth will come to light in the fulness of time.) And once this prospect of "unavailable truths" is accepted we face the fact that any question that presupposes *such* a proposition *p*—for example, "Why is it the case that *p*?"—is a question that can *never* be appropriately posed.

Someone might object as follows to this train of thought:

> At various junctures, your discussion accepts the prospect of possible but unrealized *intellectual* objects—specifically, languages, propositions, questions. But how can *such* things exist unrealized, independently of anybody's mind. (And you repeatedly reject "the myth of the God's eye view"!) To be sure, *physical* objects may well exist mind-externally; but surely such *intellectual* objects cannot do so.

While a fully adequate reply here would involve a very long story, its main thrust can be put telegraphically. One can accept the conclusion that intellectual objects have no mind-independent existence but yet locate their existential foothold in the *capabilities* of minds in their potential for conducting certain kinds of intellectual transactions. (It is perfectly unproblematic to say that a hammer has the capacity to drive in nails of a certain sort—in general, and independently of the issue of particular nails and their existence.) And this way of arriving in the sphere of "what-is-not-but-would-be-if" is a perfectly workable route to possible but unrealized intellectual objects.[15]

7. KANT'S PRINCIPLE OF QUESTION PROPAGATION

Cognitive progress is commonly thought of in terms of the discovery of new facts—new information about things. But the situation is more complicated, because not only *knowledge* but also *questions* must come into consideration. For progress on the side of *questions* is a crucial mode of cognitive progress, coorelative with—and every bit as important as—progress on the side of *information*. The questions opened up for our consideration are as crucial and definitive a facet of a cognitive system as are the theses which it endorses.

Information is developed in the context of questions. And the new theses we come to accept can bear very differently on the matter of questions. Specifically, we can discover:

(1) New (i.e., *different*) answers to old questions.
(2) New questions.
(3) The impropriety or illegitimacy of our old questions, in that they were based on erroneous or untenable presuppositions—i.e., once-purported "facts" which are no longer viewed as acceptable.

With (1) we discover that the wrong answer has been given to an old question: We uncover an error in our previous question-answering endeavors. With (2) we discover that there are certain questions which have not heretofore been posed at all: We uncover an "error of omission" in the context of our former question-asking endeavors. Finally, with (3) we find that one has asked the wrong question altogether: We uncover an "error of commission" in the context of our former question-asking endeavors. Such improper questions rest on incorrect presuppositions [and are thus generally bound up with type (1) discoveries]. Three rather different sorts of cognitive progress are involved here—different from one another and from the traditional view of cognitive progress in terms simply of an "accretion of further knowledge."

The second of these modes of question-oriented discovery is particularly interesting. The phenomenon of the ever-continuing "birth" of new questions was first emphasized by Immanuel Kant, who described it in terms of a continually evolving cycle of questions and answers:

> Who can satisfy himself with mere empirical knowledge in all the cosmological questions of the duration and of the magnitude of the world, of freedom or of natural necessity, since *every answer given on principles of experience begets a fresh question, which likewise requires its answer* and thereby clearly shows the insufficiency of all physical modes of explanation to satisfy reason.[16]

The line of thought set out in the italicized passage suggests the following: *Principle of Question Propagation (Kant's Principle)* "The solution of any factual (scientific) question gives rise to yet further unsolved questions." This principle of question-proliferation in empirical inquiry indicates a fact of importance for the theory of scientific progress. One need not claim longevity—let alone immortality—for any of the *current* problems to assure that there will be problems ten or one hundred generations hence. (As immortal individuals are not needed to assure the immortality of the race, so immortal problems are not needed to assure the immortality of problems.)

To be sure, Kant's Principle does not hold in unrestricted generality. In mathematics, for example, we can readily imagine a dialectical course of question-and-answer that runs as follows:

Question	Response
1. $\langle ? \rangle p$	p
2. $\langle \text{why?} \rangle p$	p because q
3. $\langle \text{why?} \rangle q$	q is an axiom.

(The pointed-bracket notation employed here is used to indicate the posing of a—duly indicated—question regarding the thesis to which it attaches, with $\langle ? \rangle = $ "is it the case that?".) In this sequence, we reach "the end of the line"—no further questions can validly arise because an axiom is at issue. However, in the domain of matters of objective empirical fact at the level of scientific generality, such a *cul de sac* termination in axioms or first principles or self-certifying propositions (in the sense of the Stoic *catalepsis*) seems unwarranted in theory and unattainable in practice. Here questions require answers that beget yet further questions.

On this perspective, *the interminability of the question-reply cycle is not a universal and purely theoretical fact,* but is a fact specifically about the structure of *empirical* inquiry. This opening up of new and deeper questions in the course of our inquiries into matters of empirical fact is a phenomenon that is empirically as well established as any in our study of nature itself. Insofar as the history of science has any lessons to teach us, it substantiates this operation of a conservation-law for scientific problems.

Note, however, that Kant's Principle yields an ongoing dialectical unfolding of questions and their resolution that can be construed in two ways:

(i) A *universalized* mode: EACH specific (particular) question Q that can be raised on a basis of K engenders a (Q-correlative) line of questioning that leads ultimately to a question Q' whose answer lies outside of K, a question that forces an eventual shift from K to some suitably augmented or revised modification thereof.

(ii) A *particularized* mode that arises when the capitalized EACH of the preceding formula is replaced by SOME.

Kant undoubtedly intended the principle in the first (universalized) sense. But it is more plausible by far to adopt it in the second (particularized) sense, which yields a thesis amply supported by historical experience: that every state-of-the-art condition of questioning $Q(K)$ ultimately yields somewhere along the road, a line of questioning that engenders the transition from K to a *different K'*.

Of course even if this plausible, indeed inevitable, version of Kant's principle is accepted, the matter of the comparative *significance* of the new questions still remains untouched. In theory, the prospect exists that the *magnitude of the issues* declines as scientific progress moves on to new questions. But this carries us back to the theme of the Cognitive Copernicanism of the preceding chapter. And the upshot of those deliberations, put in a nutshell, is that the successive state-of-the-art stages of science (as per the sequence $K_t \Rightarrow K_{t'} \Rightarrow \ldots$) pose issues of relatively constant *overall* importance for our understanding of the world. The progress of science confronts us with a dialectical process through which question-change is geared to cognitive change in an ongoing feedback cycle that furnishes an ever-renewed impetus to inquiry and yields, at every stage, fruits of undiminished significance.

VII

Question Exfoliation and Erotetic Dialectics

SYNOPSIS

(1) Question exfoliation and stratification: how some questions pave the way for others. (2) Question dialectics and courses of inquiry. (3) Considerations regarding the relative "importance" of questions. (4) Difficulties in predicting the development of courses of inquiry and thus in forecasting scientific innovation. (5) Some issues regarding the economic aspects of inquiry.

1. QUESTION EXFOLIATION

The state of questioning changes no less drastically than the state of knowledge. Cognitive change carries erotetic change in its wake. Any alterations in the membership of our body of knowledge will afford new presuppositions for further questions that were not available before. The question solved in one era could well not even have been posed in another. As W. Stanley Jevons put it:

> Since the time of Newton and Leibniz realms of problems have been solved which before were hardly conceived as matters of inquiry . . . May we not repeat the words of Seneca . . . *Veniet tempus, quo posteri nostri tam aperta nos nescisse mirentur.* ["A time will come when our posterity will marvel that such obvious things were unknown to us."][1]

Questions cluster together in groupings that constitute lines of inquiry, standing arranged in duly organized and sequential families; the answering of a question yielding the presuppositions for yet further questions which would not have arisen had the former questions not been answered. Collingwood offers the following example:[2] To investigate profitably the question "Has Smith left off beating his wife yet?" we must disentangle it into four issues:

(1) Has Smith a wife?
(2) Was he ever in the habit of beating her?
(3) Does he intend to leave off doing so in the future?
(4) Has he begun carrying out this intention?

Observe that this sequence is so arranged that questions (2)–(4) each presuppose an affirmative answer to its predecessor.

There is a natural stratification in the development of questions. Certain questions cannot even be posed until others have been resolved, because the resolution of these others is presupposed in their articulation: a question cannot arise before its time has come. The cognitive state-of-the-art must be conducive to the posing of a question, given the character of its presuppositions. Think here of the game of 20 questions—not until after we establish that a species of dog is at issue does it become appropriate to ask whether a large or small sort of dog is involved.

Inquiry is a dialectical process, a step-by-step exchange of query and response that produces sequences within which the answers to our questions ordinarily open up yet further questions. Such a process will issue in a regressive series illustrated by such exchanges as:

Question	Response
$\langle\,?\,\rangle\,p$	p
$\langle\text{why?}\rangle\,p$	p because q and r
$\langle?\rangle\,q$	q
$\langle\text{why?}\rangle$ q	q because s and t

Although a list of this sort looks linear and sequential (as is, of course, always the case with written exposition as well), the exfoliation of questions actually takes us into a tree-like structure, with various components of the form:

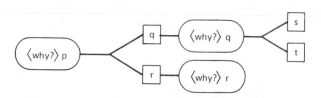

This branching exfoliation of questions makes manifest that our arguments and demonstrations setting out the reasons why behind the reasons why also have a tree like structure. And, when we have several such patterns issuing from a single question, we arrive at a structure that has a still more complex web-like form. The setting out of a sequential "course of argumentation" or "course of questioning or inquiry" always involves the reformulation (or deformation) of such a complex tree-like or web-like structure into a linear form which, however convenient, obscures the underlying complexities of the situation.

The structuring of our information as responses to a logically unfolding of questions is the most basic and doubtless the most important mode of cognitive system-building. To *systematize* knowledge is to set it out in a way that shows it to be the rational resolution of a rationally connected, sequentially exfoliated family of questions.[3]

Dialectical exchanges of questions and answers can fall victim to various technical defects such as circularity, vicious regressiveness, begging the question, etc. Circularity for example, is illustrated by the joke about the Eccentric Classicist: *Eccentric Classicist:* "Why should *anthropos* start with a *gamma*?" *Innocent Respondent:* "But *anthropos* doesn't start with a *gamma*." EC: "Well then—why doesn't *anthropos* start with a *gamma*?" IR: "But why in Heaven's name should *anthropos* start with a *gamma*?" EC: "Ha—that's exactly what I wanted to know: Why should *anthropos* start with a *gamma*?" The formal structure of this exchange is clearly circular, and serves to illustrate the fact that a sensible line of questioning should always carry us into new ground.

As the course of inquiry unfolds, the questions of the later stages are generally linked to the earlier ones in a means-ends relationship of subordination and follow-through: We resolve then in order to pave the way for the ever more satisfactory resolution of their predecessors.

The answer to a question in general sets the stage for yet further questions, providing new materials from which yet further questions can be drawn. This circumstance leads to a cyclic process whose successive transitions exhibit the structure depicted in Figure 1.

Figure 1

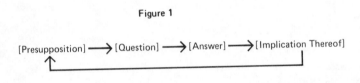

This cycle provides for a dialectical process of question-exfoliation that is exhibited (somewhat in caricature) by the example of Table 1. Observe that here the question sequence begins with a "presupposition free" question—that is, one which has no presuppositions apart from those needed to underwrite the meaningfulness of its own terms of reference. After this starting-point, the presupposition of any question in the sequence is either itself the answer of a preceding question, or else—and more generally—is something that follows from such answers.

A "course of inquiry" is thus set by an initial, controlling question together with the ancillary questions to which it gives rise and whose solution is seen as facilitating its resolution. The development of such a line of inquiry defines a direction of search—of research—in question-answering inquiry, yielding a

series of the form
$$Q_0 \Rrightarrow A_0 \Rrightarrow Q_1 \Rrightarrow A_1 \Rrightarrow Q_2 \Rrightarrow A_2 \Rrightarrow \ldots$$
where each A_i is an answer to Q_i. Once underway, we have in hand at each stage "a body of available knowledge" K_i to provide presuppositions for further question-posing, and it will always have to be the case that $Q_i \in Q\ (K_i)$.

Table 1

THE EXFOLIATION OF QUESTIONS

Presupposition	*Question*	*Answer*
(0) [See the Note]	What's become of Sir Roger?	Sir Roger was killed.
(1) Sir Roger was killed.	Who killed Sir Roger?	The cook killed Sir Roger.
(2) The cook killed Sir Roger.	How did the cook kill Sir Roger?	The cook killed Sir Roger by stabbing him with the carving knife.
(3) The cook stabbed Sir Roger with the carving knife.	Where did the cook obtain the carving knife with which he killed Sir Roger?	The cook obtained the carving knife with which he killed Sir Roger from the pantry.

Note The presuppositions of the initiating question may be based on the body of "background knowledge," which in present case must include the fact that there indeed is such a person as Sir Roger.

One question emerges from another in such a course of inquiry if it is not until we have answered the latter that the former becomes posable. (Thus Q_i emerges from Q_{i-1} iff some presuppositions of Q_i is not available until we reach K_{i-1}.) In the course of inquiry of Table 1, it is clear that the step (3) question emerges from the step (2) question in this exact sense. This process of question-emergence is a prominent feature of the real life course of inquiry.

Often, however, we reverse the direction of this means-ends sequencing, reasoning: "To resolve Q we must first answer Q' and to resolve this we need to answer Q'', etc." The operational tactics of inquiry frequently involve this sort of "working backwards" from a given question to its erotetic prerequisites. But, of course, all these questions of the series Q, Q', Q'' must belong to Q (K_n), when K_n is the *currently existing* body of knowledge. We cannot make use in framing our questions (through their presuppositions) of information we do not yet have. In this regard, "working backwards" is a more restrictive process than the standard "working forwards," which generally carries us into new informative territory.

This conception of a course of inquiry has important ramifications. For one thing, it helps us to see graphically how, as inquiry proceeds, our questions will often come to rest on an increasingly cumbersome basis, with the piling up of an increasingly detailed and content-laden family of available presuppositions.

Moreover, it is now easy to see how *a change of mind* as to the appropriate answer to some earlier question can destroy the entire structure of questions that was erected on this earlier answer. For if we change our mind regarding the correct answer to Q_i, then the whole of the subsequent questioning process may collapse. If we abandon the luminiferous aether as a vehicle for electromagnetic radiation, then we lose at one stroke the whole host of questions about its composition, structure, mode of operation, origin, etc. As further lines of questioning unfold, our old answers can come to be seen as untenable and in need of correction or replacement. The course of erotetic change is no less dramatic than that of cognitive change, seeing that the questions we pose at every stage will have to be based on the presuppositions of the existing stage of the art.

2. QUESTION DIALECTICS

Question dialectics is a formal process of information exchange, a sort of communicative game between questioner and respondent. Its fundamentals were already envisaged by Aristotle in the *Topics*. Two rules serve to define the game:

Questioner's Rule

At any juncture i you can ask any (but only) questions which are either virtually presupposition-free (vpf), or have only presuppositions that follow from the answers given at earlier stages.

Respondent's Rule

At every juncture you must candidly answer any legitimate question (i.e., any question conforming to the conditions of the Questioner's Rule).

Such a game produces a course of inquiry

$$Q_0 \Rightarrow A_0 \Rightarrow Q_1 \Rightarrow A_1 \Rightarrow Q_2 \Rightarrow A_2 \Rightarrow \ldots$$

of much the same general sort that we have been considering.

Let us examine some examples. First consider the following exchange, where $\{P\}$ is to symbolize "P is a meaningful thesis."

Q_i	Pre-suppositions of Q_i	A_i
(1) $\langle\,?\,\rangle p$	$\{p\}$	p
(2) $\langle\text{why?}\rangle p$	p	p because q and $q \to p$
(3) $\langle\,?\,\rangle r$	$\{r\}$	$\sim r$
(4) $\langle\text{why?}\rangle (q \,\&\, \sim r)$	$q \,\&\, \sim r$	$(q \,\&\, \sim r)$ because s and $s \to (q \,\&\, \sim r)$

This is a perfectly legitimate interchange. At steps (1) and (3), questions Q_1 and Q_3 pose vpf-questions, while steps (2) and (4) pose questions all of whose presuppositions are available by inference from prior answers. But for contrast consider:

Q_i	Pre-suppositions of Q_i	A_i
(1) $\langle\,?\,\rangle p$	$\{p\}$	p
(2) $\langle\text{why?}\rangle p$	p	p because q and $q \to p$
(3) $\langle\text{why?}\rangle (q \,\&\, r)$	$q \,\&\, r$	- - -

Here question Q_3 poses a query that is illegitimate because its presuppositions are *not* available from earlier answers.

As such illustrations indicate, the dialectics of question-and-answer exercises launch a process analogous to that at issue in inquiry. There is, however, one critical difference between such exercises and real-life inquiry. In such games we presuppose that once an answer is given, the facts it claims stand henceforth secure and indefeasible. The successive changes in the bodies of knowledge K_i must represent a process of strictly expansive growth, where prior answers are always retained and where change is mere supplementation, so that K_i grows cumulatively with increasing i. In real-life inquiry, of course, the answers we secure at one stage can readily be undone by results secured at later stages.

Moreover, the usual processes of question-dialectics generally envisage some predesignated basis for giving answers—some canonical source of authority that provides a court of final appeal for the issue (presumably a reference work of some sort). This too abstracts from the complexities of real life.

3. THE "IMPORTANCE" OF QUESTIONS

One question can, clearly, *include* another, as "What do dogs eat?" includes "What do schnauzers eat?" In the course of answering the one we automatically provide an answer for the other. Such relations of inclusion and dominance provide a basis for comparing the "scope" of questions (in one sense of this term) in certain cases—though certainly not in general. But this does not generalize into a concept of question-size. We surely cannot compare the "size" of "What do dogs eat?" and "What do termites eat?" The concept of "size" cannot be sensibly applied in this connection—there is no natural and generalizable measure of the magnitude of questions. And even if we could (*per impossibile*) measure and compare the size of questions in this sort of (content-volume oriented) sense, this would afford no secure guide to their relative importance. For this is something that turns on rather different sorts of considerations—fertility, for example, and systemic interlinkage with other issues—that have little or nothing to do with mere content-volume.

In resolving a factual question Q, where $Q \in Q(K)$, we must in general, transform K to K', since K as it stands will not, in general, suffice for our needs. The "importance" of a question turns on the complexity of this transformation. But two very different sorts of things can be at issue here, either a mere growth or *expansion* of K, or a *revision* of it that involves replacing some of its members by contraries thereof and readjusting the remainder to restore over-all consistency. This second sort of change in a body of knowledge (*revision*-change rather than mere *augmentation*-change) is in general the more significant mode, and a question whose resolution forces *this* sort of change is virtually bound to be of greater importance or significance than a question which merely fills in some of the *terra incognita* of our knowledge.

4. DIFFICULTIES IN PREDICTING FUTURE SCIENCE

Questions about the course of questioning itself are among the most interesting issues the factual sphere. In particular, one would like to be in a position to give some advance insight into and some advance guidance to the development of scientific inquiry. But grave difficulties arise at this point, where questions about the future, and, in particular, the *cognitive* future are involved.

When *a specific predefined occurrence* is predicted, this forecast can go wrong in only one way, by proving to be incorrect—the particular development at issue simply does not happen as predicted. But the forecasting of *a general course of developments* can go wrong in two ways, either by way of positive errors of commission (that is, forecasting something that fails to happen as predicted), or by way of negative errors of omission (that is, totally failing to foresee some significant development within the overall cause). In the first case, one forecasts the wrong thing, in the second, there is a lack of completeness, a failure of prevision, a certain blindness. In cognitive forecasting it is these errors of omission—our blind spots, as it were—that form the most serious threat.

In our present setting of cognitive forecasting it is this latter sort of error that is most prominent. For we cannot substantially anticipate the evolution of knowledge. We cannot say in advance what the answers to our scientific questions will be. In particular, it would be quite unreasonable to expect detailed prognostications about the specific *content* of scientific discoveries. It may be possible in some cases to forecast *that* science will solve such and such a problem, but *how* it will do so—in the sense of what the specific nature of the solution is—lies beyond the ken of those who antedate that discovery itself. If we could predict discoveries in detail in advance, then we could *make* them in advance.[4] In inquiry as in other sections of human affairs, major upheavals can come about in a manner that is sudden, unexpected, and sometimes unwelcome.

This circumstance that we cannot predict the answers to the presently open questions of natural science means that we cannot predict its future questions either. For these questions link to and hinge upon these yet unrealizable answers. Indeed, we cannot even say what concepts the inquirers of the future will use within the questions they will raise. Maxwell's work was directed towards answering questions that grew out of Faraday's. Hertz devised his apparatus to answer questions about the implications of Maxwell's equations. Marconi's devices were designed to resolve questions about the application of Hertz's work.

It is a key fact of life in this domain that ongoing progress in scientific inquiry is a process of *conceptual* innovation that always places certain developments outside the conceptual horizons of earlier workers because the very concepts operative in their characterization become available only in the course of scientific discovery itself. Short of learning our science from the ground up, Aristotle could have made nothing of modern genetics, nor Newton of quantum physics. The key discoveries of later stages are those of which the workers of a substantially earlier period not only have failed to make, but which they could not even have understood because the concepts for such understanding were not available to them. It is thus effectively impossible to predict not only the answers but even the questions that lie on the agenda of future science, because these questions themselves will grow out of the answers we obtain at yet unattained stages of the game.

Ironically, it transpires that, in inquiry, the unforeseeable tends to be of special significance just because of its very unpredictability, its coming upon us unsuspected. We face the circumstance that: *the more important the innovation, the less predictable because its very unpredictability is a key component of its importance.* Thomas Kuhn has interestingly distinguished between the "normal science" being developed when things go along the tracks of a well-defined tradition of thought and investigation (proceeding within an established *paradigm* as he calls it), and "scientific revolutions" in which there is massive intellectual upheaval and one paradigm is overthrown and replaced by another.[5] Science forecasting is beset by a pervasive normality bias, because the really novel seems so "far out" in prospect, with the wisdom of hindsight as yet unavailable. (Before the event, important innovations will—if imaginable at all—generally be deemed as outlandishly "wild speculation" or even mere science fiction.)

Moreover forecasts of scientific innovation conform to the perverse-seeming general principle that, other things equal, *the more informative a forecast is, the less secure, and conversely, the less informative, the more secure.*[6] If we are content to say that the solution to a problem will be of "roughly" this sort or that it will be "roughly analogous" to some mere formation process, we will be on safe ground. But science is not like that. It strives for generality, precision, detail. And this makes science forecasting a risky business. The more we enrich our forecast with the details of just exactly what and just exactly how and just exactly when, the more vulnerable it becomes.

A degradation relationship accordingly circumscribes the domain of feasible prediction. The extent (i.e., volume or range of the claims we can responsibly make) thus declines sharply with the exactness that is required of us. We are led to the situation of Figure 2 on p. 162 if one insists on resolving a predictive question with a prespecified level of exactness one's confidence in the response will have to be drastically diminished. And any exercise in science forecasting is bound to conform to this general relationship of futurological indeterminacy. The course of safety accordingly lies in degrading the informativeness of our forecasts. But this obviously undermines their utility as well and, in the case of science, renders them ineffectual.

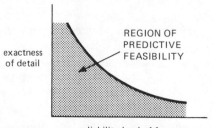

Figure 2
THE DEGRADATION OF RELIABILITY
WITH INCREASING EXACTNESS

In matters of scientific importance, then, we must be prepared for the unexpected. Not suprisingly, major scientific break-throughs often result from research projects that have very different ends in view. Louis Pasteur's discovery of the efficacy of innoculation with weakened disease strains is one of the more famous examples. While studying chicken cholera, Pasteur accidentally innoculated a group of chickens with a weak culture. The chickens became ill but, instead of dying, recovered. Pasteur, not wanting to waste chickens, later reinnoculated these chickens with fresh culture—one strong enough to kill an ordinary chicken. The chickens remained healthy. Pasteur's attention then shifted to this interesting and potentially very significant novel phenomenon, and his resulting work yielded a major medical advance. In empirical inquiry we generally cannot tell in advance what further questions will be engendered by our endeavors to answer those we have on hand. The prediction of innovation in this sphere faces insuperable obstacles.

5. ISSUES REGARDING THE ECONOMICS OF INQUIRY

The theory of search strategies in particular areas of inquiry is a large and interesting enterprise, though at present regrettably underdeveloped. Many procedures and processes can be contemplated. The resolution of questions into constituent parts is one example. Another is the process of elimination that can become operative whenever one can effectively delimit the field of possibilities in advance and make an orderly search across its range. (Twenty questions is again an example here: Knowing the answer to lie within a certain predetermined range we endeavor to get it pinned down with increasing precesion within a more narrowly delineated region.) Unfortunately, however, as we have seen, it is in general not possible in empirical inquiry to determine our question strategies substantially in advance, because later questions hinge on prior and generally unpredictable outcomes.

The "difficulty" of a question is at bottom a practical (rather than *theoretical*) issue—indeed an economic one. It is measured by the resources (time, effort, material resources etc.) that *we,* the inquiring investigators, must expend in resolving it. (Difficulty is thus something relative and not intrinsic and absolute: beings of a different constitution might find some of our hard questions simple.)

Some questions are mere reference questions—a matter of identifying an answer within a wide body of already available information that somewhere contains it. (To be sure, the "mere" here is misleading in its downplaying of the formidable challenges that arise in this problem area.) In pioneering science we face a very different situation. People may well wonder "what is the cause of X"—what causes cancer, or what produces the attraction of the loadstone for iron, to take an historical example—in circumstances where the concepts needed to develop a workable answer may still lie beyond their grasp. Such issues pose genuinely open-ended questions of original research. In general they do not call for the resolution of issues within an existing framework but for a rebuilding and enhancement of the framework itself.

The difficulty of a question can generally not be predicted in advance—save in the case of routine issues. And this condensation bears with special force upon science. With questions of pioneering research—as opposed to "mere reference questions"—we usually cannot even begin to predict how much effort we must expand on a solution. This is generally something we can tell only retrospectively, with the wisdom of the hindsight available only after an answer has been found. To be sure, in planning our inquiries we are well advised to put to good use whatever predictive foresight we can get hold of—usually by way of analogy—though this is always a risky business. The answering of a question is an achievement and the magnitude of this achievement is a function of its difficulty. In inquiry, as elsewhere we do not welcome difficulties for their own sake. We want to select what is—as best we can tell—the easiest path to the object at issue, striving towards the desideratum of an overall economy of effort.

A body of knowledge may well answer a question only provisionally, in so tentative or indecisive a tone of voice as to suggest that further information is needed to settle the matter with confidence. But even if it does confidently and unqualifiedly support a certain definite resolution, this circumstance can never be viewed as absolutely final. What is seen as the correct answer to a question at one stage of the cognitive venture, may, of course, cease to be so regarded at another.[7] Given a K-relatively appropriate answer to Q, we can never preclude the prospect that some improved K' will come about as successor to K, and that it now transpires that some other answer that is actually inconsistent with the earlier one is the correct answer to Q, relative to K'.

To be sure, all of the indications that are available from the *vantage point of a given body of knowledge K* may possibly be such that the issue is settled: that a secure answer to Q is in hand and that there is little point in extending K in its Q-relevant direction. Given our commitment to K, that is, the indications that it affords an appropriate answer to Q may be so strong that further inquiry on this issue seems a pointless waste of effort and energy because, as best one can tell, K affords us "the last word on the matter." However, experience shows that in scientific matters the cognitive present never extends absolute assurances for the future. (Cognitive Copernicanism again!) The prospect of a change of mind can never be totally precluded. To invoke Peirce's favorite dictum, one must never bar the path of inquiry.

This realization of tentativity is, to be sure, abstract and, in a sense, irrelevant and immaterial. In inquiry, as in all other human affairs, we have to proceed from where we are. Our confidence in answers forthcoming relative to K_n, the actual state of the cognitive art currently in hand, should never be impaired by the tentativity inherent in what is no more than a matter of "general principles."[8] If K_n itself gives sufficiently powerful indications on p's behalf—so powerful as to indicate the futility of wasting further resources of time and energy in pursuing the matter—then we are quite entitled to let the matter rest there for the present. Still, this is an essentially practical rather than theoretical matter. The economic aspect again comes to the fore: Where the prospect of error is sufficiently remote there presumably is no *practical* point in expending resources in an endeavor to accommodate purely hypothetical worries.[9]

VIII

Cognitive Completeness and Cognitive Limits

SYNOPSIS

(1) The notion of an *absolutely complete* body of knowledge is inherently unrealistic. (2) A look at the conception of question-answering completeness and of an erotetic equilibrium between questions and answers. (3) A consideration of eschatological issues, and, in particular, of Peirce's theory of science-in-the-limit. (4) Improper vs. intractable questions and the regulative role of cognitive completeness. (5) Limits of knowledge and different modes of cognitive incompleteness. (6) A historical illustration: the Reymond-Haekel controversy. (7) Our knowledge in the factual domain is not only incomplete but ultimately incompletable. Nevertheless, the striving for completeness remains a wholly valid cognitive ideal. And, moreover, the incompletability of science is not a matter for justified regret.

1. PROBLEMS OF COMPLETENESS

The ideal of cognitive completeness has many interesting ramifications. Let T be the set of (all) truths, so that "p is true" may be rendered as $p \in T$. On what may at first sight appear as the most straightforward construction of cognitive completeness, one may define a body of knowledge to be (absolutely) complete when it contains all truths:

K is A-complete (absolutely complete) iff $(\forall p)(p \in T \supset p \in K)$

166

This is not a very useful conception, because this sort of completeness is utterly unverifiable. We cannot determine truth independently of our inquiries and have no way to get at "the truth itself" in the absence of K-membership. We cannot get at which *is* true save *via what we take ourselves to know* to be so.

Moreover, this absolutistic mode of completeness also runs afoul of our rejection of the automatic step from K-membership to truth—our refusal to adopt the principle $(\forall p)(p \epsilon K \supset p)$. This is so because the A-completeness condition that $(\forall p)(p \epsilon T \supset p \epsilon K)$ actually entails its own converse $(\forall p)$ $(p \epsilon K \supset p \epsilon T)$ or equivalently, by contraposition, $(\forall p)(p \notin T \supset p \notin K)$. This emerges from the following argument:

Assume: $p \notin T$

$\sim p \epsilon T$ by the Law of Excluded Middle

$\sim p \epsilon K$ by the A-completeness of K

$p \notin K$ by the consistency of K.

The absolutistic construction of cognitive completeness is accordingly too hyperbolic for workaday use, since it requires the infallibility of our knowledge claims and obliterates the distinction between *real* and merely *purported* knowledge. It is thus advisable to explore the prospect of finding a more manageable conception of cognitive completeness, a prospect to which the present chapter is addressed.

2. COGNITIVE COMPLETENESS: QUESTION-ANSWERING (OR "EROTETIC") COMPLETENESS

The aim of inquiry is always to resolve our questions in terms of what is already accepted or is readily made acceptable. To be sure, this aim cannot always realized then and there. The motive force of inquiry is the existence of questions frameable relative to the "body of knowledge" of the day but not answerable within it. Inquiry sets afoot a sequential process of the cyclic form depicted in Figure 1, which gives rise to successive "stages of knowledge" K to K' to K'' etc., together with their correlative series of state-of-the-art stages with regard to questions: $Q(K)$ to $Q(K')$ to $Q(K'')$ etc.[1]

Figure 1
THE EROTETIC DYNAMICS OF INQUIRY

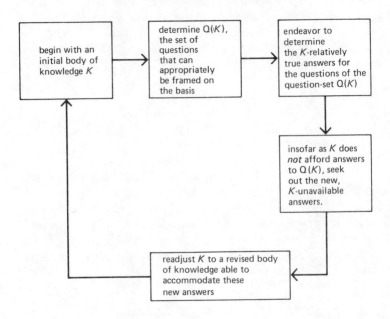

The question-and-answer relationship accordingly suggests a characteristic sense of "completeness" for bodies of knowledge, since one prime construal of the idea of cognitive completeness is that "every question is answered." To be sure, this idea of an "all-inclusively complete" state of knowledge in which literally ALL questions are answered simply makes no sense. For no matter what such a state of knowledge might be, there will, of course, be questions whose presuppositions are at variance with it—questions it does not even allow to arise, contrary to the universality hypothesis at issue. The very idea of "all questions" is thus inherently problematic in its literally universal construction.[2] The best we can do is to contemplate the K-relative range of "ALL *appropriate* questions," where the accepted body of knowledge K will itself play a key role in the determination of appropriateness.

Let us say that K_t, the "state of knowledge" at the time t, has achieved a condition of Q-*completeness* (question-answering or "erotetic" completeness) if it can furnish answers throughout $Q(K_t)$—the whole range of K_t-appropriate questions. This idea of erotetic completeness can be construed in four combinatorially available ways:

   (i) *Perceived Q-completeness*
      Every then-asked question has a then-given answer.
  (ii) *Weak Q-Completeness*
      Every then-asked question has a then-available answer.
 (iii) *Strong Q-Completeness: Completeness in Principle*
      Every then-askable question has a then-available answer:
$$(\forall\,Q)\,[Q \in Q(K_t) \supset K_t @ Q]$$
 (iv) *An Unrealistic Case*
      Every then-askable question has a then-given answer.

This last case may be dismissed as unrealistic because of the inherent discrepancy between the infinitude of the domain of the *askable* on the one hand, and on the other the inevitable finitude of actually given answers. Note, moreover, that both (i) and (iii) entail (ii). We thus arrive at only three distinct (albeit interrelated) modes of the idea of Q-completeness. Each of these alternatives reflects a way in which a family of answers can be construed as being large enough to "cover" a family of questions. But of these three modes, the strong Q-completeness at issue in (iii) is the most interesting case from an epistemological standpoint. For among the realistic cases it alone is free from the contingency of what *actually* happens to be asked.

This concept of strong Q-completeness points directly to the idea of an *equilibrium* between questions and answers, which subsists when every K-posable question is in fact answered with K: $(\forall\,Q)[Q \in Q(K) \supset K @ Q]$. Such an equilibrium subsists when the questions that can be raised on the basis of a body of knowledge can be answered with recourse to this same body of knowledge, as per the situation of Figure 2. Note the Figure 2 flow-pattern is identical with that of Figure 1 once the amplification and revision stages of the latter are deleted.

Figure 2
EROTETIC COMPLETENESS-EQUILIBRIUM

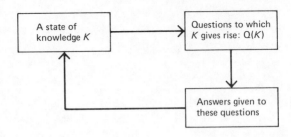

Let us define $Q\#(K)$ as the collection of all questions answered by K:

$$Q\#(K) = \text{the set of all } Q \text{ such that } K@Q$$

Then we shall have it that

$$Q \epsilon Q\#(K) \text{ iff } (\exists p)\, (p@Q \epsilon K)$$

The Q-completeness of erotetic equilibrium comes down to

$$Q(K) = Q\#(K)$$

To suppose *this* of a body of knowledge K is obviously to make a rather demanding stipulation about it.

Not only, as we have already seen, will any difference in K make itself felt in a difference in $Q(K)$-membership, but any difference in K will also make itself felt in a difference in $Q\#(K)$-membership. For with a difference in K, there must be some different K-element

p, and thus a difference in $Q\#$ as to the question "Why is it the case that p?" in which *this* particular p is presupposed. It follows that the $Q\#$-set of a body of knowledge K is a sufficient basis for uniquely determining the body of knowledge at issue:

$$K = K' \text{ iff } Q\#(K) = Q\#(K')$$

Karl Popper has suggested[3] that if the "content" of a theory T is construed as the set of all *questions* to which it can provide *answers*, then the contents of some logically incompatible scientific theories might be compared—their incompatibility notwithstanding—in point of the relation of proper inclusion with respect to this mode of "content". On this view, even if T1 is assertorically incompatible with T2, we might still be in a position to compare these question sets $Q\#(T1)$ and $Q\#(T2)$ and, in particular might have it that $Q\#(T1) \subset Q\#(T2)$. But this is nonsense. For let p be a proposition that brings this incompatibility to view, so that T1 asserts p and T2 asserts not-p. Then "Why is p the case?" is a question that the theory T1 not only allows to arise, but also presumably furnished with an answer. So this question belongs to $Q\#(T1)$. But it cannot belong to $Q\#(T2)$, because T2 (*ex hypothesi*) violates the question's evident presupposition that p is the case.[4]

The size of the gap between the set of questions K allows to arise namely $Q(K)$ and the set of questions it manages to answer namely $Q\#(K)$ indicates the extent of the erotetic inadequacy of K—the extent of perceivable ignorance of a given state of the cognitive art. The striving to close this gap is a prime motive force of scientific inquiry.

However, it is sobering to realize that the erotetic completeness of a state of knowledge K does not necessarily betoken its comprehensiveness or sufficiency, but might simply reflect the paucity of the range $Q(K)$ of questions we are in a position to contemplate. When the range of our knowledge is sufficiently restricted, then its Q-completeness will merely reflect this restrictedness rather than its intrinsitic adequacy. Our corpus of scientific knowledge could be erotetically complete and yet fundamentally inadequate. As we saw in discussing the Kantian principle of quiestion-propagation, the exfoliation of new questions from old in the course of scientific inquiry means that we cannot ever attain Q-completeness. The present line of thought goes beyond this to say that even if we could realize the Q-completeness of our knowledge, we could not be confident that we have actually brought the project of inquiry to a satisfactory conclusion.

Actually, the gap-closure at issue in erotetic completeness may accordingly indicate a defect rather than a strength. Even as its capacity to resolve our questions counts as a merit of a body of knowledge, so does its capacity to raise new questions of significance and "depth." The opening up of new lines of inquiry and the launching of new research areas qualifies among the strengths of a new state of the art in scientific inquiry, and ranks, as such, among its virtues—along with its question-resolutions. Completeness is a hallmark of pseudoscience, which is generally so contrived that the questions that are allowed to be raised are the questions the projected machinery is in a position to resolve. Real-life science is characterized by Kant's principle, and has the merit (rather than defect) of generating questions that cannot be answered in the existing state of the art. Science emerges as a project of self-transcendence, possessed of an inner drive that always presses beyond the capacity-limits of the historical present.

It is thus noteworthy that the realization of a perfect erotetic equilibrium is blocked by the very structure of science on the basis of Kant's Principle or Question Propagation. If a perfecting of knowledge is to be sought, we would have to look in very different directions.

3. SOME QUESTIONS OF ESCHATOLOGY

It is of interest in this connection to consider Charles Sanders Peirce's intriguing thesis that science is inexorably developing towards a determinable condition of "ultimate science," science in the limit:

$$K_\infty = \lim_{t \to \infty} K_t.$$

Once existence of such a limit is granted—which is in principle highly questionable, but follows from the substantive doctrines of

Peirce's metaphysics of nature—then one can take the line that all scientifically meaningful questions are (correctly) answered by "ultimate science." This position has many difficulties (see pp. 210–15). It requires three assumptions to be made:

(1) that, essentially by definition, a question is "scientifically meaningful" when (but only when) it is "posable in K_∞."
(2) that K_∞ is in erotetic equilibrium, so that "posable in K_∞" is to be equated with "actually answered in K_∞."
(3) that "the truth" in scientific matters simply IS what K_∞ asserts, so that the K_∞-delivered answer is necessarily the *correct* answer.

While (1) is forthcoming on Peirce's pragmatic theory of meaningfulness, and (3) by his long-run oriented theory of truth and reality, (2) remains highly problematic—it represents a thesis that is guaranteed neither by logic nor by any facts that we are able to get hold of. We do and can have no assurance that eventual "science in the limit" (if such there be) must needs be erotetically complete.

Instructive difficulties arise with any positivistic theory that adopts the equation:

empirically meaningful = answerable by science

For here "answerable by science" cannot mean "answerable by *our* science as it stands here and now." This, after all, is something of whose shortcomings we are only too keenly aware. It might, perhaps, be construed to mean is "answerable *in principle* by the use of scientific methods"—that is, "science as it would eventually come to be developed if we pushed far enough." But even here there are problems. For even if K_∞ is *ultimate* science—science as best we humans would be able to develop it over the long run—there can be no *a priori* guarantee that this body of knowledge will actually manage to answer to every question it allows to arise—that every question Q posable within $Q(K_\infty)$ is bound to be such that $K_\infty @ Q$. The point is simply that ultimate science (in this general sense) need by no means constitute a *completed* science, a cognitive state in which all meaningful scientific questions are indeed answerable. This is something that can be assured only by means of some rather powerful substantive assumptions. We arrive at the curious-seeming result that an essentially metaphysical supposition—and a highly dubious one at that—is needed to

undergird a positivistic doctrine of empirical meaningfulness for
questions.

One recent writer has maintained that:

> All that is requisite for science to answer every question in principle
> answerable by the scientific method is that the number of questions
> be finite and that science answer more and more questions in the
> course of time.[5]

To articulate this idea, we need to resort to the definition

M = the set of *all* (legitimate) scientific questions, all that are
"empirically meaningful," in something like the logical
positivists' sense.

There are big problems here. For one thing, the very idea of M
violates the Principle of Illicit Aggregation in its wholly unrelativized reference to "all scientifically meaningful questions."
And once we reintroduce the needed relativization, the thesis at
issue collapses. For even if the size of $Q(K_t)$ is always finite (for any
value of t), but yet grows with t, then the size of the body of actually
answered questions $Q\#(K_t)$ can grown *ad indefinitum* without
producing any diminution in the pool of questions still confronting
us unresolved at any given stage. Indeed, if we can answer 60% of
an ever-growing (but ever finite) body of questions, the *relative*
size of our "sphere of ignorance" will never diminish, but its *real*
size will itself represent an ever-growing quantity.

In sum, this entire idea of a completed or perfected state of
knowledge is an inherently problematic notion whose deployment
is fraught with puzzles and difficulties.

4. IMPROPER VS. INTRACTABLE QUESTIONS: TWO VERY DIFFERENT
    SORTS OF COGNITIVE LIMITS

It is important to distinguish between two importantly different
sorts of unanswerable questions: (1) *intractable questions* that do
arise appropriately on the basis of the cognitive framework in
hand, but that cannot be answered within it, and (2) actually
improper questions that are unanswerable because they are actu-

ally unaskable, seeing that the cognitive framework at issue effectively fails to allow such questions to arise. The question-answering completeness of a body of knowledge should accordingly be assessed in terms not of *all imaginable* questions, but of all the proper or legitimate questions, where the cognitve framework at issue is itself entitled to play a part in the determination of such legitimacy.

This perspective has important implications for the issue of the completability of science. Conceivably, if most improbably, science might reach a purely fortuitous equilibrium between problems and solutions. It could eventually be "completed" in the narrow erotetic sense—in providing an answer to every question one *can* ask in the then-existing (albeit still imperfect) state of knowledge—without thereby being completed in the larger sense of answering the questions that would arise if only one could probe nature just a bit more deeply. The erotetic completeness of a state of the cognitive art may, as we have seen, merely betoken its blindness.

All the same, this general idea of the question-answering (or *erotetic*) mode of the completeness/incompleteness of a "state of knowledge" represents a particularly attractive conception. For it does not construe completeness in terms of some state-of-knowledge external, absolutistic standard of "perfect information," comparing our "knowledge" with that of some hypothetical cognitively infalliable being. Rather, it develops a standard of completeness that is *internal* to our cognitive horizons, approaching the matter from the standpoint of the issue of whether all the questions that *we* do (or meaningfully can) pose from where we stand on the cognitive scheme of things are questions which *we* do (or can) answer. Such completeness appraises a "state of knowledge" on its own terms, and not with a view to some transcendental absolute.

5. COGNITIVE LIMITS AND THEIR RAMIFICATIONS

Having examined the idea of question-answering *completeness*, let us turn to *incompleteness* and explore the cognate issue of *cognitive* limits.

One regard in which the question-resolving capacity of our knowledge might be limited is by way of the weak limitation described in the following thesis:

Weak-Limitation (The Permanence of Unsolved Questions)
There are *always*, at every temporal stage,[6] questions to which no answer is in hand. At every juncture of cognitive history there exist then-unanswerable question for whose resolution current science is inadequate (yet which may well be answerable at some later state):

$$(\forall t)(\exists Q)[Q \epsilon Q(K_t) \ \& \ \sim K_t @Q].$$

This thesis has is that there are *always* questions within the K-correlatively posable range $Q(K)$ that fall outside of $Q\#(K)$, the sphere of what K is able to resolve. This envisages a permanence of cognitive limitation, maintaining that our knowledge is never at any state completed, because intractable (i.e., posable but unanswered) questions always remain on the agenda.

Given Kant's Principle of Question Propagation, such a situation of the permanence of unsolved questions is at once assured. For if every state of knowledge generates further new and yet unanswered questions, then we will never reach a position where all questions are resolved.

However, this condition of weak limitation is perfectly compatible with the circumstance that *every* question raisable at a given stage will *eventually* be answered. And so, a contrasting way in which the question-resolving capacity of our knowledge may be limited can envisage the following, more drastic situation:

Strong-Limitation (The Existence of Insolubilia)
There will (as of some juncture) be then-posable questions which will *never* obtain an answer, meaningful questions whose resolution lies beyond the reach of science altogether —questions that will remain ever unsolved on the cognitive agenda:

$$(\exists Q)(\exists t')(\forall t \geq t')[Q \epsilon Q(K_t) \ \& \ \sim K_t @Q].$$

Weak limitation envisages the immortality of questions; strong limitation the existence of immortal questions—permanently unanswerable questions (insolubilia). This stronger thesis has it that there are immortal problems, questions that transgress "beyond the limits" of our explanatory powers *in toto,* admitting of no resolution within any cognitive corpus we are able to bring to realization.

One can also move beyond the two preceding theses to the yet stronger principle of

Hyperlimitation (The Existence of IDENTIFIABLE Insolubilia)
Our present-day cognitive agenda includes certain specifiable questions Q_1, Q_2, etc., *whose resolution lies beyond the reach of science altogether and which are here and now identifiable as such:*

$$(\forall t \geqslant n)[Q_i \in Q(K_t) \ \& \sim K_t @ Q_i]$$

Now for there to be *insolubilia* it is certainly not necessary that anything be said about the current *availability* of the insoluble question. The prospect of its actual identification at this or indeed any other particular prespecified juncture is wholly untouched. The thesis of hyperlimitation thus makes a very strong claim—and a very implausible one. A position that holds that there indeed *are* insolubilia certainly need not regard them as being identifiable at the current stage of scientific development.

The range of issues operative in these deliberations was already mooted by Kant:

> [I]n natural philosophy, human reason admits of *limits* ("excluding limits," *Schranken*) but not of *boundaries* ("terminating limits," *Grenzen*), namely, it admits that something indeed lies without it, at which it can never arrive, but not that it will at any point find completion in its internal progress . . . . [T]he possibility of new discoveries is infinite: and the same is the case with the discovery of new properties of nature, of new powers and laws by continued experience and its rational combination . . . .[7]

The acceptance of *excluding limits (Schranken)*—of "something outside knowledge, at which it can never arrive" clearly points to the existence of insolubilia, questions we shall never be able to answer. On the other hand, the rejection of *boundaries (Grenzen)*—the denial of "a completion of knowledge in its internal progress" is clearly a matter rejecting the idea of a condition in which all posable questions are resolved:

$$(\exists\ t)(\forall\ Q)\ [Q \in Q(K_t) \supset K_t @Q]$$

Since this rejection commits us to accepting

$$(\forall\ t)(\exists\ Q)[Q \in Q(K_t)\ \&\ \sim K_t @Q],$$

it is clear that what is at issue here is simply the aforementioned principle of the permanence of unsolved questions, a condition of things that is, as we have seen, assured by Kant's Principle of Question Propagation.

The distinction between these various types of limits thus carries the important lesson—already drawn by Kant—that the resolution of all *our* scientific problems would not necessarily mean that science as such is finite or completable.

6. THE REYMOND-HAECKEL CONTROVERSY

One particular historical episode is of much interest is the present connection. In 1880, the German physiologist, philosopher, and historian of science Emil du Bois-Reymond published a widely discussed lecture on *The Seven Riddles of the Universe (Die sieben Welträtsel)*,[8] in which he maintained that some of the most fundamental problems regarding the workings of the world were insoluble. Reymond was a rigorous mechanist. On his view, the limit of our secure knowledge of the world is confined to the range where purely mechanical principles can be applied. As for all else, we not only *do not* have but *cannot* in principle obtain reliable knowledge. Under the banner of the slogan *ignoramus et ignorabimus* ("we *do not* know and *shall never* know"), Reymond maintained a sceptically agnostic position with respect to basic issues in physics (the nature of matter and force, and the ultimate source of motion) and psychology (the origin of sensation and of consciousness). These issues are simply *insolubilia* which al-

Date 6/8/00

Agency Hei

Name Joanna Collins

Address 2247700578 3705

Telephone 713-868-1141

① Title Theism and
or
Subject Empiricism

② Title Empirical Inquiry
or
Subject

Collins 6/14

l. m. or

rec. 6/9

together transcend man's scientific capabilities. Certain fundamental biological problems he regarded as unsolved, but perhaps
in principle soluble (though very difficult): the origin of life, the
adaptiveness of organisms, and the development of language and
reason. And as regards the seventh riddle—the problem of free-
dom of the will—he was undecided.

The position of du Bois-Reymond was soon and sharply contested by the zoologist Ernest Haeckel in a book *Die Welträtsel*
published in 1889,[9] which soon attained a great popularity. Far
from being intractable or even insoluble—so Haeckel
maintained—the riddles of du Bois-Reymond had all virtually been
solved. Dismissing the problem of free-will as a pseudo-
problem—since free will "is a pure dogma [which] rests on mere
illusion and in reality does not exist at all"—Haeckel turned with
relish to the remaining riddles. Problems of the origin of life, of
sensation, and of consciousness Haeckel regarded as solved—or
solvable—by appeal to the theory of evolution. Questions of the
nature of matter and force, he regarded as solved by modern
physics except for one residue: the problem (perhaps less scientific
than metaphysical) of the ultimate origin of matter and its laws.
This "problem of substance" was the only remaining riddle
recognized by Haeckel, and it was not really a problem of science:
in discovering the "fundamental law of the conservation of matter
and force" science had done pretty much what it could do with
respect to this problem; the rest that remained was metaphysics
with which the scientist has no proper concern.

Haeckel has surely had the better of this argument. The idea that
there are any now-identifiable issues that science cannot resolve
has little to recommend it—and our historical experience lies
uniformly on the other side. Never is a long time, and "never say
never" a sensible motto. The course of historical experience runs
clear against the idea that there are any identifiable questions about
the world (in a meaningful sense of these terms) that do in principle
lie beyond the reach of science.

The revelant point, to repeat, is that it is emphatically *not*
necessary for a theory of endless scientific progress—one which
envisages an unending succession of scientific problems—to
commit itself to the idea that there are any insolubilia at all, let
alone insolubilia identifiable as such *at this stage of the game*.

The thesis of incompletable scientific progress is thus wholly compatible with the view that *every* question that can be asked at each and every particular state is going to be answered— or dissolved—at some future state: it does not commit one to the idea that there are any unanswerable questions placed altogether beyond the limits of possible resolution. It thus suffices for the prospect of endless scientific progress to rely on the operation of Kant's principle to the effect that old problems when solved or dissolved give birth to others whose inherent significance is of no lesser magnitude than that of their predecessors. No recourse to *insolubilia* need be made to assure incompletability.

7. THE INCOMPLETABILITY OF "OUR KNOWLEDGE" IN THE FACTUAL DOMAIN

The desideratum of erotetic completeness nevertheless plays an important *regulative* role. The aim of inquiry is twofold: (1) to obtain answers to our questions, and (2) to do so (if possible) in such a way as to move the whole corpus of our cognitive commitments nearer to completeness. In inquiry with respect to a question Q we want not only to obtain a resolution of Q, (i.e., to have it answered or dissolved), but also to do this in a way that will shift our prior "body of knowledge" K to a successor state K' in which the *overall* range of unanswered questions is reduced or at any rate minimized insofar as possible.[10] The pursuit of systematization in science is ever guided by the desideratum of opening up the smallest volume of new problems. The quest for completeness is accordingly built into the very goal-structure of scientific inquiry as a regulative principle of the enterprise.

As we have seen, the total completion of our factual knowledge is not something one can reasonably hope ever to realize. But the fact that one cannot expect to attain this ideal fully does not annul the injunction to "strive to make your knowledge of the world as complete as you find it possible to do." The pursuit of completeness remains a perfectly legitimate and appropriate *regulative ideal* for factual inquiry, despite the fact that we do not, and cannot expect its definitive attainment.

Completeness is an ideal we cannot hope ever to bring to

completed realization, but whose pursuit pulls us towards a receding horizon that beckons ever onwards. Our old questions resolved, new ones of no lesser significance open up as per Kant's principle of question-proliferation, and this circumstance makes it impossible to realize the rational contentment of an equilibrium state where all our questions are satisfactorily resolved. This fact that science cannot be brought to an end should nevertheless be seen as rather a benefit than a source of appropriate regret. The termination of man's intellectual struggle with nature, even were it to end in a "victory" of sorts, would surely be a matter of appropriate regret. The ending of science as an inventive venture—its falling once and for all into the hands of schoolmasters and expositors—would surely spell its doom as a significant cognitve endeavor. The work of intellect would be reduced to preserving a fixed tradition, generation to generation a finished and final body of knowledge. The old dictum holds with respect to inquiry: it is better to travel than to arrive. It would be far from satisfactory to bring natural science to a satisfactory end.

With respect to the moral aspirations of man's will, Kant wrote:

> [P]erfection [of the moral will] is a thing of which no rational being in the world of sense is at any time capable. But since it is required [of us] as practically necessary, it can be found only in an endless progress to that complete fitness; on principles of pure practical reason, it is necessary to assume such a practical progress as the real object of our will. . . . Only endless progress from lower to higher stages of moral perfection is possible to a rational but finite being.[11]

Much the same story surely holds on the side of the cognitive perfecting of man's intellect. Here, comparable regulative demands are at work governing the practical venture of inquiry, urging us to the ever fuller realization of the potentialities of the human intellect. The limitations of theoretical reason make way for the demands of practical rationality.

The discontent of reason is a noble discontent. Man's commitment to an ideal of reason in his pursuit of an unattainable systematic completeness is the epistemic counterpart of our commitment to moral ideals. It reflects a striving to realize the rational ultimates of completeness, totality, and systematic finality—a striving that is all the more noble because it is not finally attainable. If the work of inquiring reason were completable, this would be something utterly tragic for us men. The crucial stimulus for our intellectual striving would be withdrawn. The day of mindless idleness—of what Kant calls *ignava ratio* ("lazy reason")—would come upon us, and we would fall into a slothful torpor, bereft of any incentive to bestir ourselves in ways befitting our characteristically human intellectual condition. Accordingly, the striving for cognitive completeness—unattainable though it is—represents a thoroughly appropriate ideal. Its validation lies not in its *achievability* but in its *utility,* its capacity to provide a motive force that powerfully facilitates the furtherance of the enterprise.

All the same, the *incompleteness* and even presumptive *incompletability* of "our (purported) knowledge" has profound and far-reaching implications for its status. For one of the clearest lessons of the history of science is that where scientific knowledge is concerned, further information does not just supplement but generally *corrects* our prior knowledge. Accordingly, we have little alternative but to take the humbling view that the incompleteness of our purported knowledge about the world entails its potential incorrectness as well—incompleteness must be presumed to carry incorrectness in its wake. It is now a matter not simply of *gaps* in the structure of our knowledge, of errors of omission. There is no realistic alternative but to suppose that we face a situation of real flaws as well, of errors of commission. This aspect of the matter endows incompleteness with an import far graver than meets the eye on first view.[12]

PART FOUR
Truth and Reality

IX

The Perspective of Science and That of Everyday-Life Common Sense

SYNOPSIS

(1)While our everyday-life talk and our scientific discourse are discontinuous in point of the meaning-content of their assertions (given the wholly distinct orientation of their respective vocabularies), there is a continuity in point of their question-answering concerns. This points to the thesis of *erotetic connectability,* which holds that the issues of science are ultimately linked to questions of ordinary life as means to ends. (2) Nevertheless, the two spheres of discourse are profoundly different, because very different levels of definiteness—of exactness and precision—are at issue. The fallability of our scientific theorizing is grounded in this pursuit of definiteness. (3) But despite the superior informativeness of scientific claims, we cannot abandon the (less precision-oriented but yet securer) conceptual scheme of everyday-life common sense, because it is the setting that provides the very reason for being of science. (4) Moreover, we need the machinery of our everyday-life, common-sense perspective to provide for the comparability that is essential to the idea of scientific *progress* (rather than mere development or change).

1. THE PERSPECTIVE OF SCIENCE AND THAT OF EVERYDAY-LIFE

The scientific view of things differs radically from that of everyday life. Consider Sir Arthur Eddington's famous example of the two tables:

[T]here are duplicates of every object about me—two tables, two
chairs, two pens . . . . One of them has been familiar to me from
earliest years. It is commonplace object of that environment which I
call the world. How shall I describe it? It has extension; it is comparatively permanent; it is colored; above all it is substantial . . . . Table
two is my scientific table. It is a more recent acquaintance and I do
not feel so familiar with it. It does not belong to the world previously
mentioned—that world which spontaneously appears around me
when I open my eyes, though how much of it is objective and how
much subjective I do not here consider. It is part of a world which in
more devious ways has forced itself on my attention. My scientific
table is mostly emptiness . . . . There is nothing *substantial* about
my second table. It is nearly all empty space—space pervaded, it is
true, by fields of force, but these are assigned to the category of
'influences', not of 'things'.[1]

One aspect of Eddington's discussion here is badly misleading. For
his formulation suggests that we are dealing with two *different and
distinct* tables, whereas what is in fact at issue (by hypothesis!) is
two different perspectives upon one selfsame table about which
different sorts of things are being said. The scientist, that is,
describes the make-up of this table in terms of reference very
different from those of common life. Everything he says about the
table—the whole complex story of protons, electrons, etc. which
he uses—is altogether different, because the conceptual framework on which such assertions are based is *toto caelo* different
from that of our everyday-life experience. Yet there is only one
table.

The vocabulary of science involves massive departures from
that of common life. When we contrast these ranges of discourse,
we cannot but remark a radical discontinuity at the level of the
semantical meaning-content of their respective descriptive and
classificatory machinery. (Furniture and gardens and rainstorms
are described in one range of vocabulary, electrons and viruses and
magnetic fields in another.) Nevertheless, while virtually everything said about the table is said by the scientist in variant terms of
reference, it is, intent of all the parties involved, the very same
object that is at issue. (Shades of communicative parallax!) Even
as the scientific discourse of one era is invariably very different

from that of another, so the scientific discourse of every era is different from that of everyday life.

The informative orientation of these two spheres is very different. The ordinary framework of experientiable thing-types with their colors, shapes, textures, etc., centers about how *we* (animate beings constituted as we are, exploring our environment with the sorts of sensors with which we have been endowed) react to and interact with nature by the use of our unaided senses. The language of science, on the other hand, introduces altogether novel conceptions based on much more sophisticated means of observation and consideration.

Nevertheless, their descriptive differences not withstanding, science and everyday discourse share a common basis of question-answering concerns. What is the table made of? What is the physical structure of the table? How does the table interact with other things? How will the table react when certain things are done to it? All these questions couched in the *lingua franca* of everyday life pose issues with which the sciences are also prepared to grapple. For, we saw in the discussion of categories, the questions of science root in and evolve from the primordial questions of everyday life, unfolding in the course of our attempts to give even more exact, detailed, and precise answers to these questions and their natural successors.

As the discussion of question-propagation of Chapter IV indicates, the questions of science are linked to and emerge from those of ordinary, prescientific common sense through chains of means-ends relationships. Our scientific questions exfoliate in means-ends sequences that ultimately trace back to issues posable at the common-sense level of everyday life—such as, for example, why does cooking render onions palatable? The questions of science arise out of those of everyday-life.

We inevitably begin with questions about the nature and explanation of the make-up of things, their composition and constitution, their comportment, their workings and activities and interrelations, etc. The answers that we get to these questions open up other questions which in their turn open up still other questions at ever greater levels of precision and systemic refinement. In this way, science comes to have a life of its own that carries it to levels of depth increasingly far away from its starting point. But the connection is always there and must always remain as long as science is what it always has been—an endeavor to answer our factual questions. Throughout the progress of inquiry, the issues of science remain linked to the unsophisticated questions posed at the everyday pre-scientific level. There is always a relationship of means to ends, because the mechanisms of science are, in the final analysis, instituted to answer questions posed at the level of rudimentary common sense. We have here to do, not with two realms, but two different ways of talking about the same realm at different levels of question-posing sophistication. We do *and must* begin with a pre-scientific or sub-scientific everyday-life picture: the sort of view of the rough essentials of our world that a child can master in its general outlines by the age of four or five.

Accordingly, the scientific perspective—notwithstanding its descriptive, taxonomic, and explanatory innovations—involves no *conflict* with our everyday-life perspective, but remains *continuous* with it precisely because of the evolutionary linkage that unites them. We arrive at the thesis of *erotetic connectability* to the effect that every scientific question arises in the endeavor to answer a question which arises in the endeavor to answer a question which . . . eventually arises in the endeavor to answer a question at the level of prescientific common sense. However differently science may proceed from everyday-life in the use of concepts and categories for fixing on its answers, there is still a continuity at the rock-bottom level of questions. We answer the technical questions of science in order to answer yet other technical questions in order *ultimately* to answer certain strictly common-sensical questions about the world—questions posable in everyday-life terms. Accordingly, the prescientific questions of everyday life play a crucial guiding role for scientific deliberations: scientific questions are always tied to ordinary ones by question-chains linked together by a series of means-ends relationships.

Could it ever happen that our interest would shift wholly and altogether to the domain of science? Yes and no. It is certainly possible for particular individuals that, with the passage of years, they should become wholly acculturated to the scientific outlook and their perspective gradually become that of science alone. But given the biological and social realities, this is not something that could happen with the whole group. For it is in the nature of things that group members have (at any rate) *to begin* their cognitive pilgrimage through life with the development of a sub-scientific world-picture learnable "at mother's knee."

This erotetic connectibility of science and everyday-life serves to assure some rough continuity of the science of one era with that of another. It is, however a continuity of erotetic concern rather than one of conceptual machinery. Very little if any of the theory-commitments of Galenic medicine are preserved in contemporary medicine. Democritus would be surprised and perhaps consternated to see the atomic theory in its present-day form, and Newton amazed at what has become of gravity. But the issues in the diagnosis, prognosis, and invervention at issue in the medical example, or those of the analysis of matter at issue in the physical ones, provide for a fundamental unity of project. This unity is readily captured by the everyday-life characterization of the projects involved in medicine and natural philosophy—projects which, when depicted in *these* terms, preserve their characteristic identity throughout the ages. It is the erotetic connectibility of a branch of science with a set of underlying subscientific issues—a connectibility that is maintained throughout the course of scientific change and remains substantially preserved throughout successive state-of-the-art configurations—that assures the integrity of the several characteristic departments of scientific inquiry, manifesting a continuity of concern throughout a discontinuity of doctrine and demarcating the branches of science from one another and science as a whole from other sorts of human activity.

2. THE DIFFERENCE IN COGNITIVE ORIENTATION BETWEEN SCIENCE
   AND DAILY LIFE

Science is the venture of providing the best available estimates of answers to our questions about the furnishings of the world and their modes of comportment.

Increased confidence in the correctness of our estimates can always be purchased at the price of decreased accuracy. We estimate the height of the tree at *around* 25 feet. We are *quite sure*

that the tree is 25±5 feet high. We are *virtually certain* that its
height is 25±10 feet. But we are *completely and absolutely sure*
that its height is between 1 inch and 100 yards. Of this we are
"completely sure" in the sense that we are "absolutely certain,"
"certain beyond the shadow of a doubt," "as certain as we can be
of anything in the world," "so sure that we would be willing to
stake our life on it," and the like. For any sort of estimate
whatsoever there is always a characteristic trade-off relationship
between the evidential *security* of the estimate, on the one hand (as
determinable on the basis of its probability or degree of acceptability), and on the other hand its contentual *definiteness* (exactness,
detail, precision, etc.). A situation of the sort depicted by the
concave curve of Figure 1 obtains.

Figure 1
THE TRADE-OFF BETWEEN
SECURITY AND DEFINITENESS IN ESTIMATION

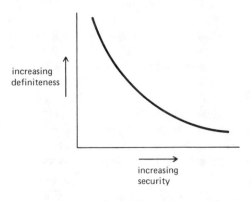

Note: Given suitable ways of measuring security *(s)* and definiteness *(d)*, the curve at issue can be supposed to be the equi-
lateral hyperbola: $s \times d = $ constant.

Now the crucial point in this regard is that natural science
eschews the security of indefiniteness. In science we always
endeavor to attain the maximal achievable universality, precision,

exactness, etc. The law-claims of science are *strict*—precise, wholly explicit, exceptionless, and unshaded. They involve no hedging, no fuzziness, no incompleteness, and no exceptions. In saying "The melting point of lead is 327.5°C," in science we mean to assert that *all* pieces of (pure) lead will unfailingly melt at *exactly* this temperature; and we certainly don't mean to assert that *most* pieces of (pure) lead will *probably* melt at *somewhere around* this temperature. By contrast when we assert in ordinary life that "Peaches are delicious" we mean to be understood as asserting something like "Most people will find the eating of suitably grown and duly matured peaches a relatively pleasurable experience." Such a statement has all sorts of built-in safeguards like "more or less," "in ordinary circumstances," "by and large," "normally," "if other things are equal," and the like. They are not really laws but rules of thumb, a matter of practical lore rather than scientific rigor. In natural science, however, we deliberately accept risk by aiming at maximal definiteness—and thus at maximal informativeness and testability. The theories of natural science take no notice of what happens ordinarily or normally; they seek to transact their explanatory business in terms of strict universality—in terms of what happens always and everywhere and in all circumstances. But in consequence we have no choice but to accept the vulnerability of our scientific statements relative to the operation of the security/definiteness tradeoff. The fact that its theoretical claims are "mere estimates" that are cognitively at risk roots unavoidably in science's inherent commitment to the pursuit of maximal definiteness, which assures its theories a modest lifespan.

The security/definiteness tradeoff is the basis of scientific fallibilism. Its cultivation of informativeness (definiteness of information) entails the risk of error in science. The increased vulnerability, the diminished security of our claims is the unavoidable other side of the coin of the pursuit of definiteness. Science operates in its upper left-hand sector of the diagram of Figure 1. The claims of science are subject to a high level of insecurity. What is learned at one level of scientific systematization is unlearned at the next.

The ground-rules of ordinary life discourse are altogether different, however. The operative injunctions here are: "Aim for security, even at the price of definiteness; don't lay yourself open to the reproach of error and the purveying of mistaken information." Ordinary-life communication is a practically oriented endeavor carried on in a social context: its cardinal maxims are "Protect your credibility; avoid misleading people, or—even worse—lying to them by asserting outright falsehoods; do not take a risk and 'cry wolf'."

The aims of ordinary-life discourse are primarily *practical* and geared to social interaction and the coordination of human effort. Through this context, it is crucial that we aim at trust and acceptance—that we establish and maintain a good reputation for reliability and trustworthiness. In the framework of common-life discourse we thus take our stance at a point of the curve of security/definiteness trade-off substantially removed from that of science, whose objectives are largely *theoretical,* and where the name of the game is disinterested inquiry. Very different probative orientations thus prevail in the two areas. In ordinary-life contexts, our approach is one of situational satisficing: we stop at the first level of sophistication and complexity that suffices for our present needs. In science, however, our approach is one of systemic maximizing: we press on towards the ideals of systemic completeness and comprehensiveness. In science we put ourselves at greater risk because we ask much more of the project.

We must recognize—without any relapse into scepticism—that the cognitive stance characteristic of science requires the acceptance of fallibility and corrigibility, and so constrains a certain tentativity, engendering the presumption of error. Because the aims of the enterprises are characteristically different, our inquiries in everyday-life and in science have a wholly different aspect, with the former achieving a stability and security at the price of sacrificing definiteness, a price which the latter scorns to pay.

A possible misapprehension arises in this connection. A view along the following lines is very tempting: "Science is the best, most thoroughly tested knowledge we have—the 'knowledge' of everyday life pales by comparison. The theses of science are really secure; those of everyday-life casual and fragile." But the very reverse is the case: our scientific theories are vulnerable and have a smallish lifespan; it is our claims at the looser level of ordinary life that are relatively secure and stable.

But, of course, the claims of everyday life readily sacrifice definiteness to gain this security and reliability. One recent writer has quite correctly written that

> we sometimes forget . . . how completely our own knowledge has absorbed what the cavemen knew, and what Ptolemy, Copernicus, Galileo and Newton knew. True, some of the things our predecessors thought they knew turned out not to be knowledge at all; and these counterfeit facts have been rejected along with the theories that "explained" them. But consider some of the facts and low-level regularities our ancestors knew, which we know, and which any astronomical theory is obligated to explain: the sky looks about the same every night; it is darker at night than during the day; there is a moon; the moon changes its appearance regularly; there is a cycle of seasons.[2]

To be sure, the sort of "knowledge" at issue here does not go very far in affording us with a detailed understanding of the ways of the world. It lacks scientific substance. But just exactly that is the basis of its comparative invulnerability.

Ongoing scientific progress is not a matter of increasing accuracy and extending the numbers in our descriptions of nature out to a few more decimal places. It will not serve to take the preservationist stance that the old theories are generally acceptable as far as they go and merely need supplementation—significant scientific progress is genuinely revolutionary in that there is a *fundamental change of mind* as to how things happen in the world. Progress of this caliber is generally a matter not of adding further facts—on the order of filling in of a crossword puzzle—but of changing the framework itself. Substantial headway is made preeminently by conceptual and theoretical innovation. And this innovation makes our entire earlier picture of natural phenomena look naive—a matter of crude trial and imperfect understanding. (No recent writer has stressed this aspect of scientific progress more persuasively than K. R. Popper.) As was already argued above (pp. 93, 156), it is gravely mistaken to think of scientific progress on the basis of an accretion-model, since the matter is one of constantly rebuilding from the very foundations. Its quest for enhanced definiteness of information is surely the prime mover of scientific inquiry. The ever-continuing pursuit of increasing accuracy, greater generality, widened comprehensiveness, and improved systematicity for its assertions is the motive force behind scientific research. And this innovative process—impelled by the quest for enhanced definiteness—drives the conceptual scheme of science to regions ever more distant from the familiar conceptual scheme of our everyday life.

3. THE INDISPENSABILITY OF THE EVERYDAY-LIFE SCHEME

But if the conceptual scheme of ordinary, everyday, common-sense discourse proves inadequate to our cognitive requirements because it is too crude and imprecise for the purposes of rigorous cognition, then why not simply abandon it altogether? Science, so we have argued, roots in common sense. Can it not also uproot common sense?

The answer is that it cannot do so, because the everyday-life scheme of things provides the very reason for being of the scheme of science. Science gives (or *purports* to give) us *theories about* these real things that we take to populate this world about us, to describe their composition, structure, operation, interaction, etc. The questions that arise in the setting of everyday life (Where does rain come from? What makes the rainbow? etc.) pose the basic task for science as a cognitive venture. The resolution of such questions constitutes the definitive task of natural science. Without the capacity to deal with them, science would lose its point, its reason for being. The erotetic connectibility of science to ordinary life is crucial to its very existence. For it is the filiation of questions generating further questions—all of them *ultimately* rooted in our initial prescientific questions about the world—that keeps science linked in an avowedly descriptive way to the characterization of the world.

To be sure, by the time its work is well under way, science no longer talks about the issues of common sense, but only about matters needed to talk about matters needed to talk about them.

But it no more *abolishes* that ultimate level of everyday-life issues than scientific medicine *abolishes* those prescientific symptoms towards whose management its efforts are in the final analysis directed. At the level of doctrine—of contentions and answers—there will be little if any conceptual connectibility between the language of science and that of everyday-life common sense, but at the level of question-resolving concern, some thread of linkage—some line of *erotetic* connectibility—will always be present between them.

Accordingly, the issues of our scientific deliberations extend and refine those of common sense but do not replace them; they are supplementary rather than competitive. The scientific framework of questions both emerges from and complements that of pre-scientific common sense. But it does not, and cannot, abolish it because, ultimately and in the final analysis, the questions of common life provide the very *raison d'être* through which the questions of science secure their very pointfulness in the intellectual scheme of things. We indispensably need the basic everyday-life terminology because it provides the terms of reference for our scientific deliberations. Means-ends connectability to these protoquestions (and thereby to the conceptual framework with reference to which they are articulated) affords the very standard of scientific relevance, i.e., relevance to the project of "describing the world we live in."

Consider the thought-experiment of imagining what would happen if this linkage were severed: if some "scientific" question proved in the end to be nowise connectible with the issues of everyday-life common sense in this sort of way. It would, clearly thereby loose all its relevance to the world and thereby its relevance to science as well, seeing that science is nothing other than the venture of securing information "about the world."

If the deliberations of science were not connectible to those of everyday-life through the processes of developmental emergence, then they would become *pointless*. For it is always these common-life questions that provide the ultimate focus and reason for being of our scientific discussions. To become ultimately disconnected here—to have no bearing whatever upon the issues that can be posed in the *lingua franca* of everyday life—would be to become *irrelevant*. Science would no longer be *natural* science: it would leave *nature* behind because one could no longer take whatever world to which it addresses itself to be identical with *our* world.

We are led back here to the identity of Eddington's two tables. Science has no world of its own. It is no abstract game with its own abstract interest—a matter of pure invention (like theoretical mathematics is sometimes thought to be). Its reason for being is to provide information about the world we live in, and without erotetic connectibility this linkage would be altogether destroyed. Without this basis of real-world purport, science would become a branch of *belles lettres* rather than a study of nature.

To be sure, science does indeed *reeducate* us regarding the sorts of questions we should ask and the sorts of answers we should expect. Slow and glacial changes also occur in our ordinary-life scheme as the progress of science exerts its feed-back pressures. But such changes tend to be relatively incidental and marginal in ways that, for the most part, leave our crude, "prescientific" questions substantially intact. The circumstances are conveniently describable in terms of Figure 2. At every stage, the "state of the art" of scientific theorizing (S_t) is correlated with, and erotetically embeddable in, a contemporaneous "world picture" of things at the level of everyday life (E_t). Even over short intervals $\triangle$, S_t can change in a dramatic, "revolutionary" way. But even over long intervals E_t will remain largely unaltered. S_t is volatile, E_t sluggish. To be sure, E_t does change over the course of time in its gradual and glacial way. Animism is long gone from the ordinary man's world picture, and the realm of magic and the occult has contracted drastically since ancient times. But nevertheless E_t changes in slow, gradualistic and marginal ways, and has a "hard core" that alters scarcely at all. A substantial section of our ordinary world-picture remains as it was in classical antiquity. (The reader should think back here to the discussion of categories in Chapter III.)

Such elemental questions as "How do birds fly" or "How do they reproduce?" etc. are issues that could not be unmade by scientific change. We could not be persuaded into withdrawing these questions; it is literally "unthinkable" that we should discover that we are mistaken about the matters at issue in their presuppositions.

Figure 1
THE STRUCTURE OF COGNITIVE CHANGE

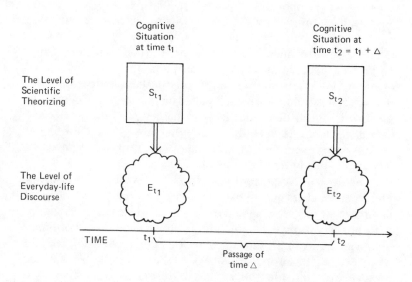

They are immune to the impetus of scientific innovation because their presuppositions are too rudimentary: the sorts of considerations that science brings on the stage come later—too late to undo the elemental presuppositions at issue with the claims that there are birds, that they fly, and the like. In the sciences, we just don't raise questions like "Are there birds?" or "Do birds fly?" Science intervenes in the cognitive scheme of things at a later stage and is thereby not in a position to uproot common sense at the rudimentary level of its most gross and molar commitments. But just exactly what sorts of creatures birds are, that they fly by means of certain particular processes, that they emerge from eggs by just exactly this or that mechanism, and the like, are all matters regarding which the progress of science could continue to reeducate us. Yet the more elemental issues of *what* rather than *how* lie at a level too basic for scientific emendation.

Much of what we hold essential at the common level is left untouched and unaltered when we do science; everything must be at once preserved and transmuted (*aufgehoben* in the Hegelian sense). Like the poor, the "low level regularities" of everyday life are always with us. Any "science" worthy of the name must be able to accomodate them and must ultimately be connectible to them. If science does not—or, rather, insofar as it does not—provide satisfactory answers to the questions that arise at the level of ordinary-life common sense, it fails in its definitive mission. Science cannot abolish what it is called on to clarify. (Of course, to say this is not to deny that its explanatory machinery may use causal mechanisms very different from those envisaged at the ordinary life level; e.g., that it might explain the phenomena of witchcraft and sorcery in terms of autosuggestion.)

In its descriptive purport science is continuous with ordinary life, from which its questions all ultimately emerge. To be sure, its commitment to precision and informativeness soon shift science onto a path of its own, where the conceptual resources of ordinary life no longer avail. But the quest for the ultimate starting point of its investigations always leads back to the issues that arise at the level of everyday-life concerns. The relevance of science as a project of affording information about the world we live in turns crucially on this connectibility to the familiar world of our common sensical experience, this realistic intent to deal in the final analysis with the issues of reality as we ordinarily encounter them in everyday experience.

4. THE COMPARABILITY OF THEORY-CONSTELLATIONS

There is yet another reason why we would (and should) be extremely reluctant to abandon the *lingua franca* of everyday life in favor of an exclusive reliance on the more sophisticated discourse of science. This roots in two circumstances. (1) We must accept the reality of scientific change: the science of our era does in fact differ, radically and fundamentally, from that of another. (2) This difference can be of *toto caelo* proportions on the side of theory-content: there just is no limit to the extent to which a scientific theory that supersedes another can differ from its conceptual orientation. These considerations indicate that a comparison of the adequacy of our scientific theories cannot be carried out on the basis of a content-analysis with respect to their assertoric substance. Indeed, once we leave the secure substratum of the everyday-life world for the more sophisticated domain of scientific theorizing, we cannot even say that where the development of science yields different theories it nevertheless continues to address "the same facts." For science can certainly change its mind with respect to the very facts themselves, seeing that theory plays a critical role in determining what is to count as a fact. The "natural motion" of a celestial body is one thing for Aristotle and another for Galileo; an evil-eye hexing is one sort of thing for a superstitious peasant and quite another for a modern psychologist. Every theory-configuration is itself allowed to determine what sorts of phenomena count as data and how these data are to be construed. This means that, in scientific contexts, we cannot ever speak unproblematically of a "better accommodation of the (theory-external) data."

Now such a radical discontinuity of meaning-shifts seems to throw the very concept of *progress* in science into question. For progress is a matter, not just of change, but of improvement, and if the later stage of discussion is conceptually disjoint from the earlier, how could one consider the later as constituting an improvement upon the earlier? The replacement of one thing by something else of a totally different sort can hardly qualify as meliorative. (One can improve upon one's car by getting a better car, but cannot improve it by getting a computer or a dish-washing machine.) Fortunately, the ongoing linkage of science to the world of everyday life enters in to save the day at this stage.

In maintaining that the successive theses of science represent not just *change* but *progress* one does indeed stand committed to the view that in some fashion or other something that is strictly comparable is being improved upon. But the items at issue need not be matters of the theory-laden substance of scientific claims, they can be matters characterizable in the *lingua franca* of our commonplace affairs. The comparabilities at issue here are not achievable at the level of scientific theorizing, but only with the phenomena and the data assessible at the level of pre- or sub-scientific common-sense affairs.

To see the eventuation of conceptual discontinuity as destroying any and all basis for scientific progress is, however, to take an unduly literary view of science. For at bottom the progress at issue does not proceed along purely theoretical but rather practical lines. The progressiveness of science hinges crucially on its *applications;* it inheres in the pragmatic dimension of the enterprise—the increasing success of its applications in problem solving and control, in its affording not only cognitive but physical mastery over nature. A new theory need not explain the purported facts of the old one it replaces, because these "facts" need not remain facts—the new theory may revise or dismiss them. (The "emission of phylogiston" disappears with the onset of Lavosier's oxydation.) But the practical successes of the old theory in enabling us to predict occurrences or to achieve control at the *grosso modo* level of the developments we can discuss in the language of everyday life is something relatively unproblematic.

In general, one cannot compare the theoretical stances of diverse state-of-the-art stages of scientific inquiry on a purely cognitive (theoretical) basis because their assertive content is too diverse—indeed incommensurable. There is no theory-neutral body of facts that makes a direct comparison possible; no neutral, science-external "higher" standpoint to provide a basis of comparison. But the case is very different as regards praxis, and, in particular, praxis at the level of everyday-life proceedings. The lab explodes; the rocket doesn't fly. Here we do indeed have theory-neutral facts for assessing the comparative merits of rival theory-systems. But such comparisons at the level of effective "control over nature" operate at the level of pre-or sub-scientific dealings and affairs as describable in the *lingua franca* of everyday life, which provides the neutral ground shared in common by different theory-postures. Application becomes the touchstone.

From where we stand in the epistemic dispensation there is no way of attaining a higher vantage point—no God's eye view for comparison. However, what we do fortunately have as common basis across the divides of scientific change is not a higher but rather a lower standpoint—the crude vantage point of the ordinary everyday-life scheme, the (relatively) theory-neutral or theory-external mechanisms of a pre- or sub-scientific instrumentality of discourse to provide an inquiry-external standard of appraisal. No sophisticated complexities are needed to say that one stage in the career of science is superior to another in point of launching rockets and curing colds and exploding bombs.

The crucial fact is that such applications are in large measure operative at the level of the ordinary, everyday concepts of natural-language discourse, concepts that remain relatively fixed throughout the ages, and lie deep beneath the changing surface of scientific sophistication. In the technological *applications* of science we come back to actions and transactions that intersect with our everyday life, sub-scientific thoughts and actions—a level which, as we have seen, is relatively stable and unchanging precisely because of the greater crudity of its concerns. This technological and applicative dimension endows science with a theory-era transcending comparability that it lacks at the level of its ideas and concepts—a comparability that finds its expression in the persistence of problem solving tasks in the sphere of *praxis* as described on the basis of everyday-life conceptions.

The ancient Greek physician and the modern medical practitioner might talk of the problems of their patients in very different and conceptually incommensurate ways (say an imbalance in humors to be treated by countervailing changes in diet or regimen vs. a bacterial infection to be treated by administering an antibiotic). But at the pragmatic level of control—i.e., a removal of those symptoms of their patients (pain, fever, dizziness, etc.) that are describable in much the same terms in antiquity as today—both are working on "the same problem." And just as the merest novice can detect a false note in the musical performance of a master player whose activities he could not begin to emulate, so malfunctioning of a missile or computer can be detected by the relative amateur. Dominance in technological power to produce intended results tends to operate across the board. (The superiority of modern over Galenic medicine requires few if any subtle distinctions of respect.)

Since Bacon's day, this idea of control over nature has been recognized as affording the touchstone of scientific progress. The question of *technological* superiority (i.e., our ability at a given state-of-the-art level to obtain desired results—never mind for the moment if they are intrinsically desirable or not) is something far less sophisticated, but also far more manageable and unproblematic than the issue of *theoretical* superiority. For the factors determiniative of *technical* superiority operate at a grosser and more rough-and-ready level than those of theoretical meaning content. At the level of praxis we can operate to a relatively large degree with the *lingua franca* of everyday affairs and make our comparisons on this basis—we simply need not worry ourselves about the unavailability of a theory-neutral perspective for appraising conceptually disjoint theories. Despite any *semantic* or *ideational incommensurability* between one stage of theoretical science and its latter-day replacements, there yet remains the factor of the *pragmatic commensurability* of a constellation of practical achievements that can (by and large) be formulated in the ordinary everyday language that antedates scientific sophistication alike in the development of the species and that of its individuals.[3]

A later and progressively superior state-of-the-art in scientific theorizing need certainly not preserve the *content* of the earlier ones; its descriptive and taxonmic innovations can make for semantical discontinuity. Nor, again, need it preserve the theoretical successes of the earlier theories, their explanatory successes at elaborating interrelations among their own elements (eg. answering questions about the *modus operandi* of the luminiferous aether). But a later and progressively superior theory must *ipso facto* preserve and improve upon the practical successes of its predecessors, when these practical issues are formulated *grosso modo* in the rough-and-ready terms of everyday-life discourse. The ultimate arbiter of scientific progressiveness is accordingly seen to lie in the sphere of praxis, at a level where effectiveness is discernible from the rude and crude posture of our ordinary-life perspective.

The fundamentally pragmatic aspect of its applications in problem-solving and control at the level of everyday life manifests those continuities and comparabilities of the scientific enterprise with reference to which the idea of progress can be invoked.[4] In this way, the applicative and technological dimensions of scientific progress can be assessed comparatively without any explicit reference to the semantical content of scientific theories or the conceptual framework used in their articulation. Once the "theory-external" element of *control over nature* is given its due prominence, the substantiation of imputations of scientific *progress* becomes a more manageable project than it could ever be on an "internal," content-oriented basis.

Accordingly, the erotetic connectibility of science to the prescientific framework of our everyday life renders the immense service of providing the basis on which alone we can secure that pragmatic comparability of diverse state-of-the-art stages in scientific history needed to implement the concept of *progress* in this domain. And this circumstance yields yet another reason why we should reject any temptation to abandon the *lingua franca* of ordinary discourse in favor of an exclusive reliance on more sophisticated mechanisms of natural science.

X

Truth and Idealization

SYNOPSIS

(1) The fragile character of our putative "knowledge" and the important distinction between "*our* (putative) truth" and "*the* (real) truth." (2) The gulf between appearance and reality cannot be averted: one cannot identify "the real truth" with "the *putative* truth of such-and-such a sort." (3) Nor can this gap be bridged by Peirce's contrivance of taking the real truth to be the apparent truth of "the long run". In the context of scientific inquiry, there is no warrant for speaking of approximation or congruence or limits. There is no reason to think that later science is lesser science: that with the ongoing progress of inquiry, the "size" of our discoveries (in terms of their fundamentality or importance) is steadily diminishing. In the evolution of knowledge, later findings are not necessarily lesser findings. (4) To be sure, this no-convergence theory must be confined to matters of factual generality at the theoretical level; the case stands rather differently with issues of the concrete details of descriptive particularity. (5) In theoretical science, however, we cannot with justification claim either to *attain* nor even to *approximate* the truth, but only to *estimate* it. (6) The upshot for science of a realistic fallibilism is not scepticism, but simply a matter of the prudent recognition of the facts of life. And this idea of defeasible claims to knowledge is a perfectly workable one. Our position does not engender abandonment of "the pursuit of truth" as a key part of the goal-structure of science. Such an abandonment would exact too high a price in its destructive impact on our conceptual scheme regarding scientific inquiry. (7) While one can never lay claim to "the real truth" in matters of scientific theorizing, this notion nevertheless serves a positive role in furnishing a contrast-conception that provides a useful reminder of the fragility of our cognitive endeavors. It establishes a

204

contrast between *our* science and the idea of an "ideal science" which alone can provedly be claimed to afford a grasp of reality, an idea which crucially regulates our view as to the nature and status of the knowledge we lay claim to and productively fosters the conduct of inquiry.

1. FALLIBILISM AND THE CRUCIAL DISTINCTION BETWEEN OUR (PUTATIVE) TRUTH AND THE REAL TRUTH

It is an important fact of epistemology—perhaps the single most important fact of the field—that we have no failproof way of securing definitive information about the world at the level of scientific generality and precision. Let us explore the ramifications of a cognitive fallibilism that holds that science—*our* science, the body of our scientific beliefs as a whole—consists largely, and even predominantly, of false beliefs, embracing various theses that we will ultimately come to see (with the wisdom of hindsight) as quite untenable.

It is useful to distinguish between potential error at the *particularistic* and *collectivistic* levels—between *thesis defeasibility* and *systemic fallibilism*. The former position makes the claim that *each* of our scientific beliefs *may* be false, while the latter claims that *many or most* of our scientific beliefs *are* false. The two theses are independent. Of the pair, "Each might be false" and "Most are false," neither entails the other. (Each of the entrants in the contest might be its winner, but it could not turn out that most of them indeed are. Again, most of the pages of the book do actually come after the tenth, but it cannot be that each of them might do so.)

Our present perspective upon the claims of science espouses both thesis defeasibility and systemic fallibilism. The first follows from the standard epistemic gap between evidence-in-hand and assertive content that obtains throughout our scientific theorizing; the second from the thesis of Cognitive Copernicanism. However, systemic fallibilism with respect to science is a more serious matter than thesis defeasibility. For it means that one must presume that our whole scientific picture of the world is seriously flawed—and will ultimately come to be recognized as such. The present chapter will consider the implications of this realization.

We admit in our heart of hearts that there is a strong prospect that we shall ultimately recognize that many or most of our current scientific theories are false and that what we proudly vaunt as "scientific knowledge" is a tissue of hypotheses—of tentatively adopted contentions many or most of which we will ultimately come to regard with the wisdom of eventual hindsight as quite untenable and in need of serious revision or perhaps even abandonment. (To be sure, this realization is something of which we can make no effective use—while we realize *that* many of our scientific beliefs are wrong, we have no way of telling *which* ones, and no way of telling *how* error has crept in.) We must temper our claims to scientific knowledge with a Cognitive Copernicanism which recognizes that the current state of "knowledge" is simply one state among others that share in the same imperfect footing in point of ultimate correctness or truth.

We learn by empirical inquiry about empirical inquiry, and one of the key things we learn is that at no actual stage does science yield a final and unchanging result. All the experience we can muster indicates that there is no justification for viewing our science as more than an inherently imperfect stage within an ongoing development. And this brings us to the realization that we have no responsible alternative but to presume the imperfection of what we take ourselves to know. We occupy the posture of the so-called "Preface Paradox"—standing in the shoes of the author who apologizes in his Preface for those errors that have doubtless made their way into his work, and yet blithely remains commited to all those assertions in the body of the work itself. We know or must presume that (at the synoptic level) these are errors, though we certainly cannot say just where and how they arise.

It goes pretty much without saying that we can never be in a position to claim justifiedly that our scientific corpus of knowledge has managed to capture "the whole truth." But the present deliberations go beyond this to indicate that we are not even in a position justifiedly to claim that we've got "nothing but the truth." Our overall picture of the real world as science delivers it into our hands is held tentatively (however deeply we may be attached to some of its details).

The relationship of "our (putative) knowledge" to "the (real) truth" has to be conceived of in terms of *estimation*. The most we can do is to take K_n (i.e., K_t with t = n for *now*) as our *best estimate* of *T*, and construe K_n membership as the imperfect best we can do here and now to establish real truth. But in viewing K_n as an estimate of *T*, we have recourse to an epistemic qualifier to mediate between the two categories. And this, indeed, is inevitable: There just is no way of bypassing such an epistemic qualification and launching into an inferential process that moves from *K-membership* on the one side *to truth* on the other. At the level of scientific theorizing the linking of K_n to *T* is always a matter of a rough rule of thumb of whose ultimate inaccuracy we are keenly aware.

It is perfectly possible—and not only theoretically but *realistically* possible—that one should play the game of inquiry correctly by all the epistemological rules and still come to a result that fails to be true. For the truth of our objective claims hinges on "how matters really stand in the world" and not on the (inevitably incomplete) grounding or evidence or justification that we ourselves have in hand. We cannot cross the epistemic gap between the apparent and the real by *logically* secure means, whatever twists and turns we may take. With respect to science, as elsewhere, we must distinguish carefully between "our (putative or ostensible) truth", WHAT WE THINK TO BE TRUE on the one hand, and, on the other, "the real truth", WHAT ACTUALLY IS TRUE—the (unqualified) truth of the matter.

To be sure, at the level of specific theses and contentions, one clearly faces difficulties in distinguishing between "what really is true" and "what one thinks to be true [here and now]." For while I can unproblematically subscribe to the generalized thesis "Various claims I think to be true are actually false," this abstract general principle is something I cannot apply concretely at the level of particular judgments—the general circumstance is one of which I can adduce no specific instances. Its critique of "our knowledge" is impotently limited to the level of generalities. We can attain this "higher standpoint" only negatively, by realizing, in the abstract, the potential deficiencies of our cognitive position, but we cannot—*ex hypothesi*—say anything positive and definite about the substantive differences between *our* truth and *the* truth of the matter. At the retail level of specific theses, we are inescapably committed to viewing "our truth" as *the truth* (and "our certainty" as *actual certainty*): it simply wouldn't be OUR truth if we didn't *regard* it as THE truth. From one's own current standpoint, it appears that there is a distinction without a difference here: the distinction is one we cannot implement ourselves at the level of our actual particular current judgments. As J. H. Newman rightly stressed, at the level of concrete detail "there is no distinct test to separate real from apparent certitude."[1]

To be sure, we stand committed to our truths; imperfect, they may be, but we have nowhere else to go. We have no alternative to proceeding on the "working hypothesis" that in scientific matters *our* truth is *the* truth. But in our heart of hearts we recognize that that's just not so—that the working hypothesis in question is no more than just that.

We recognize that the workaday identification of *our* truth with *the* truth is little more than a makeshift—albeit one that stands above criticism because no alternative course is open to us. In truth-estimation, as elsewhere, we cannot do better than the best we can. The recognition that this may well not be good enough is simply an ineliminable part of the human condition. No deity has made a covenant with us to assure that what we take to be "adequately established" theories must indeed be true in these matters of scientific inquiry.

The proper lesson here is not the sceptical conclusion that our "science" counts for naught, but simply, and much less devastatingly, the realization that our scientific knowledge—or purported knowledge—of how things work in the world is flawed; that it is replete with errors which we ourselves are impotent to distinguish from the rest. With respect to the claims of science we realize that our herd is full of goats that appear altogether sheep-like to us.

2. BRIDGING THE APPEARANCE/REALITY GAP

Already in antiquity, various philosophers were persuaded that the *apparent* truths of various individuals differ so drastically that the *real* truth must be sought elsewhere.[2] Nevertheless, since the earliest days of theorizing about knowledge philosophers have striven to find some theoretical device to bridge the epistemic gap between *our* truth—the apparent or merely putative truth—on the one hand, and the *real* truth on the other. Aristotle and some of the Stoics toyed with the equation the real truth can be identified with the putative truth of certain privileged individuals. The *privileged individuals* at issue might perhaps be "the truly wise," or "the experts" or "the vast majority of men" *(consensus gentium)*. None of these are very promising alternatives. Even Homer, nay even the whole fraternity of poets and sages, might be found nodding—to say nothing of lesser mortals.

Then, too, there is the effort of other Stoics and of Descartes and sundry others to operate the equation

the real truth = the putative truth afforded by theses that are validated by a certain privileged epistemic source or process

This line of thought motivated the perennial search for a privileged process—the *cataleptic perception* of the Stoics, for example, or the *clear and distinct perceptions* of Descartes, or the *observational protocols* of the Logical Positivists, or the like. The idea is that "the truth" is to be identified with the results attained by those using certain approved methods. But this approach shipwrecks upon our heart-of-hearts realization that we can be mistaken even in doing our best, that truth is what emerges as such, not in *our* circumstances, or *anybody's* circumstances, but only in *ideal* circumstances.

All attempts to equate the real truth with the apparent truth of some sort are condemned to failure: having the same generic structure they have the same basic defect. They all view "the real truth" as "the putative truth when arrived at under conditions C." And in each case the mooted equation is destroyed by the ineliminable possibility of a separation between "the real truth" and the *putative* truth that we ourselves reach (by *whatever* route may be at issue). There is no way of telling which of our scientific beliefs are so "cataleptic" or so "clear and distinct" they cannot run awry.

The thesis-schema

$$[p \epsilon K \ \& \ C(K)] \rightarrow p \epsilon T$$

simply cannot be implemented. No workable condition C upon the inquirers at issue enables one to move inferentially from *their pretentions* to knowledge to the actual truth of things. The principle in question will fail us no matter what constituency-correlative condition C may be laid upon K—be it the knowledge of the majority, or of the experts, or of those who prudently implement established epistemic methods. With respect to the fallibility of our claims to knowledge at the level of scientific generality and precision we are all in the same boat. There is no way in which we can effect an inferentially secure transition to the real truth from anybody's *ostensible* scientific truth (our own included). In these matters the epistemic gap between the apparent and the real is unbridgeable.

To be sure, the position at issue can be salvaged by taking God to be the "privileged individual" whose putative truth is at issue, and resorting to the Myth of the God's Eye View. With K^* as the cognitive corpus of "perfected science," we can indeed establish the equivalence: $p \epsilon K^* \equiv p \epsilon T$. But this somewhat desperate remedy is of little philosophical use. For God only knows what "perfected science" is like—we ourselves certainly do not. And the Schoolmen were right: *Non in philosophia recurrere est ad deum.* (No telephone line connects us with the Recording Angel, or even if one does, we seem to have lost the Area Code.) While the idea at issue may provide a useful contrast-conception, it is something we cannot put into concrete implementation.

3. THE PEIRCEAN STRATEGEM: AGAINST CONVERGENTISM,
   APPROXIMATION, AND THE VIEW THAT LATER SCIENCE IS LESSER
   SCIENCE

It is worthwhile to examine more closely Charles Sanders Peirce's idea of equating "the real truth" with "our *ultimate* truth"—with the true as the result that science will approximate asymtotically in the long run. On this approach we begin with the (already familiar) idea of "ultimate science" or "science in the limit"

$$K_\infty = \lim_{t \to \infty} K_t$$

and then equate the *real* truth in scientific matters with true-in-K_∞: $T = K_\infty$.

Such an approach has the immense theoretical advantage of making it possible to see the real truth not as a relation between our "domesticated" knowledge and something that lies wholly and altogether outside this sphere, but rather as something determinable *within* the sphere of our knowledge. Truth-determination is no longer a matter of relating the manifold of our knowledge K_t to an external reality, but merely having the successive K_t stages themselves converge towards a limit. (Compare pp. 172–5.)

Despite its attractions, this Peircean approach faces grave, indeed insuperable difficulties.

The first is the problem of the *existence* of such a limit. For we meet the formidable difficulty: how can one possibly define a metric to measure the "distance" between bodies of knowledge?[3] Once this idea of distance is abandoned—as it seemingly must be—the idea of a measure also goes by the board.

But even if we had such a measure, there seems precious little reason to think that the actual progress of science is such that the successive stages of knowledge will come to be less and less distant from one another. As Thomas Kuhn and Paul Feyerabend and others have argued, there is no reason to think that the successive theories of science involve an historical consilience in the theoretical accounts they give. There is no indication of practice and no reason of general principle to think that scientific progress is a matter of diminishing differences with respect to the meaning-content of the theories at issue, moving towards an ultimate limit theory. To be sure, the successive stages of science come to be more and more *successful*—in some sense of this idea they do an increasingly more *adequate* job. But this increasing success is attained across a never-lessening range of content-diversity. Our commitment to the view that later theories are better theories does *not* underwrite the idea of an ever closer approach to a position of fixity. Improvements in *grounding* do not engender improvements in *depiction*.

Moreover, even if there were a limit, we could not find it out. For we live and breathe and have our being in the short run, while limits have to do with what happens in the eventual long run. And, as the saying has it, "In the long run we are all dead." Anything we can get hold of is without implications, one way or the other with respect to what happens "in the limit."

A Peircean limit theory is thus a very doubtful proposition, to put it mildly. But the dismissal of limits means that we also abandon any temptation to speak of the progress of science in terms of a process of processively closer "approximation" of the truth. Talk of approximation is parasitic upon talk of limits, so once we abandon limits, we must also give up any temptation to discuss scientific progress in the language of approximation.

This theme of approximation and limits leads back to the late 19th century controversy between W. Stanley Jevons and those who, like John Tyndall and Charles Sanders Peirce, saw the history of science as addressing itself to issues of ever-decreasing magnitude. Thus Jevons wrote:

> Professor Tyndall . . . likens the supply of novel phenomena to a convergent series, the earlier and larger terms of which have been successfully disposed of so that comparatively minor groups of phenomena alone remain for future investigators to occupy themselves upon. On the contrary, as it appears to me, the supply of new and unexplained facts is divergent in extent, so that the more we have explained the more there is to explain. The further we advance in [developing] any generalisation, the more numerous and intricate [and significant] are the exceptional cases still demanding further treatment. . . . By . . . [numerous] illustrations it might readily be shown that in whatever direction we extend our investigations and successfully harmonise a few facts, the result is only to raise up a host of other unexplained facts.[4]

There is surely no reason whatsoever to see the *later* issues of science as *lesser* issues in the significance of their bearing upon science as a cognitive enterprise. However, we ourselves see neither a convergent nor a divergent series here, but pretty much of a steady-state condition in which every major successive stage in the evolution of science yields innovations and innovations of roughly equal *overall* interest and importance.[5]

At any rate, the oft-drawn analogy of geographic exploration is surely mistaken. It views scientific progress as a whole on the basis of one particular (and by no means typical) *sort* of advance, namely the sequential filling-in in greater and greater detail of a roughly predetermined picture—the continual working out of more decimal places to lend additional refinement to a generally known result. Scientific inquiry is conceived of an analogy with terrestrial exploration, whose ongoing pursuit yields findings of continually smaller significance, since what is at issue is the filling-in of ever more minute gaps in our information. We have here an *accretional* view of the progress of science, subject to the idea that each successive accretion inevitably makes a relatively smaller contribution to what has already come to hand. Progress, on this view, consists in driving questions down to a lesser and lesser magnitude, continually decreasing their inherent significance to a smaller and smaller scale, descending to even more fine-grained level of detail. (This at bottom is the Peircean version of ultimate convergence in scientific inquiry.)

Such a picture combines two gravely mistaken ideas: (1) that the progress of science proceeds by way of cumulative accretion (like the growth of a coral reef), and (2) that the magnitude of these additions is steadily decreasing. If the former of these ideas collapses, then so will the position as a whole. And collapse it does. For science progresses not additively but largely subtractively. As Thomas Kuhn and others have persuasively argued, today's most significant discoveries generally represent a revolutionary *overthrow* of yesterdays, the big findings of science taking a form that *contradicts* its earlier big findings and involves not just supplementation but even outright replacement on the basis of conceptual and theoretical innovation.

It will not serve to take the preservationist stance that the old views were acceptable as far as they went and merely need supplementation and refinement. Significant scientific progress is genuinely revolutionary in that there is a *fundamental change of mind* as to how things happen in the world. Relativity theory does not amend the doctrine of luminiferous either, but abandons it. The creative scientist is every bit as much of a demolition expert as a master builder. Significant scientific progress is generally a matter not of adding further facts—on the order of filling in of a crossword puzzle—but of changing the framework itself; substantial headway is made pre-eminently by conceptual and theoretical innovation. Ongoing scientific progress is emphatically not a matter of merely increasing accuracy—of pushing the numbers operative in our descriptions of nature a few decimal places further out.

It is quite wrong to think of scientific progress on the basis of an accretion-model, for the matter is one of constantly rebuilding from the very foundations. Science in the main derives its picture of the natural world not by way of cumulation but by way of substitution and replacement. To all appearances, the progress of science is a matter of discontinuous jumps. Today's major discoveries represent an overthrow of yesterday's: the big findings of science, it would appear, inevitably contradict its earlier big findings (in the absence of "saving qualifications"). Significant scientific progress is generally a matter not of adding further facts—on the order of filling in of a crossword puzzle—but of changing the framework itself. And there is no reason to think that this process need ever come to a stop.[6]

Given that science in the main develops not by way of culmination but by way of substitution and replacement, it makes no sense to think of the development of science in terms of convergence or approximation.[7] Not only are we not in a position to claim to achieve the truth in science, we cannot even say that we are drawing *closer* to it. For how could we possibly do so without knowing where it lies? We have no guarantee that we are not exchanging one somehow incorrect opinion for another that is at bottom no less so. Accordingly, we can neither claim that in inquiry we attain the truth, nor that we steadily draw nearer to this goal.

Some theorists find this prospect of science moving through an endless sequence of fundamental revisions unacceptable. Science being a matter of the pursuit of truth, its progress must—they insist—increasingly converge upon some fixed and final result.[8] But this gradual convergence doctrine faces grave obstacles. There is no reason to think that nature will be cooperative in always yielding its most important secrets early on and reserving nothing but the relatively insignificant for later on. A very small-scale effect—even one that lies very far out along the extremes of a "range exploration" in point of temperature, pressure, velocity, or the like—can force a far-reaching revision and have profound impact by way of major theoretical revisions. (Think of special relativity in relation to either-drift experimentation or general relativity in relation to the perihelion of mercury.) No preestablished harmony—no metaphysical hidden hand—is at work to assure that the *order of discovery* in our penetration of the secrets of nature replicates their *order of importance* in some ontological sense, so that later penetration of the "deeper" layers are always of lesser cognitive significance for the constituting of an adequate picture of nature.

4. ISSUES OF DESCRIPTIVE PARTICULARITY

One important qualification is in order. Our no-convergence view of scientific progress holds that science "moves through an endless sequence of fundamental revisions." But here it becomes crucial to distinguish between the level of theoretical generality and the level of descriptive particularity, between *generalized theses* and *particular facts,* between issues of explanation and issues of description.

Theoretical issues are always wide-open—there is no predeterminable limit to the range of potential variation among the hypotheses at issue here. (Think, for example, of the shift from Newtonian to Einsteinean gravity, from gravity as a kind of force to gravity as an aspect of the spatio-temporal geometry-structure of the universe.) With the descriptive specification of particulars, however, we generally confront a prespecifiable descriptive range of limited potential variation. The concrete particular, objective furnishings "the real world" must by their very nature as such have certain delineable property-determinations. And when these are of a quantitative nature, the Peircean idea of a "convergence of inquiry" takes on a more tractable aspect.

We may, for example, inquire, within the scientific framework, into such matters as: the age of man (or of the earth, or of the universe), the atomic weight of lead, the boiling point of water, the number of stars in the galaxy, or the relative positions of spectral lines of a certain substance. In each instance of such "constants of nature" we are dealing with particularizations within the manifold of a certain parametrized range that is predetermined in terms of the properties essential to a certain thing or thing-kind. (A species must have an evolutionary origin in real time; an elemental substance must have some atomic weight or other, etc.) Any if such a quantity is well-defined at all, ongoing inquiry should be able to determine it in an ultimately convergent manner. In this regard, at any rate, Peirce's theory of inquiry is fundamentally correct.

Thus let $v_t(X)$ be the best-estimate value of the parameter of X as determinable with reference to the evidence-in-hand at the time t. Then as time marches on and the course of inquiry proceeds, $v_t(X)$ must tend to some definite quantity. The limit-quantity

$$\lim_{t \to \infty} v_t(X)$$

surely *must* exist: eventually there is bound to be convergence on some definite value of X. If there is not, then we can no longer think of X as a well-defined parameter at all.

Peirce's idea of convergence in inquiry can thus be implemented unproblematically as regards a limited range comprising such issues of specifically quantitative description. That is, we can look for convergence not at the global level of knowledge-system K_t as a whole, but rather with respect to matters of concrete fact grounded in the range-coordinated properties of particulars. Thus let X represent a particular-descriptive constant quantity in nature that can be subject to meaningful inquiry: the accelleration due to gravity, for example, or the length of Saturn's year, or the melting point of lead, or the population of India 1280 A.D. Then, as Peirce insisted, if this magnitude at issue is to be a well-defined quantity at all, then ongoing inquiry about it must ultimately converge to some definite value. No matter how wildly our initial efforts at evaluation may fluctuate, still, in the end, as the volume of relevant evidence grows larger and larger, a definite result must eventually emerge—to all visible intents and purposes.

Our standard conception of objectivity and the nature of real things certainly does assume or postulate that ongoing inquiry will converge to a definite result in just exactly the Peircean manner in such descriptive contexts. We stand committed to the existence of a particular parameter-determination within a certain descriptive range—that the earth is an object that does have a certain age, which cannot be less than the roughly 1×10^8 years that organic life has existed on the planet nor greater than the roughly 2×10^{10} years of the existence of the solar system of which it forms a part. And we stand committed (within the framework of our conceptual scheme) to the idea that fuller and more sophisticated inquiry will eventually pin this value down—or, rather, would in principle do so if inquiry were pushed far enough. All these commitments inhere straightforwardly in our conceptual scheme regarding the character of inquiry into the nature of things—they are a straightforward consequence of our view of the essential properties of natural things and of the structure of inquiry regarding them.

In this regard, then, the descriptive features of concrete particulars (of which we take the view that we can fix *ab initio* certain of their essential features) and the explanatory law-structures we project at the theoretical level to account for the *modus operandi* of nature at large (where we neither can nor do claim such prior knowledge) stand on a very different footing. At the level of discriptively quantified particularity, we place *a priori* limits about the range of conceivable variation. Given our commitment to there being certain particular sorts of things at issue, we consider that the range of descriptive variation as in some ways predetermined, taking the view that the course of inquiry is thereby circumscribed and, as regards the future, ever-narrowing. But at the level of scientific generality—of science's view of the law-structure of the world—we can indeed contemplate an "endless sequence of fundamental revisions" in the course of inquiry.

5. TRUTH ESTIMATION

In empirical inquiry we seek to determine the truth about things at the level of scientific generality and precision—this is beyond question of our goal and our desire. But, of course, though we aim at this target, we do so with the full realization that we generally miss the mark. How, then, is one to characterize the relationship between the fruits of our cognitive efforts and the real truth at which they are directed, given that *identification* is out of the question here?

What we manage to do in scientific inquiry is not to *approximate* the truth but to *estimate* it—to form, as best we can, a reasoned judgment of where the truth of the matter lies. With respect to OUR truth, we have to take the stand that it represents no more (but also no less) than our *best estimate* of THE truth. With the progress of science these estimates become more surely based. Increasingly, the new estimates overcome the shortcomings—both theoretical and practical—of their earlier forbears. It is, accordingly, rational to prefer the new estimate to the old one. But the basis of this rationality does not lie in some purely theoretical consideration like "getting nearer to the truth"—in a contentual sense akin to that in which a picture made with a better camera is more accurate. At the level of scientific theorizing, our present picture of the world represents a *better estimate* than our past pictures only in the sense that it is, comparitively speaking, better based than they are; it is a matter of better grounding and not a matter of better information in some content-oriented sense.

Scientific progress thus correlates with warranted confidence, and not approximation. At the level of theory-content, science moves through a series of radical changes and discontinuities that invalidate any talk of sucessive approximation. The situation is emphatically *not* one of the Peircean picture of stable essentials, or improvements only at the decimal point. And so, while we can make content-external claims about an improved warrant for our truth-estimates, we can make no such claims at the content-internal level of "increasingly close approximation to a 'true picture of things'." There is in the circumstances of the case no way of moving from "more warranted" to "more closely approximating to the truth." In this context of empirical inquiry we must resist any temptation to think of improvement in *estimation* in terms of improvement in *approximation*.

The need for such an estimative approach is easy to see. Pilate's question is still relevant. How are we men—imperfect mortals dwelling in this imperfect sublunary sphere—to determine where "the real truth" lies? The consideration that we have no *direct* access to the truth regarding the world is perhaps the most fundamental fact of epistemology. To repeat: we have no lines of communication with the Recording Angel. We live in a world not of our making where we have to do the best we can with the means at our disposal. We must recognize that there is no prospect of assessing the truth—or presumptive truth—of claims in this domain independently of the use of our imperfect epistemic mechanisms of inquiry and systematization. And here it is *estimation* that affords the best means for doing the job. In the inescapable circumstances of the case, we have no alternative but to settle for the best available estimate of the truth of the matter.

We cannot bypass epistemic qualification in regard to the facts of inquiry—we cannot get to "is true" save *via* "is reasonably held to be true." This latter must be accounted good enough—for the simple and sufficient reason that it's the best we can possibly do. Throughout this context, one must carefully bear in mind the distinction between a *better* estimate (one that is better made, based on securer or fuller information, or the like) and a *closer* estimate (one "nearer to the real truth"). With scientific theorizing we must settle for "better" because there is no (science-independent) way of monitoring the issue of "closer."

The most we can ever realistically do in matters of theoretical science is to characterize what we do actually have as the very best that one can possibly obtain in the circumstances—as the *best estimate* of the truth. Here "best estimate" means that estimate for which the best case can be made out according to the established standards of rational cogency. This is something we must accept realistically and have no right to lament. Of course, we have, and indeed can have, no "direct access" to "the real Truth" independently of our resources of inquiry, and it could be grossly foolish to hanker after it.[9] Of course we have to come by our view of reality via the epistemic route—not "direct inspection." In human inquiry, putative or ostensible truth is all there is: the shadow of the Kantian "we think" uneliminably accompanies all of our scientific declarations. Simple realism forbids us to regret that "we can't get outside our thought and experience to compare it with reality." It is a fallacious mis-analogy of picture-taking to suppose that only in somehow direct or intuitive apprehension could we ever really know what things are like. The lesson here is not that there is no difference between "what we think we know" and "the real truth," but just that we are never entitled to do more than to view the former as our best estimate of the latter.

There is nothing absurd about our holding something to be the very best that we can possibly do to determine the truth of the matter and to recognize at the same time the possibility, the probability, nay even the virtual certainty of eventually coming to recognize its untenability and indeed falsity. There is nothing infeasible about viewing our accepted scientific "truths" as representing nothing more than the best estimates of the real truth that we are able to make in the present state-of-the-art. There is much to J. B. S. Haldane's dictum that in science "a fact is a theory in which no one has made a large hole for a long time."

6. IS A SCEPTICAL ABANDONMENT OF TRUTH POSSIBLE?

Some have been tempted by the following sort of argumentation:

> Neither can we claim to have attained the truth in scientific matters, nor can we even say that we are approaching it more and more closely. It follows then, that there simply is no such thing as "the real truth" in these matters. This whole absolutistic notion should simply be abandoned.

It must be said emphatically that the sceptical tendency of certain of our remarks does *not* underwrite such an all-out scepticism. To be sure, some of the most prominent philosophers of science of the age have accordingly given up on truth. Rudolf Carnap teaches that science should never make flat assertions but only statements of probability.[10] Again, Karl Popper has argued long and eloquently that we must abstain from staking claims to truth in the sciences; that scientists should never *believe* the theses they devise but view them as mere conjectures, which they must try (and even hope) to falsify and must never regard as claims of substantive fact. Why then not bite the bullet and follow the sceptical path in dropping all reference to "the pursuit of truth" as regards the aim of science? As one recent writer eloquently puts it,

What is the notion of "the truth of things" over and above the notion
of a "something, I know not what" (in Rorty's words, "the purely
vacuous notion of the ineffable cause of sense and good of
intellect")—that is, a mere verbal counter for which one could
equally well substitute the equally vacuous notion of the self-
actualization of the Absolute Spirit?[11]

The answer is straightforward. Recourse to "the truth" is
justified pragmatically in terms of the sort of useful work this
notion is able to accomplish in the conceptual scheme of things.

The characterizing telos of science, after all, is the discovery of
facts—the providing of presumptively true answers to what goes
on in the world calls for espousing—and rightly espousing—
various theses about it. Accordingly, if one is to hold that either
scientific or everyday inquiry yields information about the world,
one is constrained to the view that they entitle us to *accept* certain
factual theses—with "acceptance," of course, to be understood as
acceptance-*as-true*. Any view of scientific or of common-life
claims as *information*-providing proceeds on an acceptance-model
of rational inquiry into "the truth" of things. We may, of course,
not actually succeed in finding "the real truth," but unless we are
prepared to take a committal stance towards what we do find—
unless we are prepared at any rate to *claim* truth for our findings
and so to accept them (at least provisionally) as asserting what is
actually the case—we must simply abandon an information-
oriented cognitive stance toward the world. (It would not make
sense to think of scientific inquiry as a project in truth-estimation
if there were no truth to be estimated.)

If science were not an *attempt* to get at the truth of things (an
attempt this is, admittedly, imperfect and, as best we can tell,
generally ends in failure) then the aim of discerning how things
really stand in the world—of providing information about the
world and of answering our questions about how things actually
stand—would become altogether unworkable. Our whole conception of the very nature of the project would have to be
abandoned—reference to science as a process of inquiry would go
by the board. It becomes difficult to see what we would be left with.
What we think of as "scientific knowledge" would become a

matter of tribal ideology, a sociological issue of opinion research, of assessing the shared beliefs of the practitioners of scientific disciplines—an inquiry that would disintegrate into a matter of collecting opinions about opinions. Any doctrine able to avert such consequences automatically has much to be said in its favor.

The pursuit of truth is the name of the game, the definite object of the whole project of inquiry. Here as elsewhere, we must preserve a clear division between *intent* and *achievement*. It is manifestly the *intent* of science to declare the real capital-T Truth about things. The "real Truth"—authentic truth about reality—represents a conception to which we stand committed throughout the whole project of rational inquiry because it affords its aim—its target or telos—though not, to be sure, its actual achievement.

The mission of science is to obtain answers to our questions about the world and to secure information about it. To secure information about the world (which is, after all, the name of the scientific game) we must accept contentions about it. And given the standard Tarski equivalence

$$P = `P' \text{ is true}$$

we recognize that to accept *P* is to accept it *as true*. So we certainly cannot simply follow the sceptic here and drop the reference to the pursuit of truth. Our estimate is still and ineradicably an estimate of the *true answer* to the question. Without a reference to the truth we would lose our hold on the teleology of the aims that define the very nature of the enterprise of inquiry.

Moreover in abandoning our claims to truth we would also lose our hold on the *methods* of science—and in particular, its use of the machinery of logic and mathematics. Logic and deductive science in general is no more than a conduit for the transmission of truth. If one is not prepared to claim the premises to be true one cannot use logic to base any conclusions on them—the definitive characteristic of the rules of logic being that they lead from truths to truths.

Of course we aim at "the real truth" in scientific inquiry. But all this is on the side of intention, of purport. In point of actual achievement we realize (indeed presume) that our existing science falls short, that it gives us estimates of the truth rather than the truth itself. But this only means that we must treat its claims as *provisional,* not that we should abandon them altogether. To do so would, as we have seen, be to throw out the baby with the bath water: to abandon the definitive aim of science as a rational enterprise that is designed to answer our questions about the world.

As regards the issue of aim and aspiration, it is indeed "the truth" that we're after. But this is something to whose actual possession we do not now and cannot ever lay a secure claim. It is to the great credit of C.S. Peirce that he clearly saw—two millennia of skepticism from Pyrrho to Descartes notwithstanding—the fallibility of our sceptical truth claims does *not* mean that the conception of "the pursuit of truth" should be abandoned in this domain.

In abandoning our claims to the real truth we would be reduced to talking only of what we (I, you, many of us) *think* to be so. The contrast with "what actually is so"—the *real* truth of things—would no longer be available. We would now only be in a position to contrast our *putative* truths with those of others, but could no longer operate with the classical distinction between the putative and the actual, between what we think to be so and what actually is so. And at this point, the idea of *inquiry*—aimed as it is, at increasing our grasp of the truth of things—would also go by the board. It would be senseless to study an object whose very existence is in question and to endeavor to estimate something that isn't there—or at any rate presupposed or assumed or postulated to be there. In abandoning truth—in refraining from assuming or postulating that there indeed is such a theory as "the real truth of the matter" in regard to how things work in the world *sub ratione generalitatis*—we would no longer be able to conceptualize the project of scientific inquiry as we standardly do. (The argumentation is, in effect, a transcendental argument from the very possibility of science).

To be sure, we have learned in the school of bitter experience that, even as we must presume that "the real truth of the matter" exists, so there is no alternative to presuming that our science does not achieve the real Truth here and now. It is one thing to speak of truth-realization in the language of aspiration and quite another to speak of it in the language of achievement. But the whole crucial contrast between the real truths of the perfected cognitive condition of things and merely purported or ostensible truths of the cognitive state of the art as it stands would come apart at the seams if we abandoned our (regulative) commitment to the view that there is indeed such a thing as the real truth.

7. IDEAL SCIENCE

Given "the facts of life" in empirical inquiry, we have neither the inclination nor the justification to claim that the world is as our *present* science describes it to be. Nor, as we have seen, does it make sense to identify "the real truth" with "the truth as science-in-the-limit will eventually see it to be." The best that can be done in this direction is to say that the world exists as *ideal or perfected* science describes it to be. The real, which is to say, final and definitive truth about nature at the level of scientific generality and precision is something we certainly cannot assume *our* science to capture. We have no choice but to take the stance that it's not something we've got, but something which—so we must suppose—is attained only in the ideal or perfected state of things. We thus arrive at the equation:

the truth = the truth as ideal (perfected) science purports it to be

(To be sure, in espousing this conception, we intend to make "ideal science" contingent upon truth, rather than the reverse.)

The concept of science perfected—of an ideal and completed science that captures the real truth of things and satisfies all of our cognitive ideals (definitiveness, completeness, unity, consistency, etc.)—is at best a useful fiction, a creature of the imagination and not the secured product of inquiring reason. This "ideal science" is, as the very name suggests, an idealization.

We have no alternative to presuming that *our* science as it stands here and now does not present the real truth, but only *estimates* it. "Our truth" in matters of scientific theorizing is not—and may well never actually be—the real truth. However confidently science may affirm its conclusions, the realization must be maintained that its declarations are provisional, tentative—subject to revision and even to outright abandonment and replacement. But all this is not, of course, any reason to abandon the link to truth at the teleological level of aims, goals and aspirations. The pursuit of scientific truth, like the pursuit of happiness, or for that matter any other ideal in life, is not vitiated by the consideration that its full realization is not a matter of the practical politics of this imperfect world.

The ideal of a state-of-the-art in science that attains definitive finality in scientific inquiry is pie in the sky. It represents an idealization and not a matter of the practical politics of the epistemic domain. But it affords the *focus imaginarius* whose pursuit canalizes and structures our inquiry. It represents the ultimate objective (goal) of inquiry—the destination of a journey in which we are *still* and indeed are *ever* engaged. The conception of capital-T Truth thus serves a negative and fundamentally regulative role to mark the fact that the place we have attained falls short of our capacity actually to realize our cognitive aspirations. It marks a fundamental contrast that *regulates* how we do and must view our claims to have got at the truth of things. It plays a role somewhat reminiscent of the functionary who reminded the Roman emperor of his mortality in reminding us that our pretentions to truth are always vulnerable. Contemplation of this ideal enables us to maintain the ever-renewed recognition of the essential ambiguity of the human condition as suspended between the reality of imperfect achievement and the ideal of an unattainable perfection. In abandoning this conception—in rejecting the idea of an "ideal science" which alone can properly be claimed to afford a grasp of reality—we would abandon an idea which crucially regulates our view as to the nature and status of the knowledge we lay claim to. We would then no longer be constrained to characterize our truth as *merely* ostensible and purported. And then, did our truth not exhibit any blatant *inherent* imperfections, we would be tempted to view it as real, authentic and final in a manner which as we at bottom realize it does not deserve. We must presume that science cannot attain an ω-condition of final perfection. The prospect of fundamental changes lying just around the corner can never be eliminated finally and decisively.

Ideal science is not something we've got in hand here and now. And it is emphatically not something towards which we are moving along the asymptotic and approximative lines envisaged by Peirce.[12] The asymptotic theory of scientific truth runs together two things that are by no means necessarily connected: *science-in-the-limit* (K_∞ is something which, even if it exists (i.e. will eventually come to realization) need by no means conform to the conditions of an *ideal* science (K^*). Even if it made sense to contemplate the Peircean idea of an eventual completion of science, there would be no guarantee that this completed science (given it existed!) would satisfy the definitive requirements of a *perfected* science and that, in particular, it would achieve the completeness of erotetic equilibrium where every posable question is duly resolved. Peircean convergentism is geared to the supposition that ultimate science—the science of the very distant future—will somehow prove to be an ideal or perfected science freed from the sorts of imperfections that afflict its predecessors. But the potential gap that arises here can only be closed by old-style, substantive metaphysics of a most problematic sort.[13]

There is accordingly no warrant for identifying *ideal* or perfected science with *ultimate* science—science-in-the-limit. Perfected science is not something that exists here and how, nor is it something that lies ahead at some eventual offing in the remote future. It is not a real thing to be met with in this world. It is an idealization that exists "outside time"—i.e., cannot actually exist at all. It lies outside history as a useful contrast-case that cannot be numbered among the achieved realities of this imperfect world. Existing science does not and presumably never will embody to perfection cognitive ideals of completeness, unity, consistency, etc. These factors represent an aspiration rather than a coming reality: a *telos*, not a realizable condition of things—a hypothetical condition from which any and all of the negativities of the realized actual positions have been removed.

One acute commentator has recently written as follows:

> The universally acknowledged fact of the matter is that there are no compelling reasons whatever to believe that scientific theories, past or present, are true (or likely or verisimilar, or any of the other ersatz surrogates for truth). To retain the view that science aims at presumptively true theories, in the face of the admission that we would not know how to recognize a true theory if we had it, is to render science an irrational enterprise; for, on any coherent account of what *rational* behavior is, it is irrational to adopt a goal which (a)

we do not know how to achieve, (b) we could not recognize if we had achieved, and (c) was such that we could not even tell whether we were gradually moving closer to achieving it. "True scientific theories" seems to be precisely such a goal . . . It leads to the view that science represents a utopian, and therefore irrational activity whose *telos* is, to the best of our knowledge, forever beyond our grasp.[14]

This position is profoundly wrong. It fails to reckon appropriately with the standard gap between aspiration and attainment. In the practical sphere—in craftsmanship, for example, or the cultivation of our health—we may *strive* for perfection, but cannot ever claim to have *attained* it. And the situation in inquiry is exactly parallel with that we encounter in other domains—ethics specifically included. The value of a goal, even of one that is not realizable, lies not in the benefit of its attainment (obviously and *ex hypothesi!*), but in the benefits that accrue from its pursuit. The view that it is rational to persue a goal only if we are in a position to achieve its attainment or approximation is mistaken. The goal can be perfectly valid—and entirely rational—if the indirect benefits of its pursuit and adoption are sufficient—if in striving after it we realize relevant advantages in substantial degree. An unattainable ideal can be enormously productive. Perfected science is an ideal, and an ideal is not something we encounter in experience, but rather the hypothetical projection or extrapolation of what we encounter in experience. And the legitimacy of our cognitve ideals as regulators inhere in their *utility* as guides to inquiry, and specifically in their capacity to guide our thoughts and efforts in constructive and productive directions. It is fallacy to see the validity of goals and ideals to reside solely and wholly in the presumed consequence of their *realization*. The benefits may reside not in arriving but in the pursuing itself. The striving after an ideal science that affords us "the ultimate truth" about the workings of nature seems to be a *telos* of just this sort. Its legitimation lies in its facilitation of the ongoing evolution of inquiry. In this domain, we arrive at the perhaps odd-seeming posture of an invocation of practical utility for the validation of an ideal.[15]

XI

Scientific Truth and the Arbitrament of Praxis

SYNOPSIS

(1) Can anything be said about how good an estimate of the truth science actually provides? Yes, because we can monitor the adequacy of our truth-estimation methods and procedures in terms of the success of the praxis they afford us. (2) On the need for such theory-external quality-controls. (3) An explanation of the reasons for this linkage between truth and pragmatic efficacy. (4) A "Copernician Inversion" of the traditional relation between truthfulness and progress. (5) The need for the continual improvement of praxis results in an ongoing technological excalation. (6) While we can confidently anticipate progress here, we cannot expect perfection. But just how far can human inquiry reasonably be expected to go in affording us a grasp of the nature of reality? This is in the end a meaningless question, there being no workable way of defining the destination at issue.

1. SCIENCE AS TRUTH-ESTIMATOR

Any sensible attempt to determine how effective our cognitive efforts are in their intended mission of getting at the truth of things must face the fact that there is no way to assess the adequacy of our theorizing directly by seeing how well inquiry is doing in getting at the truth of things, because we have no inquiry-independent way of telling what this truth is. Any attempt to appraise the adequacy of our theorizing on its own, purely theoretical terms is ultimately futile. This clearly indicates the need for a theory-external control on the adequacy of our theorizing, some theory-external reality-principle to serve as a standard of adequacy.

228

The aim of science as a cognitive venture is to provide us with information about how matters stand in the world—with an estimate as to the truth of things. But this perspective at once poses the question: can we say anything about how good an estimate of "the real truth" science in fact provides?

Clearly we cannot determine the truth with respect to factual matters *directly,* independently of scientific inquiry, and then monitor the adequacy of our science by comparing its deliverances with this independently determined truth.[1] There just is no science-independent means at our disposal for getting at the real truth of things at the level of scientific generality and precision. This, the final analysis, is the crucial and decisive reason for rejecting the otherwise plausible-sounding view that science makes progress insofar as it succeeds in its aim of discovering the truth.

We can, fortunately, monitor the functional adequacy of our science *obliquely* by considering how well we fare when it comes to applying and implementing its resultant claims in prediction and control. The guiding idea is that the adequacy of our cognitive instruments is to be assessed pragmatically in terms of their effectiveness in helping us to navigate with affective success amidst the shoals and narrows of a hostile (or at best indifferent) environment.

The aim of science is represented by the traditional quartet of description, explanation, prediction, and control, in line with the following picture:

theoretical goals
- *description* (answering *what?* and *how?* questions about nature)
- *explanation* (answering *why?* questions about nature)

practical goals
- *prediction* (successful alignment of our expectations regarding nature)
- *control* (effective intervention in nature)

The theoretical sector concerns itself with matters of characterizing, explaining, accounting for, and rendering intelligible—with purely cognitive issues, in short. By contrast, the practical sector is concerned with canalizing expectations, guiding actions, and, in general, with achieving that control of our environment necessary to the satisfactory conduct of our affairs. The former deals with what science *says;* the latter with what it *does.*

The teleology of scientific inquiry is thus internally diversified and complex, spreading across both the cognitive/theoretical and active/practical sectors. Our truth-criteriology thus comes to be endowed with a duality of objectives, and the relevant teleology of inquiry is both cognitive and practical.[2] Truth-acceptance is, on the one hand, a determining factor for belief in purely intellectual and theoretical regards, and, on the other, a guiding standard for the practical conduct of life. The two are inseparably interrelated, and where we cannot take hold of the one we cannot grasp the other.

On this perspective, the adequacy of our predictive and interventionist praxis becomes the quality-controlling monitor of our scientific claims. It does so not because of an instrumentalistic commitment which abandons the pursuit of truth and sees prediction and control as the sole goals of science, but simply and solely because there just is no prospect of any more direct alternative, any immediate comparison of these claims with the science-independent "real-truth" of things. The practical and *purposive* aspect of cognition thus comes to the fore. The governing quality controls of our mechanisms of inquiry—its methods, concepts, etc.; the whole machinery by which we build up our world-picture (knowledge, *epistēmē*, science)—emerge as fundamentally pragmatic, a circumstance to which philosophical pragmatists have always accorded a central role on the epistemological stage. We are led to the doctrine that effective *praxis* is the ultimate quality-control arbiter of acceptable *theoria.*

To be sure, success in the domain of praxis is something very different from success in theoretical regards. For practical success lies in the *affective* order, ranging over the spectrum from physical survival and avoidance of pain and injury on the negative side, to positive satisfactions such as the satiation of physical needs on the other. Even merely intellectually rooted satisfactions, like the achievement of "predictive success," are part of the picture—

although only a small part. (After all, even a world-external, disembodied spectator can make predictions about the world and utter a pleased "aha—there it is" to himself when his predictions work out.) The key factor is that of the "success" of a creature who must intervene in the course of events to make matters eventuate so as to conduce to his survival and well-being. Success in the pragmatic sphere is a matter of avoiding the affective mishaps and affective satisfaction by guiding satisfactorily the actions of a vulnerable being emplaced *in medias res* within a difficult and generally uncooperative world.

Is success itself, however, not something merely theoretical, something that also lies in the eye of the beholder? As one recent critic has put it:

> But while the actual occurrence of happiness or unhappiness, pleasure or pain, etc., is indeed beyond our control . . . the same does not seem obviously to hold for our beliefs about such matters. . . . Thus beliefs or judgments about pragmatic success turn out not to constitute genuine input from the world, but instead . . . can . . . be arbitrarily manipulated at will, so long as the other elements are appropriately adjusted.[3]

It would thus be contended that, while *the actual occurrence* of pain, suffering, disappointment (etc.), is something that lies outside our theorizing stance, this does not hold for our convictions about the matter—our subscription to the beliefs that we are in pain, distress, (etc.). But this seems very dubious. To begin with, actual *survival* is not a matter of belief at all. Nor is actual bodily injury and physical harm something markedly susceptible to variation in the beliefs of individuals. The "power of positive thinking" is rather feeble in these regards. "Mind over matter" is a precept whose range of effectiveness has its limits. In human affairs, we are, after all dealing with a conscious being for whom the affective negativities of actual mishap—and indeed even of merely disappointed expectations—neither be overlooked nor, in the normal course of things, be appraised as other than the negativities that they are. The idea that—outside the laboratory setting of Pavlovian conditioning—we can manipulate arbitrarily and at will the sorts of things that cause people happiness or unhappiness, pleasure or pain is surely implausible. A powerful dictator can certainly get people to *do* things, but what he can get them to *like* seems to be a good deal less plastic.

In taking the praxis it underwrites as index of the adequacy of our science, it is imperative to distinguish carefully between the ontological or existence-oriented and the epistemological or cognition-oriented dimensions. In *ontological* perspective, the aim of science is undoubtedly realistic—to offer us a true account of the *what* and *why* of the real world, or at any rate a best available estimate of the correct account of these matters. At the level of aim and aspiration this is undenied and undeniable. But it is no less undeniable that, *epistemologically,* the only way we have to monitor the functional adequacy of our efforts at reality-characterization is through the efficacy of the praxis underwritten by the methods of inquiry we use in constructing our world-picture. The capacity of our cognitive tools to meet their *theoretical* goals can be controlled *obliquely,* by monitoring their realization of our *practical* goals.

This line of thought suggests our reply to the following objection:

> Your pragmatic theory exhibits the characteristic flaw of all instrumentalism, because, in effect, it simply abandons *truth* for *utility* in pivoting the issue of quality-control on goal-attainment in the practical rather than theoretical area.

This objection is gravely mistaken. At the leve of particular claims and theses our theory is not "instrumentalistic" at all: it continues the orthodox commitment to the truth as such, duly construed as the pivotal object of the enterprise of inquiry and the subject of the usual truth-criteriology of the scientific method. Only at a remove, at the methodological level, do pragmatic considerations enter in. Successful praxis is seen as adequacy-indicative with respect to our generalized criteria of acceptance and verification. The link between truth and praxis is not seen as direct, but as mediated by the methodology of inquiry. Our rule is: truth claims *via* methods; methods *via* praxis.

This *methodological* pragmatism must be distinguished carefully from a *thesis*-oriented pragmatism. The latter assesses the acceptability of individual propositions or theses. The former is oriented to the methodological and systemic level, proceeding macroscopically with regard to scientific belief-formation as a whole, and carefully refraining from offering any pragmatic justifications at the level of individual claims and contentions. Our theory thus eschews the thesis-pragmatists' attempt to assess the truth of *individual* factual theses by the pragmatic efficacy of adopting them in isolated particularity, in terms of the pragmatic benefits of their adoption. Such thesis adoption itself continues to be governed by the probative practices of scientific method, rather than by any directly pragmatic considerations. Only the adequacy of the venture as a whole—taken at the methodological, criteriological, systemic level—is monitored via the pragmatic route.

It is useful to contrast our approach with that of Hilary Putnam's explanatory realism.[4] On Putnam's approach, the veridicality of the products of our inquiry-methods turns on pragmatic argumentation of the form:

—Our epistemic criteria entitle us to assert the claims of the corpus S (i.e., of science).
—The products of our epistemic criteria are successfully implementable.

∴ The claims of the corpus S are indeed true.

Now as Putnam sees it, this is an argument of the quintessentially inductive "inference to the best explanation" mode. Its conclusion that the theses of science are veridical is seen as itself a quasi-scientific theory that effectively *explains* the successful implementability of these scientific claims in prediction and intervention. The presumptive truth of our scientific claims—their authenticity *vis-à-vis* the real world—is an inductive product, a scientific theory, an inference to the best explanation.

The present approach is quite different, however, because it casts the second premiss of the above argument in a very different role. It sees the conclusion as emerging from the first premiss alone: if our epistemic criteria authorizes us to assert a thesis, then the truthfulness of this thesis is something we stand committed to *ipso facto,* simply because that's exactly what is at issue in these epistemic criteria as standards for acceptance *as true.* But, of course, the further question of the *appropriateness or validity* of those epistemic criteria still remains. And it is on *this* issue that the pragmatic efficacy of the second premiss has a crucial bearing. The relative pragmatic efficacy of our implementation of the theses they validate is seen as index of the relative acceptability of alternative systematic methods of inquiry and substantiation.

The argument thus breaks apart into two stages, with a crucial methodological level inserted as mediating between pragmatic efficacy and truth. The mediation of methodology—of a layer of considerations at the epistemological level—always intervenes between pragmatic considerations and considerations regarding the acceptability of factual claims. To repeat: On our approach, pragmatic considerations are never brought to bear in the acceptability of factual claims directly, but only in the issue of the methods, criteria, and standards that govern the acceptability of such theses.

2. THE ARBITRAMENT OF PRAXIS

The burden of our present deliberations is that the practical element is ultimately in the controlling position; that praxis affords our quality-control monitor over *theoria,* that applied science is ultimately in command *vis-à-vis* theoretical science. Control ranging from mere prediction as minimal ("*merely* intellectual") control—the adequate alignment of our expectations with the actual course of events—to the more elaborately modifactory change in the course of nature through effective intervention in the course of things thus comes to operate as the final arbiter of cognitive adequacy. This aspect of the cognitive centrality of control over nature leads us to an *interventionist* theory of knowledge, one which sees the issues of monitoring the adequacy of our theorizing to reside ultimately on the side of efficacy in application.[5]

To be sure, one must give all due credit to the familiar spectrum of theoretical desiderata for our belief-structures: comprehensiveness, explanatory coherence, simplicity, and the other parameters of cognitive systematicity.[6] But this by itself is not enough: such factors *count,* but do not *decide.* For our inquiry procedures not only constitute neat systems of beliefs, but *thereby* lead us to stub our toes upon the harsh realities of implementing praxis. Everyone is familiar with the occasional surfacing, even today, of some occult or pseudo-scientific methodology leading to views of the world that substantiate fact-purporting theses of the strangest sort. It is often striking here how beautifully everything meshes at the theoretical level—one bit of strangeness being supported by others. A seamless fabric of self-supportive absurdities is readily imagined. The crunch comes only with the tough question: Does this approach to the warranting of claims actually enable its proponents to navigate more successfully and effectively amidst the rocks and shoals of this world?

A theory-external quality-control upon cognition is ultimately vital to our justificatory deliberations because it blocks the prospect of a futile spinning around in reality-detached cycles of purely theoretical gyrations. Someplace along the line of justification there must be provision for a correlative contact with an uncooperative and largely unmanipulable reality—an agency that operates quite independently of the drift of our theorizing. This crucial reality principle is provided for in the framework of the present approach by the factor of the success consequent upon implementing action. Goal-attainment—successful praxis (regardless for the moment of the intrinsic character of these goals)—is the ultimate guarantor of validity of the products of man's endeavors at the acquisition of empirical knowledge.

The sort of progressiveness that lies at the root of quality-control in scientific inquiry is not something arcane, sophisticated, and heavily theory-laden. It turns on the fact that *any* enhancement in control—any growth of our technological mastery over nature—will have involvements that are also discernible at the *grosso modo* level of our everyday life conceptions and dealings. *How* our control is extended will generally be a very sophisticated matter, but any fool can see *that* our control has been extended in certain ways. It is perfectly clear to even the most unsophisticated observer that as regards "control over nature" science has for centuries been moving from strength to strength. The progressiveness of science appears most strikingly and decisively in its ever-expanding predictive and physical control over nature.[7] The old conception of *scientia propter potentiam* provides a perfectly workable basis for taking the widening horizons of technological capacity as an index of scientific progress.[8]

3. WHY THIS LINK BETWEEN PRAGMATIC EFFICACY AND TRUTHFULNESS?

Just why should the pragmatic success engendered by its deliverances be taken to justify an inquiry method and be allowed to count towards establishing its legitimacy as a criterion of acceptability or verification? Why should its underwriting of a more effective praxis be pivotal when the real issue is that of a method's greater adequacy in depicting the real world?

Consider the traditional objection against pragmatism that it might well prove highly successful to act on some (quite incorrect) thesis. This perfectly possible prospect makes one rightly hesitant to maintain that the successful implementation of a thesis in practice is an adequate basis for holding it to be true. After all, action that proceeds on beliefs that are false and fail to capture "what is actually the case" can on occasion—or even frequently—eventuate as pragmatically successful, due to chance or good luck or kindly fate or whatever. Individual theses may well manage to slip through the pragmatic net singly or in groups. However, the situation must be different when what is at issue is not an isolated action or a particular believed thesis (or even a cluster of them), but rather a general, across-the-board policy of belief-validation.

One recent writer has advanced the following objection:

> No doubt a truth criterion which yielded results which were utterly discordant with reality would not lead to pragmatic success; but how close to the truth such results would have to be in order to be successful would seem to depend enormously on the particular world in question and the particular needs and purposes of the beings which inhabit it. It is far from obvious that a criterion which produced only very approximately accurate results could not, in some circumstances, be more pragmatically successful than one whose results were more accurate. . . .[9]

But this objection is far-fetched. Its force at the level of factual consideration is blunted by the generality and universality of a methodology of inquiry, and its impact severely limited by the realities of the circumstances under which we labor in carrying on our inquiries in this, the real world. The range at issue with scientific inquiry at a totally generalized systemic and methodological level is to be literally boundless: no factual issue is to lie outside its intended province. This is so comprehensive that probatively irrelevant side effects by way of fortuitous bonuses or disasters become cancelled out in the larger scheme of things. That a mistaken or unwarranted body of scientific commitments might prove really successful at this level of generality is a prospect so farfetched that it can be dismissed with confidence. Fundamental mistakes at *this* level would have repercussions across a limitless frontier and would be bound to prove ultimately catastrophic. The generality and open endedness of an inquiry-method is seen to furnish it with a capacity to wash out the influence of these fortuitous and extraneous factors.

Methods for factual inquiry operate on an endlessly broad and extensive front, and this feature of across-the-board systematicity renders them much more vulnerable. Their flaws and deficiencies are bound to manifest themselves over the vast multiplicity of their applications. Methods inherently function at a wholesale rather than retail level. The success of a method of inquiry accordingly must be construed in systematic terms: working on some limited number of occasions does not entail working in general, and failing on some occasions is not necessarily completely invalidating. Success hinges on how our science fares in *general* over the whole gamut of its applications. The range and versatility of an inquiry procedure is too obvious to need much elaboration. Generality is here tantamount to openendedness: our systematic commitments operate across the board of an enormous variety of areas of application and a literally innumerable proliferation of particular instances. Here all of the safeguards built into the statistical theory of the "design of experiences" come into play with respect to the probative significance of the number and variety of instances. It is improbable that a *systematic* success across so broad a range should be gratuitous.

To be sure, if a bounteous nature satisfied our every whim spontaneously, without effort and striving on our part, the situation would be very different. For then the beliefs which guide and canalize our activities would not come into play—they would remain inoperative on the sidelines, never being "put to the test." There would then be no need for active (and thought-guided) intervention in "the natural course of things" within an uncooperative (at best indifferent, at worst hostile) environment. But *as things stand* we are constantly called upon to establish varying degrees of "control over nature" to satisfy even our most basic needs (to say nothing of our virtually limitless wants).

We cannot reasonably look on nature as a friendly collaborator in our human efforts, systematically shielding us against the consequences of our follies and crowning our cognitive endeavors with a wholly undeserved success that ensues for reasons wholly independent of their actual adequacy. The human condition is such that active intervention in the course of events is constantly required (and even the noninterventionist process of "letting things take their course" becomes, in such a context, simply another mode of control). Moreover, human agency produces a flow of consequences that rebound back upon the agent, ultimately producing satisfaction or frustration. This interactionism is a crucial part of the justificatory background. The facilitation of purpose-guided interaction with nature—of acting so as to produce successfully the intended results of our efforts—is a vital part of the cluster of factual considerations that establish the cognitive bearing of pragmatic success. The Darwinian aspect is particularly crucial here. It is no more miraculous that the human man can *understand* nature than it is that the human eye should be able to *see* it. Peirce's insight holds true: Our cognitive methods are able to earn credit as giving a trustworthy picture of the world precisely because they evolve under the casual pressure of that world.[10]

In the circumstances of the case, the systematic success of their deliverances must be viewed as strongly indicative of methodological appropriateness. It is implausible to suppose—and eccentric to maintain—that a method of inquiry that outperforms all envisaged alternatives in facilating the prediction and control of nature's eventuations should yield results that do not merit adoption. But what is at issue here is *not* an inductive "inference to the best explanation" (based on the idea that a method's truth potential must be involved to *explain* the pragmatic efficacy of its findings). Rather, the pivotal consideration here is one of probative rationality. It is the point of Section 1 above that *the only effective way* we have of effecting rational control over the acceptability of an inquiry method is to proceed via this issue of its applicative efficacy. If this sort of efficacy cannot serve as index of methodological adequacy, then nothing can.

4. A COPERNICAN INVERSION

The present practicalist line of approach to the merit of our inquiry methods engenders an *inversion* of the orthodox view of the relationship between truth and merit in this domain. Later findings do not rest on a superior methodological basis because they are "closer to the truth"; rather they qualify to be viewed as better bets because they rest on a superior basis. In effect this "Copernican Inversion" proposes that we not evaluate an inquiry procedure by the truth of its results, but conversely, assess the truthfulness of the results in terms of rational merits of the procedure that underwrites them—as determined by factors that are in part internal, systematic, and coherentist, but predominantly external, applicative, and pragmatic.

The direction of the reasoning thus does not proceed from "greater truth" to "more adequate warrant," but the very reverse. The traditional and seemingly more straightforward view will simply not do, since vitiating circularity cannot be avoided in seeking to validate the procedure in view through its capacity to lead to the truth, given that what is to count as true is to be determined by this very procedure itself. To be sure, the linking equation between truth and warrant need not be abandoned, but it must now be viewed in a very different light. Warrant must be taken as the independent variable and truthfulness as the dependent variable, with our inquiry procedures not seen as warranted because truth-producing, but rather presumed to be truth-producing because of their rational warrant. Precisely because the later, "progressive" stages of the application of our inquiry procedures are more fully warranted on the basis of the ampler and more successful body of praxis that they underwrite, we can take the stance that is *rational to view their deliverances as better qualified for endowment with the presumption of truth.* It is on this basis alone that we can be increasingly confident that our picture of nature affords a comparatively *better estimate* than our past pictures do. Accordingly, our scientific commitments are seen as having two interrelated aspects: on the one hand, they are *mere* estimates of the truth and not definitive demonstrations thereof, but on the other hand they are *responsible* estimates of the truth that rest on a duly authenticated methodological basis.

There is thus an inversion in the order of precedence here. Ontologically, in the order of *rationes essendi,* there is no question that inquiry is correct because it yields truths. (This just is how things stand in the conceptual order, given the content of our very concept of *correct inquiry.*) But epistemically, in the order of *rationes cognoscenti,* truths appear as those results that properly conducted inquiry yields, and we are rationally entitled to endorse as putative truths those these yielded by our most conscientiously conducted inquiries: to view theses as truths *because* they are what such inquiry yields. In the order of *being,* inquiry hinges on the truth; in the order of *knowing,* the reverse relationship holds. To its detriment, pragmatism has generally run these two together. It fails to recognize that while we can only *determine* truths through appropriate inquiry, that nevertheless the *meaning* of "being true" also has more ambitious ontological ramifications. (The issue of truth-conditions vs. use-conditions looms up once more.)

Our Copernican inversion sees any effort to validate the propriety of our inquiry procedure in terms of the truthfulness of its products as picking up the wrong end of the stick—one does not approach warrant by way of truthfulness, but truthfulness by way of warrant. The claims of later science are justifiedly taken to afford better estimates of the truth because of their enhanced epistemic grounding: they are ruled to be more acceptable by a method of inquiry whose credentials—relative to all envisaged alternatives are substantially superior.

Progress thus correlates with warranted confidence. But *this* augmentation in our level of confidence moves—at the level of theory *content*—through a series of radical changes and discontinuities. (The situation is emphatically *not* one of the Peircean picture of stable essentials, of improvements only at the decimal point.) With the transition from a corpus of scientific knowledge to a successor we get neither more of the truth, nor draw nearer to it, rather, we get a better based estimate of the truth—one that gives us a firmer warrant for our claims. Accordingly, while we can make content-external method-oriented claims about "improving correctness," we can make no such claims at the content-internal substance-oriented level of "increasingly close approximation to a 'correct picture of things'." Our talk of progress cannot bypass the epistemic and regulative aspect and move directly to a descriptive and constitutive result. To reemphasize: One must resist any temptation to think of improvement in *estimation* in terms of improvement in *approximation*.

5. PERFECTION NOT ATTAINABLE: TECHNOLOGICAL ESCALATION

On the pragmatic standard envisaged in the preceding discussion, the scientific method affords a picture that is neither all white nor all black, but is painted in various shades of gray. Viewed in the perspective of its applicative success, science is very much of a mixed bag—a compound of solid strengths and signal weaknesses. A hundred years ago, the English physicist and chemist George Gore did his sums on the negative side of the ledger in a way that still holds good:

> Another reason for concluding that the future of science is immense is because, in a very large proportion of new experiments, we are unable to predict the results successfully. Knowledge of principles and laws enables us to predict effects; and the extent to which we are *unable* to predict successfully indicates, in a rough sort of way, the proportionate amount of such principles and laws yet to be found. If . . . in 100 proposed new experiments we can only predict successfully the result of 10, the knowledge necessary to enable us to predict successfully the remainder has yet to be obtained. . . .[11]

The situation we face today is different from that described by Gore only in degree, and not in kind.

Our procedures of inquiry can be enhanced not only on the side of theoretical resources but preeminently on the side of the technological instrumentalities of observational and experimental intervention. Successful praxis is a matter of "power," but the power at issue is not *merely* practical—it is not wholly overted towards meeting our familiar everyday-life requirements in production, transport, communication, etc. Its main manifestation is at the level of the technological frontier, and, in particular, with the technology of observation and experimentation used in the context of the man-nature interactions of science. The impetus to augment the adequacy of our science—to enhance ever more the extent to which we can have a rationally warranted confidence in its deliverances—is a crucial aspect of the project of rational inquiry. It demands an unending effort to improve the range of effective experimental intervention, because only by operating under new and heretofore inaccessible conditions of observational or experimental systematization—attaining extreme temperature, pressure, particle velocity, field strength, etc.—can we realize those circumstances that enable us to put our hypotheses and estimates to the test, and thereby to monitor the adequacy of those probative methods which have vouched for them.

We arrive in this context at that drive towards ever-increasing capability in inquiry-relevant technology which may be characterized as *technological escalation*. As one acute observer has rightly remarked: "most critical experiments [in physics] planned today, if they had to be constrained within the technology of even ten years ago, would be seriously compromised."[12] This technology of inquiry falls into relatively distinct levels or stages in sophistication—correlatively with successively "later generations" in the state-of-the-art of instrumentative and manipulative machinery. These levels reflect the performance capacity of a technology to set up experiments (to create specified temperatures, pressures, voltages, etc.), to determine the quantities in such situations (to yield exact measurement, sensitive detection, etc.), or to process the data (to deploy mathematical technique, computers, etc.). Once the major findings accessible at a given data-technology level has been attained, the very structure of scientific inquiry forces us into the situation of an arms-race reminiscent technological escalation where the frontier equipment of today's research becomes the museum piece of tomorrow under the relentless pace of technical obsolescence.[13]

Without developing technology, scientific progress would grind to a halt. The discoveries of today cannot be advanced with yesterday's instrumentation. To secure new data, to test new hypotheses and to detect new phenomena, an ever more powerful technology of inquiry is needed. Throughout the natural sciences, technological progress is an intrinsic dimension of cognitive progress. This circumstance has far-reaching implications for the perfectibility of science.

6. HOW FAR?

While we can confidently anticipate improvement in the capabilities of science we cannot expect ever to attain perfection. A vista of ongoing potential improvements in effecting "control over nature" spreads unendingly before us. And, in this domain, there is no reason to think that we will ever reach "the end of the line." There is always more to be done. The accessible pressures and temperatures can in theory always be increased; the low-temperature experiments brought closer to absolute zero, the particles accellerated closer to the speed of light, etc. Every successive level of capability has its inherent limits and limitations whose over-coming opens up yet another more sophisticated level of the technological state-of-the-art. Any such enhanced practical mastery carries along—so experience teaches—new phenomena and an enhanced capability to test yet further hypotheses and discriminate between alternative theories conducive to deepening our knowledge of nature.

We must, accordingly, come to terms with the fact that we cannot realistically expect that our science will ever—at *any* given stage of its actual development—be in a position to afford us more than a very partial and incomplete control over nature. The achievement of control over nature requires not only intellectual instrumentalities (concepts, ideas, theories, knowledge), but also physical resources (technology and "power"). And the physical resources needed for the development of technical instrumentalities are restricted and finite. It follows that our control is bound to be imperfect and incomplete, with much in the realm of the doable always remaining undone. Our capacity to effect control is inevitably limited. As best we can tell, there is certainly no basis for an optimistic expectation that we can travel down this route as we might ideally like to do.

Moreover, this issue of "control over nature" involves more complexities than may appear on first view. For just how is this conception to be understood? Clearly in terms of bending the course of events to our will, of attaining our ends within nature. But this involvement of "*our* ends" brings to light the prominence of our own contribution. On the one hand, if we are inordinately modest in our demands (or very unimaginative) we may even achieve "complete control over nature" in the sense of being in a position to do *whatever* we want to do, but yet attain this happy condition in a way that betokens very little real capability. On the other hand, if our understanding of nature is suitable bizarre, we will "ask the impossible" by way of accomplishment (e.g., putting spaceships into an "overdrive" that accellerates them to speeds exceeding the velocity of light), and thus complain of incapacity to achieve control in ways that put unfair burdens on this conception.

Power is a matter of the "effecting of things possible," and it is clearly science itself (the cognitive "state-of-the-art") which, in teaching us about the limits of the possible, shapes our conception of this issue. As science grows and develops, it poses new issues of power and control, reformulating and reshaping those demands whose realization represents "control over nature." Science itself brings new possibilities to light. (At a suitable stage, the idea of "splitting the atom" will no longer seem a contradiction in terms.)

Seen in this light—with predictive and physical control as arbiters of progress—the idea of *improving* our science is workable and unproblematic—as is the correlative regulative ideal of "working to perfect" our science. But the idea of "*achieving* a perfected science" is inherently problematic. Our standards of assessment and evaluation are such that we can realize the idea of improvements, of progress, but not of completion, of realized perfection. We know what it is to *enlarge* our technological mastery, but we cannot meaningfully say what it would be to *perfect* it. (Our conception of the *doable* keeps changing with changes in the cognitive state of the art, a fact which—in its futuristic and potentialistic bearing—does not, of course, alter our view of what already *has been* done in the practical sphere.) The question "How far?" accordingly makes no sense—it would be appropriate only if there were a determinable destination, and there just simply is not.

Even if (per impossibile) a "practical equilibrium" between what we can and what we wish to do in science came to be realized, we could not rest totally confident that this circumstance will remain unchanged. The possibility that "just around the corner" things will become unstuck can never be eliminated. Even if we "achieve control" to all extents and purposes, we cannot be sure of not losing our grip upon it—not because of a loss of power, but because of cognitive changes that produce a broadening of the imagination and a widened apprehension as to what "having control" involves. The project of achieving practical mastery can never be accomplished in a satisfactory way. We thus have no alternative but to *presume* our knowledge (i.e., purported knowledge) to be inadequate at this and indeed at any other particular stage of the game. Here, then, we are once more brought back to the preceding chapter's theme of the inevitable presumption of cognitive incompleteness and cognitive limits.

XII

Scientific Realism

SYNOPSIS

(1) Critique of a doctrine of scientific realism which claims that science correctly describes the real world. This is clearly not a claim we are minded (or entitled) to advance for *our* science—science as it currently stands. (2) Realism is nevertheless an inherent aspect of the goal-structure of science. While it is not a descriptive feature of science as it exists, it is a crucial constituent of the teleology of scientific aspirations. (3) The facts of life regarding scientific change indicate that realism is a plausible doctrine only with respect to *ideal* science, and certainly not for science as we actually have it—now *or ever*. (4) A critique of instrumentalism as an unwarranted abandonment of the characteristic aims of the scientific enterprise.

1. THE THESIS OF SCIENTIFIC REALISM AND THE FACT OF SCIENTIFIC FALLIBILISM

On the traditional and established view of the matter, the aim of empirical inquiry is to answer our factual questions as to how things work in the world. It is, accordingly, expedient to consider the issue of goal-attainment in this regard. Exactly how are we to conceive of the relationship between the answers we give to our factual questions and the reality they purport to depict?

To begin with, let us explore the implications of these present deliberations for the currently fashionable theory of scientific realism.

Scientific realism is the doctrine that *science describes the real world:*[1] that the world actually is as science takes it to be and that its furnishings are as science envisages them to be.[2] If we want to

246

know about the existence and the nature of heavy water or quarks, of man-eating molluscs or a luminiferous ether, we are referred to the natural sciences for the correct answer. The stance is that the theoretical terms of natural science refer to real physical entities and describe their attributes and comportments; for example, the "electron spin" of atomic physics refers to a behavioral characteristic of a real albeit unobservable object—an electron. On this realistic construction of scientific theorizing, the declarations of science are factually true generalizations about the actual behavior of objects that exist in the world. Is this a tenable position?

It is quite clear that it is not. For as was already argued above (pp. 205–208), there is insufficient warrant for and little plausibility to the claim that the world indeed is as our science claims it to be—that we've got matters altogether right, so that *our* science is *correct* science and offers the definitive "last word" on the issues. We really cannot reasonably suppose that science as it now stands affords the real truth as regards its creatures-of-theory.

The characteristic genius of scientific realism is inherent in its equating of the resources of natural science with the domain of what actually exists. But this equation would work only if science, as it stands, has actually "got it right." And this is something we are certainly not minded—and not entitled—to claim. The postulation as real of the commitments of our science is viable only if done *provisionally,* in the spirit of "doing the best we can now do, in the current state-of-the-art" and giving our best estimate of the matter. The step of reification is always to be taken provisionally, subject to a *reservatio mentis* of presumptive revisability. We do and must recognize that we cannot blithely equate *our* truth with *the* truth. We do and must realize that the declarations of science are inherently fallible and that we can only "accept" them with a certain tentativity, subject to a clear realization that they may need to be corrected or even abandoned.

These considerations must inevitably constrain and condition our attitude towards the natural mechanisms envisaged in our science. We certainly do not—or should not—want to reify (hypostasize) the "theoretical entities" of current science—to say flatly and unqualifiedly that the contrivances of *our* present-day science correctly depict the furniture of the real world. We do

not—or at any rate, given the realities of the case, should not—
want to adopt categorically the ontological implications of scientific theorizing in just exactly the state-of-the-art configuration
presently in hand. Scientific fallibilism precludes the claim that
what we purport to be scientific knowledge is in fact *real* knowledge, and accordingly blocks the path to a scientific realism that
maintains that the furnishings of the real world are exactly as our
science state them to be.

The world *that we describe* is one thing, the world *as we describe
it* is another, and they would coincide only if our descriptions were
totally correct—something that we are certainly not in a position to
claim. The world-as-known is a thing of our contrivance, an
artifact we devise on our own terms. Even if the "data" uniquely
determined a corresponding picture of reality, and did not under-
determine the theoretical constructions we base upon them (as
they always do), the fact remains that altered circumstances lead to
altered manifolds of "data." Our recognition of the fact that the
world-picture of science is ever-changing blocks our taking the
chance that it is ever *correct*.

According to one expositor, the scientific realist:

> maintains that, if a theory has scientific merit, then we are thereby
> justified in concluding that . . . the theoretical entities characterized
> by the theory really do exist.[3]

But this sort of position has its difficulties. Philologiston, caloric,
and the luminiferous ether all had scientific merit in their day but
this did not establish their existence. Why, then, should things be
all that different with us, and *our* "scientific merit" now suddenly
assure actual existence? What matters for real existence is clearly
(and only) the issue of truth itself, and not the issue of what is
thought to be true at some particular stage of scientific history.
And here problems arise. For its changeability is a fact ABOUT
science that is as inductively well established as any theory OF
science itself. Science is not a static system but a dynamic process.

The "that's how it is" of our scientific declarations must always
be qualified by an "as we shall view the matter until further notice"
at the level of the epistemological stance that underlies them.

The following objection might be attempted:

In *accepting* something, one accepts it *as true*. And so once we accept the contentions of science, there is no alternative to also accepting all of their correlative existential commitments.

However, the basic premiss of this line of argumentation ignores the fact that the matter of "acceptance" is not all that simple. It overlooks that scientific acceptance is not just acceptance (any more than a stuffed owl is not *just* an owl). What is at issue is not just acceptance as such, but a tentative or provisional acceptance, predicated on the idea that what is being "accepted," rather than being the definitive truth of the matter, is simply the best estimate of the truth that can be made in the present state-of-the-art.

2. REALISM AND THE AIM OF SCIENCE

We must maintain a clear distinction between *"our conception of reality"* and *"reality as it really is."* Given the equation,

Our (conception of) reality = the condition of things as seen from the standpoint of "our *putative* truth" (= the truth as we see it = the science of the day)

we realize full well that there is little justification for holding that our present-day science indeed describes reality and depicts the world as it really is. In our hearts of hearts, then, our attitude towards our science is one of *guarded* affirmation. We realize that there is a decisive difference between what science *accomplishes* and what it *endeavors* to do.

The posture of scientific realism—at any rate of a duly qualified sort—is nevertheless built into the very goal-structure of science. The task of science—the definitively characteristic mission of the enterprise,—is to respond to our basic, pre-systematic interest in getting the best answers we can to our questions about the world. On the traditional view of the matter, this question-resolving concern is the *raison d' être* of the project. To be sure, we have no advance guarantee of success in this venture, and may well in the end have to recognize our limits and limitations in this regard. But this consideration affords no reason for abstaining from the endeavor to do the very best we can.

It is accordingly useful to draw a clear distinction between a *realism of intent* and a *realism of achievement*. We are certainly not in a position to claim that science as we have it achieves a characterization of reality. In *intent or aspiration,* however, science is unabashedly realistic: its *aim* is unquestionably to answer our questions about the world *correctly* and to describe the world "as it actually is." The orientation of science is factual and objective: it is concerned with establishing the *true* facts about the *real* world. The theories of physics purport to describe the actual operation of real entities—the Nobel prizes awarded for discovering the electron, the neutron, the pi meson, the anti-proton, etc., were intended to recognize an enlargement of our understanding of nature, not to reward the contriving of plausible fictions or devising clever ways of relating observations.

The language of science is descriptively committal. At the semantical level of the content of its assertions, science makes firm claims as to how things stand in the world. Scientific realism skates along a thin border between patent falsity and triviality. Viewed as the doctrine that science *indeed describes* reality, it is utterly untenable, but viewed as the doctrine that science *seeks to describe* reality, it is virtually a truism. For there is no way of side-stepping the conditional thesis:

> IF a scientific theory regarding heavy water or electrons or quarks or whatever is correct—if it were indeed to be true—THEN its subject materials would exist in the manner the theory envisages and would have the properties the theory attributes to it: the theory, that is, would afford descriptively correct information about the world.

But this conditional relationship reflects what is, in the final analysis, less a profound fact about the nature of science than a near truism about the nature of truth as *adaequatio ad rem*. The fact remains that "our reality"—reality as we conceive it to be—goes no further than to represent our best estimate of what reality is like.

When we look to *WHAT science declares,* to the content and substance of its declarations, we see that these declarations are realistic in intent, that they *purport* to describe the world as it really is. But when we look to *HOW science makes its declarations* and note the tentativity and provisionality with which they are offered and accepted, we recognize that this realism is of an abridged and qualified sort—that we are not prepared to claim that this is how matters actually stand in the real world. Despite a commitment to realism at the semantical level of assertion-content, there is no longer a commitment to realism at the epistemological level of assertoric commitment. Realism prevails with respect to the *language* of science (i.e., the content of its declarations); it is abandoned with respect to the *status* of science (i.e., the ultimate tenability or correctness of these assertions). What science says is descriptively committal in making claims regarding "the real world," but the tone of voice in which it proffers these claims always is (or should be) provisional and tentative.

All the same, commitment to a realism of intent is built into science because of the genesis of its questions. The ultimate ground of the factually descriptive status of science lies in just this erotetic continuity of the issue of science with those of "prescientific" everyday life. We begin at the prescientific level of the paradigmatic realities of our prosaic everyday-life experience—the things, occurrences, and processes of our everyday world. The very reason for being of our scientific paraphernalia is to resolve our questions about this real world of our everyday-life experience. Given that the teleology of the scientific enterprise roots in the "real world" that provides the stage of our being and action, we are committed *within its framework* to take the realistic view of its mechanisms.[4] Natural science does not address itself to some world-abstracted realm of its own. Its concern is with this familiar "real world" of ours in which we live and breathe and have our being—however differently science may characterize it. However gravely science may fall short in performance, nevertheless in aspiration and endeavor it is unequivocally committed to the project of depicting "the real world," for in this way alone could it realize its constituting mandate of answering our questions as to how things work in the world. This perspective reinforces the previous contention that we are irrevocably committed to viewing the lineaments of the world as depicted by science as an at any rate tentative or aspiring depiction of how things actually work in the world.

3. SCIENTIFIC REALISM AT THE LEVEL OF IDEAL SCIENCE

With respect to the issue of truth and reality, all we can and should say is that current science affords our *best estimate* of the makeup of the world. Scientific progress is *not* of a nature that encourages us to reify (hypostasize) the furnishings of present-day science. Once we have taken a careful and realistic look at the history of science, it is scarcely an appealing proposition to maintain that *our* science as it stands here and now, depicts reality actually and correctly. Here one is led back to the deliberations of the preceding chapter. The *mission* of science is indeed to describe the real world, but its *actual accomplishment* lies in its merely affording us "the best estimate" of reality that can be had in the present state of the art. Thus if we were "forced to say" what the world is really like, then of course science yields the substance of our response because that is (*ex hypothesi*) the best we can do. But we realize full well that this is no more than a matter of estimation and of doing the best we can.

In sum, we cannot say that the world *is* such that the paraphernalia of our science actually exist as such. Given that we must recognize its claims to be tentative and provisional, one cannot justifiably take the stance that our science *depicts* reality; at best one can say that it affords an *estimate* of it, an estimate that will presumably, stand in need of eventual revision and whose creatures-of-theory may in the final analysis not be real at all. This feature of science must crucially constrain our attitude towards its deliverances. Depiction is in this regard a matter of intent rather than one of accomplishment. Correctness in the characterization of nature is achieved not by *our* science, but only by *perfected* or *ideal* science—only by that (ineradicably hypothetical!) state of science in which the cognitive goals of the scientific enterprise are fully and definitively realized. There is no plausible alternative to reality depicted by *ideal* (or perfected or "completed") science, and not by the real science of the day, which, after all, is the only one we've actually got—now or ever.

A viable scientific realism must therefore turn not on what *our* science takes the world to be like, but on what *ideal or perfected* science takes the world to be like. The thesis that "science describes the real world" must be looked upon as a matter of intent rather than as an accomplished fact, of aspiration rather than achievement, of the ideal rather than the real state of things. Scientific realism is a viable position only with respect to that idealized science which, as we full well realize, we do not now have—regardless of the "now" at issue. We cannot justifiably be scientific realists—or rather, ironically, we can be so only in an idealistic manner, namely with respect to an "ideal science" that we can never actually claim to possess.

4. INSTRUMENTALISM AND THE DESCRIPTIVE PURPORT OF SCIENCE.

Should this fact that we cannot claim that *our* science, as it stands, depicts reality correctly be construed to mean that science has the status of a merely practical device—a mechanism of prediction and control that is (or properly should be thought of as being) devoid of any actually descriptive purport? Does science perhaps afford no focus for belief at all, but merely a guide to action? Such a stance is embodied in the doctrine of instrumentalism, which embraces roughly the following position:

> Science has no descriptive or existential import. It is simply an organon of prediction, a device for calculating what observational consequences will ensue (or will probably ensue) if certain things are done (or left undone)—above all, what results will be obtained when certain measurements are taken under certain conditions. It is an instrument for generating reliable predictions and guiding effective control. It is a "black box," as it were, into which we put some information (data or assumptions) and get out predictions about events or instructions for modes of intervention. But the propositions that figure in the contents of this black box must be construed as devoid of any claims to describing the world. As an instrumentality of prediction and control, science is wholly free of commitment that certain sorts of things really exist and actually have such-and-such a nature. The theories adopted by science are not to be construed as assertoric propositions. They are mere rules for drawing inferences to actual or possible observations. These rules themselves are neither true nor false; they are ways of dealing with the phenomena which work or do not work, are or are not successful and fruitful as guides to prediction and control.

The instrumentalist sees our scientific theories as no more than a practical device—than a set of rules for effective interventions and verifiable predictions.

Such a position gravely misconceives the character of the scientific enterprise. Admittedly, it is interested in prediction and control, but that's only a small part of it. What we seek above all, nay what constitutes the very reason for being of science, is *information*—description and classification and explanation, getting answers to our questions about how things go in the world. The statements of science are always made with descriptive and informative intent. And its descriptive orientation creates an unavoidable linkage between the assertions of science and objective reality—at any rate on the side of aim and aspiration.

Scientific inquiry, as we have argued, is a matter of achieving the very best estimate of the real truth that is available in the circumstances. And the idea of an "estimate of the truth" cannot be stripped of descriptive purport. The contentions of our science may not be—nay presumably are not—adequate to reality itself, but they would not be what they are if one refrained from recognizing their descriptive intent and failed to acknowledge their purporting (although perhaps failing) to depict matters as they stand in the real world. The intention to describe the world (however much our performance may fall short of its realization) is a crucial aspect of the goal-structure of science. To fail to recognize this fundamental fact is to go badly awry in our understanding of the definitive nature of the enterprise—to fail to recognize what is the very reason for being of the venture (however far our actual performance may fall short of its realization).

To be sure, science cannot be dogmatic in regard to its descriptive mission. It must, no doubt, refrain from claiming definitive correctness for the descriptive picture of the world it puts before us. But while science cannot be dogmatic here, it can, nevertheless, unhesitantly claim to do the very best that can be done in the circumstances at hand. And while we recognize that we cannot claim *correctness* for the descriptive claims of our science, we nevertheless do—and can—view them as the best estimate of the matter that can be made with the cognitive technology of the day. It is of the very essence of an estimate that it should seek to estimate *the truth of the matter*.

Instrumentalism insists that it is necessary to reorient the goal structure of science away from its traditional teleology of question-answering. On its basis, our scientific theories are to be viewed as a contentless black box—a mere computing device that provides a calculating mechanism that mediates between data-inputs and data-out-puts, but itself is a mere instrument of conveniences devoid of any descriptive import, a useful fiction that produces results. But why should one take this stance? What we have here is clearly no more than a fall-back position that would only make sense if the traditional descriptive goals of science could be shown in some decisive way to be, in principle, improper and illegitimate. But there is no good reason for taking this line. The legitimacy of the traditional ideal of "the pursuit of truth" is something we have already considered at length. Moreover, as was argued in the last chapter, the pragmatic successes of science give persuasive augury for regarding its information-providing methods as being able to afford us with a relatively respectable estimate of the truth of things.

Instrumentalism draws wrong conclusions from the undoubted fact of the fallibility and corrigibility of science. This corrigibility does not mean that we cannot make existential and descriptive claims; it merely means that we must make them provisionally, talking in the hypothetical mode: *if* "our science" is correct, *then* electrons exist and have such-and-such features, etc. We must acknowledge that our science is ontologically committed in its ontological and descriptive *purport*—in its aim or intention— though doubtless imperfect in its executions of this mandate. Admittedly, at the level of existing science, our explanatory and descriptive claims must be viewed as no more than corrigible estimates of the truth. But to say this is not to say that we should not make them at all. It is clear that the level of perfected science we clearly would want to make such claims, and this very fact shows how our intentions are directed.

A commitment to realism is thus inherent in the very teleology of science. In abandoning realism we would turn our back on the definitive aims and tasks of the scientific enterprise. In attempting answers to our questions about how things stand in the world, science offers (or at any rate, *endeavors* to offer) information about the world. The extent to which science succeeds in this mission is, of course, discussible. (And no doubt in this discussion the issue of success in prediction and control will have to play a central role.[5]) But this does not alter the fact that science both endeavors and purports to provide realistically authentic description of what the world is actually like.

To be sure, here as elsewhere one must be mindful of the distinction between aim and achievement, between what we set out to do and the extent to which we've actually done it. But, clearly, the fact that science's goal of a correct description of natural processes is something that we can never claim to have realized in full does not constitute a sufficent reason for abandoning this goal altogether. In inquiry, as in the moral life, we can never attain perfection. But this is surely no reason for abandoning the endeavor.

XIII

Reality and Realism

SYNOPSIS

(1) A consideration of the pivotal contrast between "our picture of reality" and "reality itself." (2) Realism as the doctrine that the world is what it is independently of our cognitive endeavors. To motivate this doctrine little more is necessary than to recognize the pervasive changeability and fallibility of the theorizing through which we shape our (confessedly inadequate) picture of reality. (3) Why not simply drop our commitment to the conception of "reality itself"? Because we need it (i) to maintain the linkage between truth and reality, (ii) to check any unrealistic pretentions regarding the current state of the cognitive art, and (iii) to operate the causal model of inquiry. The realistic conception of a shared world of "real things"—a world into which we inquire, but about which we presumably manage to secure only imperfect information—is basic to the whole process of human communication. (4) The doctrine of metaphysical *realism*—of a commitment to a wholly knowledge-in-hand transcending and thought-independent Reality that affords the telos and the source of empirical inquiry—is only tenable on an essentially *idealistic* basis.

1. REALITY

Reality (on the traditional metaphysicians' construction of the concept) is the condition of things answering to "the real truth"; it is the realm of what really is as it really is. The pivotal contrast is that between "our picture of reality" and "reality itself," between what actually is and what we merely think (believe, suppose, etc.) to be. And our allegiance to the conception of reality, and to this contrast that pivots upon it, roots in the fallibilistic recognition

257

that, at the level of the detailed specifics of scientific theory, anything we presently hold to be the case may well turn out otherwise. Our commitment to the mind-independent reality of "the real world" stands coordinate with our acknowledgement that in principle any or all of our *present* ideas as to how things work in the world, at *any* present, may well prove to be untenable —our recognition of the ever-present and ineliminable possibility of a slip between "what we think things to be like" in our scientific theorizing and the "way things actually are" in nature. Our conviction in a reality that lies beyond our imperfect understanding of it (in all the various senses of "lying beyond") roots in our sense of the imperfections of our world-picture—its tentativity and potential fallibility.

We need the notion of reality to operate the conception of truth. The statement "There are pi mesons" is true if and only if the world is such that—really and truly—pi mesons exist within it. True claims *ex hypothesi* state facts; they state what really is—which is exactly what it is to "characterize reality." The conceptions of *truth* and of *reality* come together in the notion of *adequatio ad rem*—the venerable principle that to speak truly is to say how matters stand in reality, in that things actually are as we have said them to be.

Unfortunately, however, these truisms nowise help us towards getting a cognitive grip on reality. In our own case, here and now, we have no decisive way of discriminating real from apparent truth, of distinguishing between *our* truth and *the* truth. And far-reaching implications issue from this absence of any inquiry-independent access to reality, and the circumstance that in empirical inquiry, as in his other endeavors, man's proceedings are imperfect.

The ineliminable prospect of error—the recognition of the potential corrigibility of all our scientific theorizing, and the unavoidable acknowledgement that we are not in a position to claim that in this domain *our* truth is *the* truth—mean that we cannot ever lay claim to a definitively correct and final picture of reality. Once we acknowledge that a prospect of incompleteness and a presumption of at least partial incorrectness attaches to our present picture of the world, we can no longer subscribe to the idea that the world really exists as we conceive of it. And so we can no longer adopt the view that, at the level of scientific theorizing, "our world picture" depicts "the real world"—the world as it actually is.

The fact is that we have no choice but to view what we do get hold of by way of "scientific truth" about the world—now, or ever—as being (at the synoptic, systemic level) *imperfect:* incomplete, incorrect, perhaps even inconsistent. The gulf between Appearance (= our *putative* reality) and the Reality portrayed by a body of capital-T Truth that satisfies all of the traditional ideals of completeness, consistency, finality, etc., is—and ever shall remain—every bit as wide as F. H. Bradley envisaged it to be.

Throughout scientific inquiry, the prospect of a gap between "what *we think* the real to be" and "what reality is *actually like*" is absolute and insuperable: we are never in a position to claim it to be closed. It is clear that we have—and can have—no cognitive access to reality except through the epistemic route that our mechanisms of inquiry afford us. Our scientific endeavors provide us no way to determine what reality is like save through the fallible epistemic process of deciding which theories about it we are to accept. We have no way of coming to cognitive grips with reality apart from the laborious, and inherently error-prone, empirical and inductive process of constructing our "picture of the world." The *character* of the world is no doubt independent of our cognitive devisings, but its *characterization* emphatically is not, but is something supervenient and description-relative. And *for us*—and this is the key point—there is no cognitive access to character save via characterization. There is no royal road to knowledge of reality save through the mediation of imperfect inquiry.

We recognize, or at any rate have no alternative but to suppose, *that* reality exists (that there is such a thing "as the real truth" about the things of this world), but we are not in a position to stake any final and definitive claims as to *what* it is like. Historical experience and consideration of the theoretical general principles of the matter combine to indicate that at the level of scientific generality and precision, our "knowledge of reality" is always *putative* knowledge. Not only are we not in a position to claim that our knowledge of reality is *complete* (that we have gotten at the *whole* truth of things), but we are not even in a position to claim that our knowledge of reality is *correct* (that we have gotten at the *real* truth of things). To close the gap between "the world as we ourselves picture it" (our *putative* truth) to "the world itself" (the *real* truth), we would have to suspend our clear recognition that our present picture of the world—as best we can now form it in the existing cognitive state-of-the-art—must be presumed to be gravely deficient.

The Kantian distinction between the empirically and the transcendentally real can be adapted to do useful work at this juncture. To be transcendentally real is to be real, period. *Empirical* reality, on the other hand, is *our* reality: to be empirically real is to be real under the belief-contravening supposition that "our truth" is "the truth." Now, to be sure, we almost always and everywhere can and must adopt the working hypothesis that we've got it right; we have no alternative to proceeding on the basis of the over-optimistic supposition that the best that we can do is good enough. And so at the level of concrete detail we subscribe for the most part to the working hypothesis that in the factual domain *our* truth may be taken to be *the* truth. Yet we cannot but recognize that this "empirical reality" is a fiction—a mind-devised, man-made artifact that cannot be identified with actual reality because we full-well realize that reality is *not* actually as we picture it, that our truth is not the real truth, that we are probably quite wrong in supposing that the furnishings of "our science" actually exist as we currently conceive of them.

Once we "distance" ourselves from our epistemic commitments and recognize that they can, nay presumably *do* go awry, we realize that "our reality" is not reality *per se,* and that we have neither the inclination nor the warrant for claiming that reality actually is as we picture it to be. And given this presupposition or presumption, we have no alternative but to suppose reality to have a character regarding which we are only imperfectly informed.

Committed to the unproblematic claim *that* reality exists, we are nevertheless equally committed to a standing (and surely correct!) presumption that its nature is in various not unimportant ways different from what we think it to be. We can make no confident claims in this matter of "describing reality"; the most we can do is to give our best estimate of its descriptive constitution. We recognize that "our picture" of reality is no more than an estimate of the truth. We are constrained to acknowledge that it is not *our* science, or even *future* science, but only *ideal* science that correctly describes reality.

To be sure, "our world" (= "the world as we picture it") and "the real world" (= "the world as 'ideal science' pictures it") are *not* distinct worlds: there is just *the world* (the actual, extant one), of which we on the one hand, and "ideal science" on the other, draw rather different pictures. It would be a grave mistake of illicit hypostatization to reify "the world as we see it" into a *thing* distinct from the real world (just as it would be a mistake, as we have seen, to populate the world with two Harrys, "Harry as I picture him" and "the real Harry"). "The world AS it is depicted" from the vantage point of a certain state of science may differ from one time to another, but not "the world THAT is so depicted." It is not a matter of plurality of worlds, but of a single world conceptualized differently—and, *by us,* imperfectly. (This is how we can know *that* the world of ideal or perfected science exists, while yet being ignorant with respect to what it's actually like; for, of course, we can make no substantive assertions whatsoever regarding reality itself as *contradistinguished* from reality as we picture it.)

To say all this is not, of course, to say that reality is inherently unknowable. Such mystification is not at issue: our claims to factual knowledge are always and inevitably claims to factual knowledge *of reality.* The point is merely that, at the level of scientific theorizing, our knowledge of reality is always *purported* knowledge; it is knowledge that cannot be claimed with dogmatic finality, but to which an element of tentativity and provisionality must always be attached.

2. REALISM

Metaphysical Realism is the doctrine that the world exists independently of the thinking beings that inquire into it, that its nature (its having whatever characteristics it does have) is also comparably thought-independent. The fundamental idea of this realism is that the existence and nature of the world are separate from our

thinking about it: that the world is what it is without any reference
to our cognitive endeavors, and that, the things of nature are—in a
sense—quite *impervious* to the state of our knowledge or belief
regarding them. One recent expositor formulates this idea as
follows:

> Even if there were no human thought, even if there were no
> human beings, whatever there is other than human thought (and
> what depends on that, causally or logically) would still be just what it
> actually is.[1]

Such a realism is based upon a commitment to the notion that
human inquiry addresses itself to what is really and truly the
condition of things whose existence and character are altogether
independent of our cognitive activities. Reality is not subject to the
operations of the human mind; *au contraire,* man's mind and its
dealings are but a minuscule part of reality.

Given an understanding of reality along the lines expounded in
our earlier discussion, such a position seems wholly correct and
unexceptionable. For what *really is* true is obviously nowise
affected or determined by what *we think to be* true. And so, since
reality, as the condition of things answering to the *real* truth, is
clearly not something we are going to alter or modify by changes in
what we think about it, it is bound to be unaffected by any
developments with respect to what we purport to be true through
cognitive endeavors in the course of inquiry. On the contrary, a
proper view of these endeavors is unavoidably conditioned by our
acknowledgement that a full and final knowledge of reality is
something we cannot justifiably claim to have—now or ever.
Reality is recognized as being essentially cognition-transcending.

Accordingly, our conception of the nature of inquiry involves
recognition of the following facts: (1) That the world (existence,
reality) has a nature whose characterization in point of description,
explanation, and prediction is the object of empirical inquiry. (2)
That the real nature of the world is in the main independent of the
process of inquiry which, however, it (the real world) canalizes or
conditions. Dependency is a one-way street here: reality shapes or
influences inquiry, but not conversely. Our opinions do not affect

the real truth but, rather, our strivings after the real truth engender changes in our opinions. (3) That, in the face of (2), we can stake neither total nor final claims for our purported knowledge of reality. Our knowledge of the world must be presumed incomplete, incorrect, and imperfect, with the consequence that "our reality" must be considered to afford an inadequate characterization of "reality itself." As concerns our cognitive endeavors, "man proposes and nature disposes," and it does so in both senses of the term: it disposes *over* our current view of reality and it will doubtless eventually dispose *of* it as well.

3. THE REGULATIVE ASPECT

Given that even our most exactingly contrived scientific view of the nature of reality is—and must always be—provisional and tenative, why not abandon the whole notion? Why endorse the conception of "reality" at all—why postulate something to which we can never stake a secure and final claim?

The answer here lies in considering the price that such an abandonment would exact from us.

To begin with, we indispensably require the notion of reality to operate the classical concept of truth as "agreement with reality" *(adaequatio ad rem)*. Once we abandon the concept of reality, the idea that in accepting a factual claim as true we become committed to the proposition that that's how the facts actually stand—"how it really is"—would also go by the board. Semantics constrains realism: we have no alternative but to regard as real those states of affairs claimed by the contentions we are prepared to make. (That is, once we put a claim forward by way of serious assertion, we must view as real the states of affairs it purports.) The nihilistic denial that there is such a thing as reality at all would destroy once and for all the crucial Parmenidean divide between appearance and reality. And this would exact a fearful price from us: we would now be reduced to talking only of what we (I, you, many of us) *think* to be so. The crucial contrast notion of the *real* truth would no longer be available: we would only be able to contrast our *putative* truths with those of others, but could no longer operate the classical distinction between the putative and the actual, between what we think to be so and what actually *is* so. We could not take the stance that, as the Aristotelian commentator Themistius put it, "that which exists does not conform to various opinions, but rather the correct opinions conform to that which exists."[2]

Second, the issue of cognitive coordination comes into play. Communication and inquiry, as we carry them on, are predicated on the fundamental idea of a real world of things existing and functioning "in themselves," without dependence on us and so equally accessible to others. Underlying and underpinning our discourse is the commitment to the realistic idea of "real things" whose being and comportment is quite independent of whatever thoughts about them we ourselves may (very possibly) have quite the wrong conception. Only through reference to the real world as a *common object* and shared focus of our diverse and imperfect epistemic strivings are we able to effect communicative contact with one another. But if reality were dispensed with, the whole notion of person-indifferent facts—on the basis of which alone any real communication is possible—would also go by the board. And at this point, the idea of *inquiry,* of seeking after the objective truth of things, would also run into difficulty. Inquiry, like communication, is geared to the conception of an objective world: a communally shared realm of things that exist strictly and "on their own," comprising an enduring and impersonal realm within which and, more importantly, with reference to which inquiry proceeds. Inquiry, as we standardly conceive it, is predicated on the commitment to an inquiry-independent reality; it is a quest for information about "the real world" with respect to which our own conceptions of things are nowise definitive, and into which others can accordingly enter unproblematically. We could not operate the notion of inquiry as aimed at estimating the character of the real if we were not prepared to presume or postulate a reality for these estimates to be estimates of. It would clearly be pointless to devise our characterizations of reality if we did not stand committed to the proposition that there indeed is a reality to be characterized.

Last but not least, we need the conception of reality to operate the causal model of inquiry about the real world. Our standard picture of man's place in the scheme of things is predicated on the fundamental idea that there is indeed a real world (however imperfectly our inquiry may characterize it) whose causal operations produce *inter alia* those impacts upon us serve as the basis of our world-picture. Reality is viewed as the causal source and basis of the appearances, the originator and determiner of the phenomena of our cognitively relevant experience. "The real world" is seen as causally operative in serving as the thought-external moulder of thought and as constituting the ultimate arbiter of the adequacy of our theorizing.

The conception of Reality thus plays a triple role in our thinking. It is seen as the epistemological *object* of veridical cognition, in the context of the contrast between "the real" and its "merely phenomenal" appearances. Again, it is seen as the target or *telos* of the truth-estimation process at issue in inquiry, providing for a common focus in communication and communal inquiry. (The "real world" thus constitutes the "object" of our cognitive endeavors in both senses of this term—the *objective* at which they are directed and the *purpose* for which they are exerted.) Finally, reality is seen as the ontological *source* of cognitive endeavors, affording the existential matrix in which we move and have our being and whose impact upon us is the prime mover for our cognitive efforts. All of these facets of the concept of reality are integrated and unified in the classical doctrine of truth as *adaequatio ad rem*.

As these deliberations show, we are committed to the idea *that* there is a thought-independent reality even though we are not in a position to stake any claims to definitive knowledge about *what* its nature is. We know *that* there is a real and definitive truth of things, but not *what* it is. And any rejection of this commitment to Reality *"an sich"* (or to the actual Truth about it) exacts an unacceptable price. For in abandoning this commitment we also loose those regulative contrasts that canalize and condition our view of the nature of inquiry (and indeed shape our conception of this process as it stands within the framework of our conceptual scheme). We would no longer be able to use the idea of inquiry as truth-estimation if there were no real truth to be estimated, and we could no longer assert "What we have here is good enough as far as it goes, but it is presumably not 'the real truth' of the matter." Not only are such claims intelligible, but we in fact stand committed to them as facts that constitute a crucial part of the conceptual scheme within whose orbit we operate our concept of inquiry. The very conception of inquiry as we conceive of it would have to be abandoned if the contrast conceptions of "actual reality" and "the real truth" were no longer available.

Towards Reality itself, transcendental reality ("as it actually is") as contradistinguished from our empirical reality ("as we think it to be"), we must accordingly take much the same stance that Kant took towards his "thing in itself." As such, there is nothing we can say about it; its character is fundamentally a matter of *je ne sais quoi,* because we recognize that definitive and error-immune claims to knowledge cannot be substantiated at the level of scientific theorizing. On the other hand, we stand committed to the idea that there must indeed be such a thing as knowledge-transcending reality, because only in this way can we operate our conceptual scheme with respect to inquiry and communication, with its inherent dedication to the conception of an objectivity which recourse to "the real world" can alone sustain. Negative and regulative though the conception may be, we nevertheless require it as a tool of indispensible utility. (Compare pp. 120–21 above.)

4. REALISM AND IDEALISM

On the position put forward here, the conception of reality accordingly affords a fundamental presupposition for the entire network of ideas relating to communication and inquiry as we traditionally understand them. In communication and inquiry alike we seek or offer answers to our questions about how matters stand in this "objective realm."

To be sure, such an account does not show that realism is correct—that there indeed is a Reality that is wholly thought-independent and transcends all of our knowledge of it. All we have done is to argue that just such a realism underlies our conceptual scheme—that a real-world matrix of Truth and Reality that is at once the subject of our inquiry and the determiner of its results must be assumed or postulated to operate this scheme. This approach places Reality in the light, not of a discovered fact, but in that of a fundamental presupposition that governs and undergrids the framework of our thought about the world. Its status is not that of a discovery or finding but of a governing assumption. Its existence is a matter not of demonstration but of postulation or presupposition.

The information that we have about a thing—be it real or presumptive information—is always just that, viz. information that WE lay claim to. We cannot but recognize that it is person-relative and in general person-differentiated, with Tom, Dick, and Harry generally thinking rather differently about the nature of things. But our ventures at communication and communal inquiry are predicated on an information-transcending stance: the stance that we communally inhabit a shared world of objectively existing things—a realm of "real things" amongst which we live and into which we inquire, but about which we ourselves presumably have only imperfect information. This is not something we *learn* in the course of inquiry. The "facts of experience" can never reveal it to us. It is something we postulate or presuppose from the very outset. Its epistemic status is not that of an empirical discovery, but that of a regulative presupposition needed to underwrite the very possibility of communication or inquiry as we standardly conceive of them.[3]

Of course, what *is* learned by experience is that in proceeding on this prejudgment our attempts do, by and large, work out pretty well *vis-à-vis* the purposes we have in view for inquiry and communication. This success of our objectivity-presupposing proceedings shows that they are in a sense warranted. But this legitimation through the retrospective revalidation of experience does not alter their status as presuppositions and transmute them instead into established inductive conclusions. It does no more than to justify our reliance on a picture of the world that is geared to—but still transcends—the products of inquiry.

The existence of a mind-independent reality that is at once the object of and the operational stage for our cognitive endeavors is thus by no means the discovery of an objective fact, a finding as to the nature of things. Far from it. A commitment to the idea of reality is an *inherent presumption* of our conceptual scheme. We have here to do not with an objective *discovery* about the descriptive constitution of nature, but rather a formative presupposition that is part and parcel of the conceptual machinery that we ourselves bring to the process of inquiry. The reality of this mode of realism is a scheme-internal one, and not a supervenient *ab extra* addition to the commitment of our conceptual scheme. What we have here is a "transcendental argument" from the character of our conceptual scheme to its inherent presupposition.

Now if realism stands on *this* basis, then it is clear that we have a realism whose rationale is ideal. It clearly does not rest on substantive considerations about how things stand in the world, but rather is established by talking about how people think about the world within the orbit of the conceptual scheme they employ for its characterization. Realism in sum, is not a fact about the world, but a facet of how *we conceive* of the world—not a discovered fact, but a methodological presupposition of communication and inquiry: an input into our investigation of nature rather than an output thereof. Such a position sees this commitment to a mind-independent reality in an essentially regulative role—as a functional requisite or presupposition for our intellectual resources, our conceptual scheme. What we have here is an object-level realism that rests on a presuppositional idealism at the justificatory metalevel. We thus arrive, paradoxical as it may seem, at a realism that rests on a fundamentally idealistic basis.

Notes

CHAPTER ONE (pp. 3–26)

1. See Ludwig Wittgenstein, *On Certainty,* §18.
2. Cf. the author's *The Primacy of Practice* (Oxford, 1973), pp. 107–123.
3. W. V. Quine, "Epistemology Naturalized" in *Ontological Relativity and Other Essays* (New York, 1969), pp. 69–90 (see p. 83).
4. C. S. Peirce, *Collected Papers,* vol. I, sect. 1.145.
5. Even an *infinite* volume of phenomenal claims would not suffice (phenomenalism to the contrary not withstanding). For the dispositions at issue in objective claims are not only dispositions *vis-à-vis* perceivers, but also dispositions *vis-à-vis* other sorts of thing.
6. Compare the author's *Conceptual Idealism,* (Oxford, 1973), pp. 86 ff.
7. For a fuller development of the relevant issues see the author's *Methodological Pragmatism* (Oxford, 1973) and *Induction* (Oxford, 1980).
8. Donald Davidson, "On the Very Idea of a Conceptual Scheme," *Proceedings and Addresses of the American Philosophical Association,* vol. 47 (1973–74), pp. 5–20 (see p. 19).
9. A. J. Ayer, *Metaphysics and Common Sense* (London, 1967), p. 74.

CHAPTER TWO (pp. 27–60)

1. *The Structure of Scientific Revolutions* (Chicago, 1962), chap. X.
2. Georg Simmel, "Ueber eine Beziehung der Selektionslehre zur Erkenntnistheorie," *Archiv für systematische Philosophie und Soziologie,* vol. 1 (1895), pp. 34–45 (see 40-1).
3. *Pragmatism* (New York, 1907), p. 171. The basic line of thought goes back to the ancient sceptics. Compare Sextus Empiricus, *Outlines of Pyrrhonism,* I, 54, 59–60, 97, *et passim.*
4. See for example: Barry Stroud, "Conventionalism and the Indeterminacy of Translation," in D. Davison and J. Hintikka (eds.), *Words and Objections: Essays on the Work of W. V. Quine* (Dordrecht, 1969); Richard Rorty, "The World Well Lost," *The Journal of Philosophy,* vol. 69 (1972), pp. 649–665; and Donald Davidson, "On the Very Idea of a

Conceptual Scheme," *Proceedings and Addresses of the American Philosophical Association,* vol. 47 (1973–74), pp. 5–20.

5. Donald Davidson, *op. cit.*

6. Donald Davidson, *op. cit.*, p. 6.

7. Donald Davidson, *op. cit.*, pp. 14–15.

8. Moreover, overt and explicit theorizing, as carried on from an external vantage point, need not ever come into it. Language attribution can be based simply on the understanding gained by learning from within. As one recent writer helpfully put it:

> But while translatability of Galactic into English is not a require-ment for Galactic's being a language, *learnability* of Galactic by English-speakers *is*. What will be the case, of course, is that Galactic cannot be learned as one typically learns a *second* lan-guage, that is, *by* learning to translate Galactic locutions into our native tongue. Rather, Galactic must be learnable by us as it is learned by *its* native speakers, as a (second, in our case) *native* language . . . . Only if one implicitly espouses a view which equates language-learning with *translation* of the target language into a (perhaps innate) language already possessed will the non-learnability of Galactic by English-speakers be thought of as a consequence of the *non-translatability* of Galactic into English. (Jay F. Rosenberg, *Linguistic Representation,* (Dordrecht and Boston, 1974), p. 140.)

9. Bronislaw Malinowski, Supplementary Essay to C. K. Ogden and I. A. Richards, *The Meaning of Meaning,* fourth (revised) edition (London, 1936), pp. 300–301. As Malinowski justly observes, "Instead of translating, of inserting simply an English word for a native one, we are faced by a long and not altogether simple process of describing wide fields of custom, of social psychology and of tribal organization which corre-spond to one term or another." (*Ibid.,* p. 301–2.). Compare the discussion of these issues in John Dewey, *Reconstruction in Philosophy* (New York, 1920).

10. We can, of course, exchange them for our money by buying them. But *that* can't be what makes them money. One can buy virtually any sort of thing.

11. Donald Davidson, *op. cit.*, pp. 18–19.

12. Writers on the theory of rationality often stress that whatever we can validly acknowledge as constituting a reason for "them" is something that would also have to count as a reason for *us*. (See, for example, Martin

Hollis, "Limits of Irrationality" in B. R. Wilson [ed.], *Rationality* [Evanston and New York, 1970], pp. 214–220.) But this fact, that what's sauce for the goose is sauce for the gander where "the reasonable" is concerned, can be construed in terms of *functional* equivalency considerations and does not hinge on considerations of linguistic *modus operandi* and translational equivalency. Hollis' indispensable "bridgehead hypothesis" ("first that the native perceive more or less what he [the investigator] perceives and secondly that they say about it more or less what he would say") clearly turns on functional rather than translational considerations (else why that "more or less"?), and in fact is—as he points out—an underlying presupposition essential to the substantiation of any translational hypotheses.

13. Richard Rorty, "The World Well Lost," *The Journal of Philosophy,* vol. 69 (1972), pp. 649–665 (see p. 659).

14. C. I. Lewis put the point at issue in a way that cannot be improved upon:

> Categories and concepts do not literally change; they are simply given up and replaced by new ones. When disease entities give place to mere adjectival states of the organism induced by changed conditions such as bacteria, the old description of the phenomena of disease does not become false in any sense in which it was not always false. All objects are abstractions of one sort or another; a disease entity is found to be a relatively poor kind of abstraction for the understanding and control of the phenomena in question. But in terms of this abstraction any interpretation of experience which ever was correctly made will still remain true. Any contradiction between the old truth and the new is *verbal only,* because the old word "disease" has a new meaning. The old word is retained but the old concept is discarded as a poor intellectual instrument and replaced by a better one. (*Mind and the World Order* [New York, 1929], pp. 268–269.)

15. Donald Davidson, op. cit., p. 15.

16. The crucial point at issue is reminiscent of Leibniz' contention that minds that cannot communicate live in different natural spheres, and that "whoever asks whether another world or another space, can exist is asking to this extent whether there are minds that can communicate nothing to us." ("On Existence, Dreams, and Space" in Ivan Jagodinsky [ed.], *Leibnitiana elementa philosophiae arcanae de summa rerum* [Kazan, 1913], p. 114.)

17. This latter way of approaching the issue invites the very proper complaint that: "Different points of view make sense, but only if there is a common coordinate system on which to plot them." (Davidson, *op. cit.*, p. 6).

18. Compare Nelson Goodman's criticism of this view in "The Way the World Is" in his *Problems and Projects* (Indianapolis and New York, 1972), pp. 24–32.

19. See Donald Davidson, *op. cit.*, p. 11. The fundamental idea here goes back to Kant. For modern variations cf. C. I. Lewis, *Mind and the World Order* (New York, 1929), and H. H. Price, *Perception* (London, 1933).

20. Donald Davidson, *op. cit.*, p. 6.

21. On these issue cf. the writer's *Conceptual Idealism* (Oxford, 1973).

22. Richard Rorty, *op. cit.*, p. 650.

23. A. J. Ayer, *Metaphysics and Common Sense* (London, 1967), p. 76.

24. Chapter XIII deal at greater length with these issues.

25. One should perhaps be prepared to make an exception of "the world" or "the universe" or "the true facts" or "reality" or "existence" in this regard. But these, after all, only present a vacuous unifier: an inherently empty container into which we can pour anything and everything. This is not a *materia prima*—or indeed any kind of material—but a mere placeholder. For an interesting discussion of relevant issues, see Justus Buchler, "On the Concept of 'The World,'" *The Review of Metaphysics*, vol. 31 (1978), pp. 555–579.

26. Donald Davidson, *op. cit.*, p. 11.

27. Cf. W. V. Quine, "On Carnap's View of Ontology" in his *The Ways of Paradox* (N.Y., 1966), pp. 126–134.

28. To be sure, someone might ask: Why then bother with this conceptual detour at all? Why not simply operate with the notion of different theoretical stances. What work does the idea of "different schemes" do for you that that of "different theories" does not? The answer here lies in the consideration that it is not the generic fact that theories are at issue, but the special facts as to the *sorts* of theories that are involved, which makes it appropriate and helpful to speak of "conceptual schemes" in this connection.

29. Such equivalency hypotheses emerge—as do all our theories in factual matters—from our "inference to the best systematization." This means, *inter alia*, that we need not think of a *dog* in the same terms in which the Romans thought of a *canis*—fortunately so, since the gulf of the Darwinian revolution stands between us. Compare the discussion of communicative parallax at pp. 115–117 below.

30. Donald Davidson, *op. cit.*, p. 6.

31. Paul Feyerabend, "Problems of Empiricism," R. G. Colodny (ed.), *Beyond the Edge of Certainty* (Englewood Cliffs, 1965), p. 214.

32. C. I. Lewis, *Mind and the World Order*, (op. cit.), pp. 271–272.

33. It is, of course, possible that the appeal to praxis may prove indecisive—that in respect of certain ranges of purpose the one scheme is superior and that other schemes in respect of other purposes. Indeed just this seems to be the case with respect to the schemes of natural science and of ordinary life, where evolution has equipped us with a highly effective organon for social interaction.

34. These themes are developed more fully in the writer's *The Primacy of Practice* (Oxford, 1973) and *Methodological Pragmatism* (Oxford, 1976).

CHAPTER THREE (pp. 61–79)

1. To say that this is how these categories in fact arose is not to say that this is how they are invariably viewed in philosophical theorizing about the nature of categories. On the interesting and diversified situation that obtains here see Adolf Trendelenburg, *Geschichte der Kategorienlehre* (Berlin, 1846). What is at issue in our present discussion is a matter not of *historical* but of *functional* reconstruction: the proposed account of the categories is intended as a close functional equivalent in *our* conceptual scheme of what the traditional theorists were up to in *theirs*.

2. On this topic of category mistakes cf. Gilbert Ryle, *Dilemmas* (Cambridge, 1954).

3. John Dewey, *Reconstruction in Philosophy* ("Enlarged Edition," Boston, 1957), p. 153.

4. Compare the author's *Cognitive Systematization* (Oxford, 1979).

5. Some of the issues of this section will be dealt with from another perspective (and at greater length) in Chapter XII below.

6. *The Writings of William James,* ed. J.S. Mc Dermott (Chicago and London, 1977), p. 453. It would, however, be preferable to speak here of *natural science* rather than of *nature itself*.

CHAPTER FOUR (pp. 83–100)

1. Compare Nicholas Rescher and Robert Brandom, *The Logic of Inconsistency* (Oxford, 1980), sect. 11.

2. On the issues of this paragraph see "On Alternatives in Epistemic

Logic" in the author's *Studies in Modality* (Oxford, 1979; APQ Monograph Series No. 8).

3. George Gore, *The Art of Scientific Discovery*, (London, 1878), pp. 19–20.

4. Such revisions are, in general, not unique: there will be various alternatives. On the issues that arise here, see the author's *Plausible Reasoning* (Assen, 1976).

5. The background of Peirce's position will be described more fully in the next chapter. See also the author's *Peirce's Philosophy of Science* (Notre Dame, 1978).

6. Henri Poincaré, *Science and Hypothesis* tr. by W. J. Greenstreet (London and New York, 1907), p. 160. Poincaré thinks to meet this circumstance by an instrumentation that abandons the *content* of theories as a significant consideration and focuses upon their numerical predictions, at which level he holds to something like a Peircean convergentism.

7. The issues of this paragraph are explored in fuller detail in the author's *Scepticism* (Oxford, 1980).

8. A detailed exposition and defense of this view of cognitive progress will be presented in Chapter X below.

9. This formalization is a close paraphrase of the characterization of *historical* relativism given in Maurice Mandelbaum, *The Problem of Historical Knowledge* (New York, 1938), p. 19.

10. Compare Kant, *Critique of Pure Reason*, A497=B525ff.

11. On all these issues see once more Section 11 of Chapter II, pp. 57–60.

12. In this regard there is a crucial difference between classical historicism and the present position. Traditional historicists hold that history presents changing views with respect to which we ourselves are not in a position to say whether the change was sound or whether the rejected view deserved to be rejected. (Cf. R. G. Collingwood, *The Idea of History* [Oxford, 1946],pp. 229–30.) On the present position, scientific change is seen as generally warranted and well-advised, albeit not in a way that renders the new position inherently less vulnerable or more definitive than the old. Change is seen as rational, and yet not as "drawing near to the truth."

CHAPTER FIVE (pp. 101–128)

1. For a useful survey of philosophical issues located in this general area see Vincent Julian Fecher, *Error, Deception, and Incomplete Truth* (Rome: Catholic Book Agency, 1975).

2. To be sure, *abstract* things—such as colors or numbers—will not have dispositional properties. For being divisible by 4 is not a *disposition* of 16. Plato got the matter right in Book VII of the *Republic*. In the realm of *abstracta,* such as those of mathematics, there are no genuine *processes*. And process is a requisite of dispositions. Of course, there may be dispositional truths in which numbers figure (e.g., 4 may be my favorite number, or it might remind Henry of his old flame who lived at Number 4, Fourth Avenue). But a convincing case can be developed for saying that *such* dispositional truths in which numbers (or colors, etc.) figure do not issue in any dispositional properties of these numbers (or colors, etc.) themselves. For if a truth (or supposed truth) does no more than to convey how someone *thinks* about a thing, then it does not indicate any property of the thing itself. In any case, however, the subsequent discussion will focus on *realia* (in contrast to *fictionalia*) and *concreta* (in contrast to *abstracta*). (Fictional things, however, *can* have dispositions: Sherlock Holmes was addicted to cocaine, for example. Their difference from *realia* is dealt with below. [See p. 111.])

3. This aspect of objectivity was justly stressed in the Second Analogy of Kant's *Critique of Pure Reason,* though his discussion rests on ideas already investigated by Leibniz (*Phil. Schriften,* ed. by C. I. Gerhardt, vol. VII, pp. 319 ff.)

4. See C. I. Lewis, *An Analysis of Knowledge and Valuation* (La Salle, 1962, pp. 180–181.

5. Our position thus takes no issue with P. F. Strawson's precept that "facts are what statements (when true) state." ("Truth," *Procedings of the Aristotelian Society,* Supplementary Volume 24 [1950], pp. 129–156; see p. 136.

6. Note, however, that if a Davidsonian translation argument to the effect that "if it's sayable at all, then, it's sayable in *our* language" were to succeed—which it does not (cf. pp. 30–35)—then the matter would stand on a very different footing. For it would then follow any possible language can state no more than what can be stated in our own (actual) language. And then the realm of facts (= what is [correctly] statable in some *possible* language) and of that of truths (= what is [correctly] statable in some *actual* language) would necessarily coincide. Accordingly, our thesis that the range of facts is larger than that of truths hinges crucially upon a failure of the Translation Argument.

7. But can any sense be made of the idea of *merely* possible (i.e. possible but nonactual) languages? Of course it can! Once we have a generalized conception (or definition) of a certain kind of thing—be it a language or a golf club—then we are inevitably in a position to suppose the

prospect of things meeting these conditions that in fact do not do so. The prospect of mooting certain "mere" possibilities cannot be denied—that, after all, is just what possibilities are all about.

8. One possible misunderstanding must be blocked at this point. To learn about nature, we must interact with it. And so, to determine some feature of an object, we may have to make some impact upon it that would perturb its otherwise obtaining condition. (The indeterminacy principle of quantum affords a well-known reminder of this.) It should be clear that this matter of physical interaction for data-acquisition is not contested in the ontological indifference thesis here at issue.

9. This somewhat telegraphic discussion is developed more fully in the author's books on *Scientific Progress* (Oxford, 1977) and *Cognitive Systematization* (Oxford, 1978). Cf. also Chapter X below.

10. This provides a basis for multiplying conceptions—e.g., by distinguishing between the *scientifically* important facts and those important in the context of *everyday life*. Think of Eddington's distinction between the scientists' table and the table of our ordinary experience.

11. Compare F. H. Bradley's thesis: "Error *is* truth, it is partial truth, that is false only because partial and left incomplete." *Appearance and Reality* (Oxford, 1893), p. 169.

12. While this account of communicative parallax is written with a view to *particulars* (such as the moon or the Great Pyramid), much of it will also hold, *mutates mutandis,* for diffused thing-kinds (water or copper) and thing-types (books or cows). What alone matters throughout is that there must be some objective item at the pre-or sub-theoretical level of which we can say that different accounts give different accounts of IT. (This is why the *lingua franca* of everyday life is critical.) The approach does not work for creatures-of-theory, however. We cannot say of Democritean atoms that Rutherford's theory is giving an alternative account *of them.* Creatures of theory cannot exist outside the confines of their particular theoretical habitat; subtheoretical things, however, can survive changes in the theoretical environment.

13. The point is Kantian in its orientation. Kant holds that we cannot experientially learn through our perceptions about the objectivity of outer things, because we can only recognize our perceptions as perceptions (i.e. representations of outer things) if these outer things are given as such from the first (rather than being learned or inferred). As Kant summarizes his "Refutation of Idealism":

> Idealism assumed that the only immediate experience is inner experience, and that from it we can only *infer* outer things—and

this, moreover, only in an untrustworthy manner. . . . . But on the above proof it has been shown that outer experience is really immediate . . . . (CPuR, B276.)

14. The issues which this paragraph treats telegraphically are developed in more substantial detail in the author's *Induction* (Oxford, 1980).

15. It is thus perfectly possible for two people to communicate effectively about something that is wholly nonexistent and about which they have substantially discordant conceptions (for example, X's putative wife, where X is, in fact, unmarried, though one party is under the misimpression that X is married to A, and the other under the misimpression that X is married to B). The common focus is the basis on which alone the exchange of information (or misinformation) and the discovery of error becomes possible. And this inheres, not in the actual arrangements of the world, but in our shared (conventionalized) intention to talk about the same thing— about X's wife or, rather X's *putative* wife in the case at hand.

16. The justification of such imputations is treated more fully in Chapter IX of the author's *Induction* (Oxford, 1980). Cf. also pp. 15–18 above.

17. Benedictus de Spinoza, *Ethics,* Bk. 1, axiom 6.

18. Compare the interesting paper by Michael E. Levin, "On Theory-Change and Meaning-Change" in *Philosophy of Science,* vol. 46 (1979), pp. 407–424.

CHAPTER SIX (pp. 131–150)

1. A pioneering work in this area is Nuel D. Belnap, Jr. and Thomas B. Steel, Jr., *The Logic of Questions and Answers* (New Haven and London, 1976). This book contains an extensive annotated bibliography on the subject.

2. Belnap and Steel, following Harrah, call this a *direct* answer (ibid., p. 13). This terminology seems suboptimal, seeing that "direct" usually contrasts with "oblique" or "evasive" in this context.

3. Compare the pioneering discussion of R. G. Collingwood, *An Essay on Metaphysics* (Oxford, 1949), chap. IV, "On Presupposing."

4. Belnap and Steel suggest that proper yes-or-no questions (such as "Is glass a liquid at 70°F?") "are presupposition-free in the sense that it is a logical truth that at least one of their (possible) answers is true." (*Op. cit.*, p. 114.) But this is predicated on taking an ineradicably two valued view of the situation. If the very existence of glass at certain temperature ranges were a moot issue, for example, (which it indeed is), then presuppositions come in once more.

5. Belnap and Steel, *op. cit.*, p. 115.

6. Compare Belnap and Steel, *op cit.*, p. 5. They adopt this alternative characterization of presupposition.

7. On these issues see the author's *Hypothetical Reasoning* (Amsterday, 1964).

8. Belnap and Steel, *op. cit.*, p. 131

9. Adolf Grünbaum "Can a Theory Answer More Questions than One of its Rivals?," *British Journal for the Philosophy of Science,* vol. 27. 1976, pp. 1-22.

10. At this step we use an argument of the form

$$p \in K$$
$$\underline{p \to q}$$
$$p \in K$$

This, of course, does *not* work in general, but only if the implicational step from p to q that issues in $p \to q$ is sufficiently short and direct to qualify as "perfectly obvious." See "Inferential Myopia in Epistemic Logic" in the author's *Essays in Modality* (Oxford, 1974; *American Philosophical Quarterly,* Monograph No. 8), pp. 134–142 (see pp. 139–142). We can take this condition to be met in the present circumstances.

11. See footnote 10.

12. Compare Adolf Grünbaum, *op. cit.*, p. 17.

13. Kant was perhaps the first thinker who gave serious attention to developing the theory of questions and to exploit it as an instrument of philosophical method. Cf. the author's paper on "Kant and the Epistemology of Questions," in J. Kopper and W. Marx (eds.), *200 Jahre Kritik der reinen Vernunft* (Hildesheim, 1981). However Kant's démarche proved infertile and the topic of questions was put on the agenda of 20th century philosophy by R. G. Collingwood. (Cf footnote 3 above.)

14. See the author's *Hypothetical Reasoning* (Amsterdam, 1964) and *Plausible Reasoning* (Assen, 1976).

15. On the issues of this paragraph see the author's *Conceptual Idealism* (Oxford, 1973).

16. Immanuel Kant, *Prolegomena to any Future Metaphysic* (1783), sect. 57.

CHAPTER SEVEN (pp. 151–165)

1. W. S. Jevons, *The Principles of Science* (2nd ed., London, 1877), p. 759.

2. See R. G. Collingwood, *An Essay on Metaphysics* (Oxford, 1962), pp. 38–40.

3. For fuller treatment of the relevant issues see the writer's *Cognitive Systematization* (Oxford, 1979).

4. As one commentator has sagely written:

> But prediction in the field of pure science is another matter. The scientist sets forth over an uncharted sea and the scribe, left behind on the dock, is asked what he may find at the other side of the waters. If the scribe knew, the scientist would not have to make his voyage. [Anonymous, "The Future as Suggested by Developments of the Past Seventy-Five Years," *Scientific American* vol. no. 123 (1920), pp. 320–321 (see p. 321).]

5. See Thomas Kuhn, *The Structure of Scientific Revolutions* (Chicago, 1962).

6. Consider some applications of this principle: (1) It is easier and safer to forecast general trends than specific developments; (2) It is easier and safer to forecast over the near future than over the longer term; long-range forecasts are inherently more problematic; (3) The fewer and cruder the parameters of a prediction, the safer it becomes: it is easier and safer to forecast aggregated phenomena than particular eventuations (e.g., how many persons which will live in a certain city 10 years hence as compared with how many will belong to a particular family); (4) The more extensively it is laden with a protective shield of qualifications and limitations, the safer the prediction; (5) The more vaguely and ambiguously a prediction is formulated, the safer it becomes; particularly equivocal predictions have an inherent advantage; (6) The prediction of possibilities and prospects is more safe and secure than that of real and concrete developments. (It is one thing to predict what will be *feasible* at a given "state-of-the-art" and another to predict what will be *actual*.)

7. The progress of science offers innumerable illustrations of this phenomenon, as does the process of individual maturation:

> After three or thereabouts, the child begins asking himself and those around him questions, of which the most frequently noticed are the "why" questions. By studying what the child asks "why" about one can begin to see what kind of answers or solutions the child expects to receive . . . A first general observation is that the child's whys bear witness to an intermediate precausality between the efficient cause and the final cause. Specifically, these questions seek reasons for phenomena which we see as fortuitous but which in the child arouse a need for a finalist explanation. "Why are there two

Mount Salèves, a big one and a little one?'' asked a six-year-old boy. To which almost all his contemporaries, when asked the same question, replied, ''One for big trips and another for small trips.'' (Jean Piaget and B. Inhelder, *The Psychology of the Child*, tr. by H. Weaver [New York, 1969], pp. 109–110.

8. Compare the critique of doubts based on general principles in the author's *Scepticism* (Oxford, 1980), p. 97–108.

9. On the economic aspects of inquiry see also the author's *Peirce's Philosophy of Science* (Notre Dame and London, 1978), and in particular the last chapter ''Peirce and the Economy of Research.''

CHAPTER EIGHT (pp. 166–182)

1. Cp. pp. 149–152.

2. These considerations bear the lesson that we must think of Q not as a *variable* (with a correlative range over ''all questions''), but as a *notational device* that acquires this status only in the context of a specification of a determinate range.

3. Karl R. Popper, *Objective Knowledge* (Oxford, 1944) pp. 52–53.

4. See Adolf Grünbaum, ''Can a Theory Answer More Questions Than One of its Rivals?'' *British Journal for the Philosophy of Science,* vol. 27 (1976) pp. 1–22.

5. Larry Laudan, Unpublished preprint (Pittsburgh, 1979) p. 20. Compare also his ''Two Dogmas of Methodology,'' *Philosophy of Science.* vol. 43 (1976) pp. 585–597, and *Progress and Its Problems* (Berkley, 1978).

6. Or perhaps alternatively: always after a certain time—at every stage subsequent to a certain juncture.

7. *Prolegmena to any Future Metaphysics,* sect. 57. Compare the following passage from Charles Sanders Peirce:

> For my part, I cannot admit the proposition of Kant—that there are certain impassable bounds to human knowledge. . . . The history of science affords illustrations enough of the folly of saying that this, that, or the other can never be found out. Auguste Comte said that it was clearly impossible for man ever to learn anything of the chemical constitution of the fixed stars, but before his book had reached its readers the discovery which he had announced as impossible had been made. Legendre said of a certain proposition in the theory of numbers that, while it appeared to be true, it was most

likely beyond the powers of the human mind to prove it; yet the next writer on the subject gave six independent demonstrations of the theorem. (*Collected Papers,* Vol. VI, sect. 6.556.)

8. This work was published together with a famous prior (1872) lecture *On the Limits of Scientific Knowledge* as *Ueber Die Grenzen des Naturerkennens: Die Sieben Welträtsel—Zwei Vorträge* (11th ed., Leipzig, 1916). The earlier lecture has appeared in English tr. "The Limits of Our Knowledge of Nature," *Popular Scientific Monthly,* vol. 5 (1874), pp. 17–32. For Reymond cf. Ernest Cassirer, *Determinism and Indeterminism in Modern Physics: Historical and Systematic Studies of the Problem of Causality* (New Haven, 1956), Part 1.

9. Bonn, 1889. Tr. by J. McCabe as *The Riddle of the Universe—at the Close of the Nineteenth Century* (New York and London, 1901). On Haeckel see the article by Rollo Handy in *The Encyclopedia of Philosophy* (ed. by Paul Edwards), vol. III (New York, 1967).

10. The qualification "insofar as possible" may not prove trivial here—it may, of course, prove quite impossible.

11. Immanuel Kant, *CPrR,* p. 122 [Ak.].

12. Some of the issues of this discussion are developed at greater length in the author's *Methodological Pragmatism* (Oxford, 1977), and in *Scientific Progress* (Oxford, 1978), and in *Cognitive Systematization* (Oxford, 1979).

CHAPTER NINE (pp. 185–203)

1. A. S. Eddington, *The Nature of the Physical World* (Cambridge, 1929), pp. ix–xi.

2. Michael E. Levin, "On Theory Change and Meaning Change," *Philosophy of Science* vol. 46 (1979), pp. 407–424 (see p. 418).

3. Practical problems have a tendency to remain structurally invariant. The sending of messages is just that, whether horse-carried letters or laser beams are used in transmitting the information.

4. On this approach it is easy to account for the contrast between the growth of consensus in science and the cumulative progressivism of the enterprise on the one hand, and on the other the endless disagreements regarding most questions of philosophy, ethics, or religion. The difference lies precisely in this, that the latter fields are so little subject to the controls of pragmatic efficacy.

CHAPTER TEN (pp. 204–227)

1. J. H. Newman, *A Grammar for Assent,* Chap. VII, Sect. 6, paragraph 6.

2. See Sextus Empiricus, *Outlines of Pyrrhonism,* where this theme is prominent. The sceptical tradition owes much to Plato in this connection.

3. This point if forcibly pressed by W. V. Quine in *Word and Object* (New York, 1960), p. 23. Quine argues that talk of the limit of theories is based on an inappropriate mathematical analogy.

4. W. Stanley Jevons, *The Principles of Science* (2nd ed., London, 1877), pp. 753–754.

5. The ideas of this paragraph are developed at greater lengths in the author's *Scientific Progress* (Oxford, 1978).

6. E. P. Wigner puts the matter as follows:

> . . . in order to understand a growing body of phenomena, it will be necessary to introduce deeper and deeper concepts into physics and that this development will not end by the discovery of the final and perfect concepts. I believe that this is true: we have no right to expect that our intellect can formulate perfect concepts for the full understanding of inanimate nature's phenomena ("The Limits of Science," *Proceedings of the American Philosophical Society.* vol. 94 (1950), pp. 222–227 [see p. 424])

7. This shibboleth of the contemporary philosophy of science is not all that new. Already at the turn of the century, Sir Michael Foster wrote:

> The path [of progress in science] may not be always a straight line; there may be swerving to this side and to that; ideas may seem to return again and again to the same point of the intellectual compass; but it will always be found that they have reached a higher level—they have moved, not in a circle, but in a spiral. Moreover, science is not fashioned as is a house, by putting brick to brick, that which is once put remaining as it was put to the end. The growth of science is that of a living being. As in the embryo, phase follows phase, and each member or body puts on in succession different appearances, though all the while the same member, so a scientific conception of one age seems to differ from that of a following age. . . . ("The Growth of Science in the Nineteenth Century," *Annual Report of the Smithsonian Institution For 1899* [Washington, 1901], pp. 163–183 [as reprinted from Foster's 1899 presidential address to

the British Association for the Advancement of Science]; see p. 175.)

8. E.g. William Kneale, "Scientific Revolutions for Ever?" *British Journal for the Philosophy of Science*, vol. 19 (1967), pp. 27–42.

9. *Est ridiculum quaerere quae habere non possumus*, as Cicero wisely observed (*Pro Archia*, 10)

10. See Rudolf Carnap, "The Aim of Inductive Logic" in *Logic, Methodology, and Philosophy of Science*, ed. by E. Nagel, P. Suppes, and A. Torshin. (Stanford, 1962), pp. 308–318.

11. Jay Rosenberg, "In Search of an Authentic Pragmatism," unpublished lecture presented at the annual meeting of the Western Division of the American Philosophical Association, delivered April 26, 1980.

12. Cf. the author's *Peirce's Philosophy of Science* (Notre Dame and London, 1978).

13. Peirce verged on seeing this point; but his latter-day congeners do not, and try to get by with wholly transcendental argumentation from the possibility of science. Cf. Wilfrid Sellars, *Science and Metaphysics: Variations in Kantian Themes* (London, 1968).

14. Larry Laudan, "The Philosophy of Progress", mimeographed preprint (Pittsburgh, 1979), p. 4. Cf. *idem, Progress and its Problems* (Berkeley, 1977).

15. Note however, that to say that some ideals can be legitimated by practical considerations is not to say that all ideals must be legimated in this way.

CHAPTER ELEVEN (pp. 228–245)

1. Compare the discussion of the so-called Wheel Argument *(diallelus)* in the author's *Methodological Pragmatism* (Oxford, 1977), pp. 15–17 *et passim*.

2. A fuller development of these considerations regarding the teleology of inquiry is given in the author's *Scientific Explanation* (New York, 1970).

3. This objection is raised in Laurence BonJour, "Rescher's Idealistic Pragmatism," *The Review of Metaphysics*, vol. 39 (1976), pp. 702–726, (see p. 721).

4. See Hilary Putnam's *Meaning and the Moral Sciences* (Oxford, 1978).

5. The line of reasoning operative here is set out in Chapter VI, "Why

Relate Success and Truthfulness?'' of *Methodological Pragmatism, (op. cit.)*. This whole book is relevant to the discussions of the present chapter.

6. See Chapter I of the author's *Cognitive Systematization* (Oxford 1979) for a fuller development of these issues.

7. This idea that control over nature is the pivotal determinant of progress—in contrast with purely intellectual criteria (such as growing refinement, complication, precision; let alone cumulation or proliferation)—has been mooted by several writers in response to Kuhn. See, for example, Peter M. Quay, "Progress as a Demarcation Criterion for the Sciences," *Philosophy of Science,* vol. 41 (1974), pp. 154–170 (see especially p. 158). See also Freidrich Rapp, "Technological and Scientific Knowledge" in *Logic, Methodology, and Philosophy of Science: Proceedings of the Vth International Congress of DLMPS/IUHPS: London (Ontario) 1975* (Toronto, 1976). The relevant issues are treated in depth in the author's *Methodological Pragmatism (op. cit.)*.

8. This view of science was a philosophical commonplace in the era spanned by the work of Bacon, Hobbes, and Leibniz.

9. Laurence BonJour, "Rescher's Idealistic Pragmatism," *The Review of Metaphysics,* vol. 39 (1976), pp. 702–726 (see p. 720).

10. Admittedly, this line of reasoning involves factual considerations for the validation of our inquiry methods in the factual domain. But no vitiating circularity is involved here. For the reasons why see the author's *Methodological Pragmatism* (Oxford, 1976), which sets out in fuller detail the evolutionary dimension of this pragmatic approach.

11. George Gore, *The Art of Scientific Discovery* (London, 1878), pp. 26–27.

12. D. A. Bromley, *et al., Physics in Perspective: Student Edition* (Washington, D.C., 1973; NRC/NAS Publication), p. 23.

13. Cf. chaps. VIII–X of *Scientific Progress* (Oxford, 1978).

CHAPTER TWELVE (pp. 246–256)

1. This sort of *descriptive* realism has nothing to do with traditional *ontological* realism: the doctrine that the world exists independently of the thinking beings that inquire into it and that its nature (its having whatever descriptive characteristics it does have) is also comparably thought-independent. Ontological realism contrasts with ontological *idealism;* scientific realism contrasts with scientific *instrumentalism:* the doctrine that science nowise describes reality, but merely affords a useful organon of prediction and control.

2. For some recent discussions of scientific realism see: Wilfred Sellars, *Science, Perception and Reality* (London, 1963); E. McKinnon (ed.), *The*

Problem of Scientific Realism (New York, 1972); Rom Harré, *Principles of Scientific Thinking* (Chicago, 1970); Frederick Suppe (ed.), *The Structure of Scientific Theories* (2nd. ed., Urbana, 1977).

3. Keith Lehrer, "Review of *Science, Perception and Reality* by Wilfred Sellars," *The Journal of Philosophy,* vol. 63 (1966), pp. 266–277 (see p. 269).

4. Recall the discussion of Chapter III, which argued that the protocategories can never ben entirely abandoned in favor of the scientific categories of thought because the latter get their point through their exfoliative origin in our protoquestions.

5. Compare the author's *Methodological Pragmatism* (Oxford, 1977).

CHAPTER THIRTEEN (pp. 257–268)

1. William P. Alston, "Yes, Virginia, There is a Real World." *Proceedings and Addresses of the American Philosophical Association,* vol. 52 (1979), pp. 779–808 (see p. 779). Compare: "[T]he world is composed of particulars [individual existing things or processes] which have *intrinsic characteristics*—i.e., properties they have or relationships they enter into with other particulars independently of how anybody characterizes, conceptualizes, or conceives of them." Frederick Suppe, "Facts and Empirical Truth", *Canadian Journal of Philosophy,* vol. 3 (1973), pp. 197–212 (see p. 200).

2. Maimonides, *The Guide of the Perplexed,* I, 71, 96a.

3. At the present time of day, this view seems sheer heresy. We are told on all sides that the concepts of "the world" and of "the truth of things" and of "reality itself," viewed in explicit separation from any relationship to the practices and processes of inquiry, are simply empty and altogether vacuous. Arguments to this effect are nowadays almost commonplace. We find them in W. V. Quine's *Word and Object* (Cambridge, Mass; 1960) and in "Ontological Relativity" in *Ontological Relativity* (New York, 1969), in Nelson Goodman's "The Way the World is" in *Ways of World Making* (Indianapolis, 1978), in Richard Rorty's "The World Well Lost" (*The Journal of Philosophy,* vol. 69 [1972], pp. 649–666). in Donald Davidson's "The Very Idea of a Conceptual Scheme" (Proceedings of the American Philosophical Association, vol. 47 [1973–4], pp. 5–20) in Hilary Putnam's "Realism and Reason" in *Meaning and the Moral Sciences* (London, 1978), and in Jay Rosenberg's *Linguistic Representation* (Dordrecht, 1974). But none of these assaults on truth/world/reality deal adequately with (or indeed even address themselves to) the need for this conception as a negative contrast and as a regulative principle. A notion that has an important work to do cannot be dismissed as vacuous or superfluous.

Name Index

Subject Index